A Celebration of Wellness

A cookbook for vibrant living

Over 300 heart healthy, no dairy,
no cholesterol, nonfat & lowfat
inspired recipes

James Levin, M.D. and Natalie Cederquist

Avery Publishing Group
Garden City Park, New York

Library of Congress Catalog Card Number 92-094325
ISBN 0-89529-684-5

Printed in the United States of America

10   9   8   7   6

A Celebration of Wellness

A cookbook for vibrant living

1 cup = 16 tablespoon = 230 ml

½ cup = 8 tablespoon = 165 ml

¼ cup = 4 tablespoons = 82.5 ml

A Celebration of Wellness *was created by the authors of* A Vegetarians Ecstasy *to provide an expanded variety of unique new lowfat/nonfat/ cholesterol-free recipes for health conscious people.*

This easy-to-use cookbook includes:

- *Large and simple to read type*
- *Step-by-step easy recipes*
- *An illustrated cooking utensils guide*
- *Inspirational illustrations*
- *Sample menus; featuring breakfasts, picnics, Worldly Evenings, Seasonal Meals, Holiday Feasts, and Live Energy Meals*
- *A cross-referenced alphabetical index*
- *Tastes of Life, bite-sized morsels of nutritional and environmental information.*

Food of the highest degree for both body and mind await you. We invite you now to enjoy these heart healthy recipes ... A Celebration of Wellness!

Wishing you, "Health, Wealth and Vitality,"

James Levin, MD

Natalie Cederquist

*W*hen trying new ingredients, please keep in mind that each person has different needs and that some people have particular sensitivity to certain foods. If you are not certain about whether any of the ingredients mentioned in this book are right for you, please consult with a nutrition expert or health professional to assure yourself a proper diet in connection with making any dietary changes.

Table of Contents

- **Introduction** . . . *ix*
- **Healthy Choices — Food for Thought** . . . *x*
- **Do You Want More Energy in Your Life?** . . . *xi*
  Energy Zappers/Energizers
- **Which Foods Make You Feel Good?** . . . *xii*
- **The Feel Good Food Chart** . . . *xiii*
- **Fat Facts:** *Saturated and Unsaturated Fats* . . . *xiv*
- **Cholesterol** . . . *xv*
- **How to Sauté Safely without Fat or Oil** . . . *xvi*
- **Cleansing Fasts** . . . *xvii*
- **Vibrant Breathing with an Herbal Steam** . . . *xviii*
- **A Plentiful Pantry** . . . *xix*
  Stock up on these healthful dry goods for time-saving meal preparations, substitutions for ingredients.
- **Substitutions for Ingredients within This Book** . . . *xx*
- **Wellness Cookware Illustrated** . . . *xxiii*
  A visual guide to the basic utensils you will need to create recipes from this book.
- **Recipes**
  1. Liquid Delights . . . *3*
     Orange Flush, Spritzers and Smoothies
  2. Breakfast Ecstasies . . . 17
     Breakfast Burritos, Pancakes, Muffins and more
  3. Snacks and Sandwiches . . . 33
     Kids' Stuff to Salad Rolls
  4. Salads . . . 51
     Appetizers, Light Salads, and Hearty Salads featuring Fruits and Vegetables
  5. Salad Dressings . . . 91
     Simple to Exotic
  6. Sauces, Dips and Condiments . . . 105
     Including Pestos, Seed Cheeses, Cheezy Sauces, Mousses and Patés
  7. Soups . . . 147
     Live Energy Soups, Cleansing Purees, and Hearty Soups
  8. Hot Side Dishes . . . 187
     Vegetables, Beans and Grains
  9. Entrees . . . 211
     International Main Dish Extravaganzas
  10. Desserts . . . 257
      The Grand Finale, Fruit Sweetened Tortes, Sprouted Wheat Cookies and Celebration Cakes
- **Heart Healthy Menus** . . . 287
- **Bibliography** . . . 285
- **Index** . . . 295-306

Journey with us into a conscious approach to your diet. Your food choices do affect our entire planet. Vegetarianism is a lifestyle choice that leads to:

- ◆ *Cleaner air and water*
- ◆ *An increase of topsoil, fossil fuels and trees*
- ◆ *Improved personal health*
- ◆ *Enough food for all people on this Earth*
- ◆ *Honoring the lives of animals*
- ◆ *A gentler and more compassionate society*

If this kind of world appeals to you, then wait no more. Becoming conscious of our food choices is a first step. We can go beyond our cultural programming to face realities we are now living with. By living in harmony with our Earth, we can turn our precious shrinking global resources into an abundant natural supply. We hold the future of Mother Earth in our hands.

Open your heart, as we guide you through the doorway of wellness with delicious recipes, inspired ideas of health care, Earth facts and nutritional information.

There is only one time, and it is now ...

Your wellness is <u>our</u> cause for celebration!

Healthy Choices — Food for Thought

How do *you* want to feel?

. . . this question should replace the ever-popular "What would you like to eat?", because our food choices are directly related to how we look and feel. A trim body, glowing complexion and shiny eyes come from inner health, which cannot be bought at a beauty counter.

Ask yourself "How great do I want to feel?" If you want to feel vibrant, young and flexible, crystallize in your mind a clear picture of a healthy, radiant you, then take action to feel that way. .

Learn to eat vibrant, live, whole foods. Make your body happy by eating less and stop eating when you begin to feel full. Drinking eight glasses of pure filtered water a day will help to keep you full while flushing away toxins from your body. Make the healthy choice of replacing all fatty snacks with foods that have a high water content; such as, fresh squeezed juices, pure mineral water, herbal teas, fresh cut fruit or vegetable sticks.

Once you empower yourself with a healthful choice — don't stop. Healthy ways of eating, thinking, exercising, and behaving will reward you throughout your entire life. With each beneficial practice you acquire, free yourself of an unhealthy one. All it takes is self-love. We always have a choice . . . how would you like to feel?

Do You Want More Energy in Your Life?

There are many things you can do to bring more zest and vitality into your life.
You will radiate a glowing vitality by eating high quality foods in
combination with regular exercise, getting enough sleep, fresh
air, and sunshine; plus keeping a positive outlook on life.

Naturally, there are foods that give you an energy lift
(see "Energizers" below), and others which may make you sleepy.
Eliminate the foods in the "Zapper" category below and
see the difference it makes in how you feel.

Energy Zappers

Alcohol

Dairy Products
(they contain tryptophan — a sedative)

Soft drinks

Coffee and caffeinated drinks

Sugary foods

Glutinous grains
(wheat, rye, oats)

Common allergy foods
(eggs, corn, dairy, wheat, pine nuts)

Energizers
*(The right mix of energizers is specific
to each individual.)*

Live foods
(fresh fruits and vegetables)

Vitamin C
(citrus, peppers, chiles)

Iron-rich foods
*(dried prunes, figs, raisins, leafy greens,
lima beans, nutritional yeast)*

Vitamin B-rich foods
*(brown rice, leafy greens, nutritional
yeast, bee pollen, nuts, legumes)*

Complex carbohydrates
*(squash, potatoes, rice and whole grains,
sweet potatoes, yams)*

Potassium/Magnesium
*(flax seeds, beans, potatoes, melons,
nuts, whole grains, leafy greens,
pineapples)*

Which Foods Make You Feel Good?

If we listen to our body after consuming various foods, our body will tell us what it likes and what it dislikes. Foods create different chemical reactions and sensations as they are broken down and utilized by the body. What works for some people, doesn't work for others.

Get in touch with what agrees with *your* body. Choose not to consume those foods that make you feel lethargic or dull. Often, out of convenience, habit or stress, we reach for the foods that consistently make us feel lousy afterward. Once you've determined what those foods are for you, replace them with foods that lift you up, and make you feel good after eating them.

An excellent way to become aware of your emotional involvement with food is to take an active, conscious approach. Record what you eat during the day and how you feel 2 to 4 hours afterward. Writing down how you feel makes you more conscious of your food choices and eating habits (see the chart on the next page). Once you become aware of the after effects of your food choices, and what state of mind you are in when you eat, you have taken a step toward improving your life.

Taking control of what you put in your mouth leads to greater personal power and enhanced vitality.

The Feel Good Food Chart
"Your Personal Vitality Barometer"

Time of Day	Food Item Consumed	Quantity	How do you feel? 1 hr. later/Several hrs. later

Conscious eating will make you more aware of what your body needs and likes. Follow what you eat on a daily chart to examine how your body responds to what you are feeding it. Listen to the wisdom of your body if you want to improve your health.

Fat Facts

A Description of Fats:
- The most concentrated form of energy in the diet.
- The major structural components of the membranes which surround each of our cells, as well as all subcellular membranes.
- Insulate the body from environmental temperature changes, and aid in preserving body heat.
- When oxidized, fats furnish twice the number of calories per gram that carbohydrates or proteins do: 1 gram fat = 9 calories of heat energy.
- Carriers for the fat soluble vitamins A, D, E and K.
- Aid in absorption of vitamin D, thus making calcium available to body tissues (bones and teeth).
- Important for the conversion of carotene into vitamin A.
- Surround, protect, and hold in place our body's organs (kidneys, liver, heart, etc.)

Sources of fats:
- Meat, poultry, fish, eggs, dairy products, vegetable oils, nuts and seeds. (Avocados and coconuts are also high in fat content.)

Types of fat:
- Saturated   ♦ Unsaturated

Saturated Fats

DESCRIPTION
- Those fats that are usually hard at room temperature and body temperature.
- Fatty acids whose molecules are fully loaded with hydrogen atoms.

SOURCES
- All animal products, plus coconut and palm kernel oils.

Adverse effects:
- Excess dietary saturated fat is known to interfere with the healthy function of the entire cardiovascular system.

Unsaturated Fats

DESCRIPTION
- Usually liquid at room temperature and body temperature.
- Fatty acids whose molecules contain one or more double bonds between its carbon atoms so that hydrogen atoms can be added.
- Include the Essential Fatty Acids: linoleic and linolenic acids.
- There are two types of unsaturated fats: monounsaturated and polyunsaturated, which simply refer to their molecular structure.
  - Monounsaturated fats contain 1 carbon double bond
  - Polyunsaturated fats contain many carbon double bonds.

SOURCES
- Vegetables, vegetable oils, nuts and seeds. Most fruits have less than 1 percent fat by weight.

Types of unsaturated fat:

MONOUNSATURATED
◆ Found in olive, almond, canola and other seed oils, which contain oleic acid.

POLYUNSATURATED
◆ Found in corn, safflower, flax and cottonseed oil.
◆ Flax seeds are the only source of both of the Essential Fatty Acids.
◆ Safflower oil only contains the Essential Fatty Acid linoleic acid.
◆ Pumpkin seeds, walnuts, and soybeans are other sources.

Beneficial effects:
◆ Necessary for the proper growth and function of: healthy blood, arteries and nerves.
◆ Promotes proper moisture and texture of the skin.
◆ The Essential Fatty Acids serve as an "oxygen magnet"[1] that facilitates the transfer of oxygen in the lungs into the bloodstream, to the red blood cells, and across all the necessary cellular membranes to transport oxygen to all of the cells of the body.
◆ Beneficial in the function and structure of all cellular membranes in the body and in the creation of necessary cellular electrical potentials.[2]

Cholesterol

DESCRIPTION
◆ A hard, fatty, waxy substance, essential for physical health.
◆ Not required in the diet.
◆ Our body manufactures cholesterol from the breakdown of sugars, fats and proteins.
◆ The more sugars and fats (especially saturated and non-Essential Fatty Acids) that are present in our diets, the more cholesterol the body is required to produce to metabolize them.[3]

DIETARY SOURCE
◆ All animal products.

Functions[4]
◆ Keeps the membranes of our cells functioning properly.
◆ Steroid hormones are made from cholesterol.
◆ Adrenal corticosteroids are made from cholesterol (for example, regulation of water balance in the kidneys).
◆ Vitamin D is made from cholesterol.
◆ The bile acids (which emulsify the fats in food in the intestines to make them easier to digest) are derived from cholesterol.
◆ Performs vital functions in the digestion and absorption of fats and oils and fat-soluble vitamins.
◆ Secreted by the glands of the skin and aid in protecting the skin from dehydration and cracking.

Adverse effects:
◆ Excess cholesterol is known to interfere with the healthy function of the entire cardiovascular system.

1. Udo Erasmus, *Fats and Oils*, page 38; 2. Ibid., page 8; 3. Ibid., page 63; 4. Ibid., page 55-68.

How to Sauté without Fat or Oil

You can create a wonderful fat-free sauté in your skillet or wok without the use of oils or fats.

Lemon juice (or citrus juices) and vegetable broths are good basic sauté liquids. You can create easy broths by adding a bit of "lite" soy sauce, Dr. Bronner's Bouillon, or liquid aminos to water. Cooking wines like mirin or cooking sherry are also nice to try. Add minced ginger, garlic, or onions and herbs for variations of flavor. You truly won't believe how delicious non-fat cooking is!

To Celebrate Your Wellness:

Your choice of dietary fats is a major factor in the optimum functioning of the miracle of your body. Celebrate the miracle that is you by:

1. Eliminating all saturated fats in your diet.

2. Limiting your dietary fat to 10 to 15 percent or less of your daily calories.

3. Make certain that your diet includes foods rich in the dietary Essential Fatty Acids: flax seeds, pumpkin seeds, walnuts, soybeans, dark green leafy vegetables and seaweeds.

   (Helpful hint: Take either 1 to 2 tablespoons of pure flax seed oil daily, or put 1 to 3 tablespoons of flax seeds into a blender when making a breakfast smoothie, or, grind the flax seeds in a food mill and sprinkle them raw on salads, grains or soups. Do not heat them.)

How to Sauté Safely

If you decide to use oil in your saute or wok, remember that vegetable and seed oils need to be protected from light, air and heat. Heating oils at high temperatures (above 120º to 160º C) in the presence of light, oxygen or air, oxidize the oils and destroys their nutritional value (specifically the Essential Fatty Acids). Follow either of these cooking methods to promote health and well-being:

1. **Traditional Chinese Method:**

   Put water in the wok first, before adding oil. The water keeps the temperature down to 100º C and the water vapor (steam) protects the oil from oxidation.

2. **European Method:**

   Place your vegetables into the pan first, before adding oil. The vegetables protect the oils from overheating and oxidation.

The best way to use oils is fresh and unheated on salads. Or, try the Orange Flush on page 5.

Cleansing Fasts

As the need arises to awaken your true self and feel as if you've just been born, a detoxifying cleanse is your radiant ticket to inner paradise. Letting go of accumulated wastes and impurities is liberating, both physically and psychologically.

Since eating occupies so much of our energy (in the form of digestion) and thought processes (what to eat, where to eat, when to eat), when we don't eat, our awareness is freed from our basic needs. It is as if your entire perspective of life changes. In fact, we undergo a cellular transformation and regeneration. Our bodily energy and organs are freed from their daily chores of digestion, and instead, focus on "cleaning house."

Try a one day a week cleanse or a 1 to 3 day cleanse to start. The first 3 days take the most self-discipline, for the stomach is shrinking and we are still operating in the "cephalic phase" of digestion — our minds are telling us that we need to eat. Once this phase is over, we experience more energy and find it easy not to eat. Be sure you cleanse as long as you feel comfortable, and drink lots of filtered water. Herbals teas and vegetable broths may provide warming comfort as well during a cleansing fast.

There are many ways to fast effectively. One method is to drink only fresh squeezed vegetable or fruit juices, which can be diluted with water if desired. Our favorite cleanse is with "The Master Cleanser" (see side bar). Be sure to nourish yourself daily with walking, yoga, deep breathing, meditating, dry body brushing and rest.

Taking the time to do this special type of cleansing will increase your health and vitality.

The Master Cleanse

This was developed by Stanley Burroughs and is a great way to fast, drinking 1 gallon of this a day, along with herbal teas and water.

1/4 c	Lemon juice
1/4 c	Maple syrup
1/2 tsp	Cayenne
1 qt	Water (pure)

The lemon acts as a purifier and toner, the cayenne increases the circulation, and the maple syrup supplies the necessary glucose to keep your energy up.

Vibrant Breathing with an Herbal Steam

The inhalation of an herbal steam is a simple breathing exercise that facilitates the lungs' ability to transfer oxygen to the hemoglobin molecule in our red blood cells, which then serve to carry the oxygen via the bloodstream and then to deliver it on a cellular level to all of our organs and tissues.

To the degree that we enhance the lungs' ability to transfer the oxygen to our red blood cells, to that degree we maximize our sense of vitality throughout our body. This increased vitality may be noticed in the improved quality of the texture, moisture and color of our skin; flexibility of our joints; clarity of our thoughts; and ultimately, the quality and vibrancy of our life.

The herbal steam cleanses, warms and moistens the linings of the respiratory sinuses in the head (A), the back of the throat (B), the trachea as it enters the upper chest (C) before dividing into its right and left lung branches (D), on its way to the alveoli (E), which are the tiny end pockets of the lungs where the miraculous transfer of oxygen to the red blood cells takes place *(see diagram at left)*. The herbal steam mobilizes and facilitates all of the dynamic forces involved in establishing the maximum vibrant environment for this transfer of oxygen.

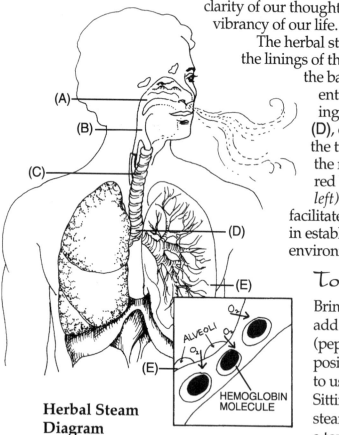

Herbal Steam Diagram

Oxygen is transferred from the alveoli in the lungs to the hemoglobin molecule of the red blood cells, which then transport the oxygen to the cells of the body.

To Prepare an Herbal Steam

Bring a pot of 4 cups of water to a boil, add 2 tablespoons of mixed dried herbs (peppermint, chamomile, eucalyptus), position the pot on a table. You may wish to use a trivet because the pot will be hot. Sitting comfortably, bend over the steaming pot as you cover your head with a towel. Inhale and exhale slowly (as described in "Deep Breathing," page 5) for a minimum of 5 minutes. Do this in the evening before retiring and in the morning upon awakening for your maximum benefit.

Remember, vibrant breathing leads to vibrant living!

A Plentiful Pantry

Here is a list of frequently called for food items required in our recipes. For your convenience, the pantry items are broken down into categories: dry goods, packaged and canned goods, supplements, liquid seasonings, herbs and spices, sweeteners, and baking essentials.

The packaged and prepared canned goods can certainly save time in meal preparations, but they aren't as alive or vital as fresh or frozen foods. Healthier options of packaged foods continue to expand store shelves as people become more conscious of what they put into their bodies. Now there are organically grown canned or bottled beans and vegetables, soups and sauces; which can create a nice meal in a pinch.

Having a well-stocked and organized kitchen is more efficient and will expedite your food preparation time, and expand your options when deciding what to make. It also makes it easier to know when you are low or out of a certain ingredient.

For shelf organization, nothing compares to the "lazy Susan." This rotating tray holds all liquid seasonings and spices, saving both cupboard space and the time trying to locate that item — just spin the shelf until you see what you need.

Save money by buying all your beans, grains, pastas, herbs and seasonings from bulk bins. By doing so, you can purchase only the quantity you need, and then can try out a new item for only a few cents rather than having to buy a whole pound or box. Label small jars for herbs and larger jars for the food staples that you use continually and refill them when they are empty. Buying in bulk is definitely environmentally friendly, no need to throw away boxes and packaging, even if they do get recycled.

Grind up whole herbs and seeds to make fresher, tastier spices at home. Immediately store them in airtight glass jars after grinding, and store them away from the light. You can grind cumin seeds, chile pods, cinnamon sticks and cardamom pods for sensational flavors. Remember that some spices are very strong and their volatile oils can leave lingering impressions in your grinder. It is best to wash out the grinder with soapy water, or use baking soda to remove odors and make it fresh for the next use. The flavor and potency of herbs and spices last about six months.

Keep flours, nuts and seeds in the refrigerator to retain their freshness. Almonds, sunflower seeds and dried fruits should be soaked in water for best assimilation and digestion; keep some submerged in a jar of water in the fridge for snacking pleasure.

Remember, the "juicier" it is, the better it is for you. If the almonds or sunflower seeds soak more than a few days, you can turn them into sprouted seed sauces, or use them in dressings and stuffings.

Most sprouted beans and peas are best digested when they are cooked or steamed first. The only exceptions are mung and lentil sprouts, which are juicier than the others. See your legumes, nuts, seeds and dried fruits as storehouses of life force, waiting to be awakened by the angel of water. Water will transform them into super nutrients.

Substitutions for Ingredients within this Book

If there are ingredients called for within this book that you cannot find, here are ideas on substitutions.

Agar Flakes — There are no healthy substitutes for agar, which is a sea plant thickener that gives a gelatinous body to foods. Agar flakes are a healthy substitute for gelatin, which is made from ground up cow hooves and bones.

Bean Thread Noodles — Also known as "sai-fun" noodles, can substitute a light noodle such as angel hair pasta (although they aren't transparent or jelly-like). Available in oriental markets, or in the oriental section in supermarkets.

Dr. Bronner's Bouillon — Try "Quick Sip," liquid aminos, miso mixed with water, tamari or "lite" soy sauce, or other concentrated vegetable bouillon liquid. Available in health food stores.

Dried Red Chiles — Use red chile powder, which is powdered dried red chiles. Do not use chili powder, which is a seasoning blend of oregano, chile, onion, and spices.

Egg Replacer — This potato starch and tapioca-based flour holds baked goods together as an egg would. You may also try blending soft tofu mashed with water or arrowroot powder as an egg replacer.

Green Chiles (Fire-roasted) — Most markets carry them canned whole or diced.

Jalapeño or Serrano Chiles — Hot green chiles can be found canned or dried if the fresh ones aren't available.

Kuzu/Arrowroot Powder — Both are herbal thickeners. Arrowroot can be purchased in bulk bins in health food stores or co-ops. It is less expensive than kuzu. Both powders are a healthier substitute for corn starch, which creates a pasty, glue-like coating in your intestines and should be avoided.

Liquid Aminos — A mineral rich soy bouillon. Use 1/2 soy sauce or miso paste mixed with 1/2 water for designated quantity. Available in health food stores.

Rice Pancakes — If you don't have an oriental market in town, try using Nori sushi or lettuce leaves to roll up salad stuffing.

Silken Tofu — Although silken tofu can be found in supermarkets, you can use soft tofu, though the texture will not be quite as silky.

A Plentiful Pantry

Dry Goods *(buy organically grown)*

Legumes
- ☐ Beans
  aduki, Anasazi, black, garbanzo, kidney, mung, navy, pinto, white, soy (see also tofu, tempeh)
- ☐ Lentils
- ☐ Peas
- ☐ Other _____

Grains
- ☐ Corn/Cornmeal
- ☐ Kasha
- ☐ Millet
- ☐ Oats/Oat Bran
- ☐ Quinoa
- ☐ Rice
  brown, basmati, jasmine, wild rice
- ☐ Rye
- ☐ Wheat Berries
  bulgar (cracked wheat), bran, cous-cous
- ☐ Pasta/Noodles *(whole grain)*

Seeds
- ☐ Alfalfa Seeds
- ☐ Flax Seeds
- ☐ Pumpkin
- ☐ Sesame
- ☐ Sunflower

Nuts
- ☐ Almonds
- ☐ Cashews
- ☐ Peanuts
- ☐ Pecans
- ☐ Pine Nuts
- ☐ Walnuts

Nut Butters
- ☐ Raw Sesame Tahini
- ☐ Peanut Butter *(or other nut)*

Dried Fruits
- ☐ Prunes
- ☐ Raisins
- ☐ Apricots
- ☐ Figs

Natural Packaged Goods
- ☐ Cereals
- ☐ Instant Beans and Grains
- ☐ Instant Soups
- ☐ Instant Noodles
- ☐ Ramen Soups
- ☐ Hummus
- ☐ Tabouli
- ☐ Instant Seitan Mix
- ☐ Silken Tofu
- ☐ "Lite" Soy Milk

Bottled and Canned Goods

Make sure they contain no preservatives, fat, or sugar, and are organic if possible.
- ☐ Beans
- ☐ Green Chiles *(fire roasted)*
- ☐ Peeled Pear Tomatoes
- ☐ Tomato Paste
- ☐ Tomato Sauce
- ☐ Pumpkin
- ☐ Vegetable Juices
- ☐ Fruit Juices
- ☐ Mineral Waters
- ☐ Eggless Mayo
- ☐ Mustard/Ketchup
- ☐ Pineapple Chunks *(canned)*

Supplements
To mix in foods and juices
- ☐ Bee Pollen *(fresh is best)*
- ☐ Lecithin Granules
- ☐ Nutritional Yeast
- ☐ Spirulina *(dried algaes or grasses)*
- ☐ Vitamin C Powder
- ☐ Soy Protein Powder

Liquid Seasonings

Oils:
- ☐ Extra Virgin Pure Olive Oil
- ☐ Flax Seed Oil
- ☐ Toasted Sesame Oil
- ☐ Chile Sesame Oil
- ☐ Canola or Safflower Oil

Vinegars:
- ☐ Cider Vinegar
- ☐ Herbed Vinegar
- ☐ Brown Rice Vinegar
- ☐ Balsamic Vinegar

Broths:
- ☐ Dr. Bronner's Bouillon
- ☐ Liquid Aminos
- ☐ "Lite" Soy Sauce/Tamari

- ☐ Miso
- ☐ Vegetable Broth *(concentrate)*

Other Condiments:
- ☐ Curry Paste
- ☐ Chile Paste *(hot sauce)*
- ☐ Horseradish

Sweeteners *(Use sparingly)*
- ☐ Raw Honey
- ☐ Pure Maple Syrup
- ☐ Barley Malt Syrup
- ☐ Applesauce
- ☐ Frozen Fruit Juice Concentrates
- ☐ Fruit Sweetened Jams & Jellies
- ☐ Frozen Fruits
- ☐ Dried Fruits

Baking Essentials
- ☐ Arrowroot Powder/Kuzu
  (natural thickeners)
- ☐ Agar Flakes *(gels)*
- ☐ Egg Replacer
- ☐ Baking Powder/Baking Soda *(leaven)*
- ☐ Vanilla Extract
- ☐ Almond Extract/Maple Extract
- ☐ Flour *(whole wheat pastry, rice flour, etc.)*
- ☐ Bran *(wheat, oat)*
  (See also Grains & Sweeteners)

Herbs and Spices
(Good for 6 months)
Savory
- ☐ Sea Salt, Vegetable Salt *(salt free)*
- ☐ Onion Powder/Garlic Powder
- ☐ Basil
- ☐ Dill Weed
- ☐ Celery Seed
- ☐ Cumin
- ☐ Oregano
- ☐ Cayenne Pepper *(hot)/* Paprika *(mild)*
- ☐ Dried Red Chile *(powder & whole)*
- ☐ Red Chile Flakes
- ☐ Chile Powder Seasoning
- ☐ Curry Powder
- ☐ Black Peppercorns
- ☐ Thyme
- ☐ Rosemary
- ☐ Kelp/Dulse Powders

- ☐ Sage
- ☐ Saffron
- ☐ Coriander
- ☐ Cajun Spice
- ☐ Other _____

Sweet
- ☐ Cinnamon
- ☐ Allspice
- ☐ Cloves
- ☐ Nutmeg
- ☐ Orange/Lemon Zest *(page 277)*
- ☐ Vanilla Beans
- ☐ Cardamom
- ☐ Chinese 5-Spice

Herbal Teas
- ☐ Chamomile
- ☐ Peppermint
- ☐ Dessert Tea
- ☐ Other Tonics *(ginseng, gotu cola, etc.)*

The Oriental Pantry Additions
(If not at your local natural foods store, these can be found at a supermarket, specialty or oriental market)
- ☐ Shiitake Mushrooms *(dried)*
- ☐ Wood Ears *(dried)*
- ☐ Spring Roll Wrappers
  (rice pancakes, dried)
- ☐ Toasted Nori Sheets
  (sushi rolls)
- ☐ Seaweeds *(excellent source of vitamin B_{12})*
  - Kombu *(for soup stock)*
  - Hiziki, Dulse, Arame
- ☐ Noodles
  - Rice/Glass Noodles
  - Soba *(buckwheat)*
  - Ramen
- ☐ Canned Goods
  - Bamboo Shoots
  - Water Chestnuts
  - Baby Corn
  - Palm Hearts
- ☐ Frozen Edamame Beans
- ☐ Mochi *(a starchy rice cake you bake)*
- ☐ Sauce Condiments
  (See also Liquid Seasonings)
  - Wasabe Paste *(hot)*
  - Umeboshi Paste *(salty)*

Wellness Cookware Illustrated

If you really enjoy cooking, you probably already have an entire collection of cooking gear. Thanks to the proliferation of specialty cook shops, there is a wonderful supply of cooking products from all over the world. Here are some basics for preparing the foods in this book.

Avoid aluminum — instead use glass, cast iron, ceramic, stainless steel or enamel pots and cookware. Research the best brands and buy quality, you'll have them for a lifetime if they are taken care of properly.

Food Processor

A must have! Essential for fancy gratings, fine minces in a flash, and for pureeing large quantities of vegetables. Its uses seem endless.

Bean/Seed Grinder

We use our grinder to pulverize spices and to prepare seed/nut milks and seed cheeses. It creates the creamiest lentil patés by grinding the lentils to a fine powder. A super-powered machine!

Blender

The ol' standby for making drinks and smoothies, salad dressings and sauces.

Pots • Pans • Baking Dishes

Flat/Round-bottom Wok
All-purpose quick cooker

3-Quart Pan
For sauces and reheating small portions

7-Quart Pan
For large ratatouilles and stews

10" Skillet
For larger sautes and rice, get one with a lid

7" Skillet
For small sautes

Steamer Basket
Vegetable steamer fits inside a medium or large pan

Mixing Bowl Set
Small, medium and large, preferably ones that have rubber lids to save leftover batters and salads in fridge

Casserole Dishes
Oven-proof for reheating

Pyrex Pie Dishes
For quiches and pies

Rectangular Dishes
For enchiladas, lasagne, baking squash and roasting potatoes

Bread and Muffin Pans

Round or Flat bottom Wok

3 QRT pot

7 QRT pot

7" skillet

Pyrex pie dish and baking rectangle

muffin pans and bread pans

Utensils and Serving Vessels

Tongs

For removing hot tortillas, potatoes.

Spoons

For stirring everything.

Slotted Spoons

For removing vegetables from liquids.

Ladles

Are a must for spooning out purees and soups.

Pasta Spoon

Looks more like a spoon with fingers, but holds pasta perfectly.

Wooden Utensils

For wok use and for stirring soups.

Whisk

For lump-free sauces.

Kitchen Scissors

Multi-use for opening packages, trimming food and cutting cheesecloth.

Garlic Press

Our favorite; gets daily use, also use with ginger root.

Teaspoon Measuring Set

Cup Measuring Set

Knives

Buy the best! One large knife to cut roots and vegetables, one small knife to core fruits. Large utility knife for cutting squash or cubing eggplant.

Sauce and Gravy Boats

Have assorted sizes. Use to hold salad dressings too.

Serving Platters

For salads, pastas, steamed veggies and other great presentations.

There are some ingredients that must be in every successful recipe for vibrant living, yet they are not listed as essential ... They hold everything together and assure a meaningful outcome.

Found only in the Pantry of the Heart,
  they are love,
    friendship,
      consideration,
        tenderness,
          and most special of all ...
            the all embracing guiding light
              that illuminates the path of success.

We invite you now,
to Celebrate your Wellness ...
Through these heart-healthy recipes,
inspired illustrations,
and Tastes of Information,
we send you
Health, Wealth and Vitality!

Let your love flow
into your meal preparation
and remember,
real flavor comes from the heart.

Liquid Delights

Morning Cleanser   5

Orange Flush   5

Juice of Life   6

Juice Combos   7

Herbs and Herbal Brews   8

Cranberry Gingerale   9

Fresh Ginger Concentrate   9

Apricot Spritzer   10

Strawberry Spritzer   10

Fairy Tea   10

Orange Banana Flips   11

Fruity Flax Smoothie   11

Banana Blueberry Shake   11

Strawberry Nut Milk Smoothie   12

Almond Milk   12

Fresh Fig Vanilla Shake   13

Pineapple Date Shake   13

Mocha Date Shake   14

Iced Mochas   14

Classic Cashew Nut Milk   15

Hot 'Eggless' Nog   15

A Celebration of Wellness

Morning Cleanser

Begin your day by drinking a cup of warm water with 1/2 a lemon juiced into it. This restores the acidic balance in your body, and is a very cleansing and purifying way to start your day.

Lemon juice flushes out impurities and excess mucus, cleans the liver and acts as a natural appetite suppressant. Wait 15 to 30 minutes before consuming other beverages or foods, so the lemon has a chance to do its magic.

Orange Flush

This liver flush was designed by Dr. Stone and has super cleansing, strengthening and invigorating properties for your liver and whole system in general. You can add the garlic and cayenne according to taste. The Purifying Diet by Dr. Stone is a wonderfully gentle way to heal and cleanse. It consists of this flush every morning and eating only fruits and vegetables (raw or steamed), plus herbal teas throughout the day.

2 c	**Fresh squeezed orange/grapefruit juice**
1/2	**Lemon, juiced**
1 tsp	**Olive oil — extra virgin pure**
1 tsp	**Ginger, chopped fresh**
1	**Garlic clove**
Dash	**Cayenne**

Blend everything in blender first on low, then on high till frothy.
Strain into goblets.

SERVES: 1

Deep Breathing

Pranayama is the ancient Indian term for deep breathing exercises. These oxygenating practices encourage inner peace, health and well being through centering your mind on one thing: the rhythm of your breath bringing fresh oxygen to every cell of your body.

To begin, put yourself in a relaxing environment, sit upright and inhale slowly through your nose for a count of 5. Hold the breath in for 5 counts, then empty your lungs, slowly exhaling out through your mouth for 10 counts.

These exercises should be done daily for 10-20 minutes for optimal benefit. Remember, adequate and effective oxygenation of your body's cells is essential for the process of cellular rejuvenation.

Juice of Life
... Freshly Squeezed Juices

Freshly squeezed juices are the highest quality concentrated vitamin, mineral, and energy drinks your body can readily assimilate. Few natural sources have as much nutritional value and offer such a high vibrational frequency of life energy (which only comes from unpasteurized, raw sources). Freshly squeezed juices are natural nutritional supplements, carrying lots of nutrients directly to your cells. No extended digestive process is necessary.

Considering that it takes 1 pound of carrots to make 10.5 ounces of juice, just imagine all the vitamins and minerals that you assimilate by drinking carrot juice. How often do you chew a pound of carrots?

Do your body a favor and include a glass of freshly squeezed orange or grapefruit juice in the morning, a glass of carrot (or carrot-veggie blend) in the afternoon or evening. Your body will be ever so grateful for the care you give it!

If you don't have a juicer, be sure to find "fresh squeezed" juice (juiced the same day), at the local health store or "juice stand." Store bought freshly squeezed juices still have many nutrients and will make a considerable improvement on your health and energy level.

Preparation

Be sure to buy organically grown produce, if possible, and use only the freshest quality available. If concerned about pesticides or parasites, you can soak your food in a sink of cold water that has 4 Tbl of salt and 2 Tbl lemon juice added or 1 Tbl white vinegar. Soak for 5 to 10 minutes, then rinse in cool water.

Juice Combos

These juices can become your meals on cleansing days or fasts.

The Carrot Classic

Carrots give you energy! They have a natural sweetness and are good for your digestion, eyes, skin and hair. An excellent source of beta-carotene.

For 1 serving, juice:
8 carrots

Apple-Lemonade

This is an intestinal broom. The flavor is bright, sweet and refreshingly tart. The lemon heightens the apple flavor, and acts as a cleansing agent for your liver and gallbladder. The apple removes impurities from your digestive tract.

For 2 servings, juice:
12 apples
add 2-3 Tbl **lemon juice**,
to taste

The Carrot Cleanser

Carrot and apple juices make for a delicious, sweet and cleansing drink.

For 1 serving, juice:
8 carrots
1 apple

Veggie Delight

This is a fortifying drink. It energizes, cleanses, and tones your system. Beet juice stimulates the liver, parsley purifies the blood and acts as a diuretic, spinach acts as a laxative and is good for the liver also. In combinations involving carrot juice, carrots should comprise 50% of the juice content.

You may also add tomato, cucumber, cabbage or bell pepper.

50% carrot juice
20% beet
10% each spinach,
parsley, celery
add **dill, cayenne, garlic**
or **lemon** to taste

"The Detoxifier"

Wheatgrass Juice
A powerful purifier, oxygenator, liver cleanser and cellular healer. Add 1 oz. of wheatgrass juice to 8 oz. apple, carrot or pineapple juice for an instant energy boost. Or, mix the wheatgrass juice into a glass of water.

Herbal Brews

So many to choose from! There are herbal blends for weight loss, increasing energy, easy breathing, a good night's rest, calming and cleansing — you name it! Here is a simple list of some herbs and their uses.

Energize
    Peppermint
    Spearmint
    Ginseng
    Gotu Kola

Dispel Gas
    Anise
    Ginger
    Fennel
    Parsley

Calming
    Chamomile
    Nettle
    Skullcap
    Catnip

Digestion Stimulant
    Cinnamon
    Nutmeg
    Cloves

Healing
    Goldenseal

Nutritional
    Comfrey
    Alfalfa

Bowel Stimulant
    Licorice
    Cascara
        Sagrada

Menstrual Anti-cramping
    Raspberry Leaf

Herbs

The use of herbs as daily beverages, and as tonics or medicines to rebalance and heal the body is thousands of years old.

Various parts of the plant are used, depending on wherein its specific healing benefits reside. It may be the bark (as in cinnamon and sassafras), the root (ginseng, licorice, ginger and goldenseal), the stems (lemon grass and alfalfa), the leaves (peppermint, rosemary and strawberry), or the flowers (chamomile, lavender and linden).

There are many herbs that we use daily as seasonings that have healing properties (such as thyme, mint and basil); others are powerful disinfectants which strengthen our immune system (for example, golden seal).

The new frontier of herbal discovery lies within the rain forests. Thousands of plants exist there that we know nothing about. From less than 1 percent of the plants tested so far, we have derived 25 percent of our modern medicines. Hopefully, we will recognize the incredible value in protecting our rain forests! Over 1,000 species of plants become extinct every year due to tropical rain forest destruction.

Herbs are a blessing from Mother Nature; they are a truly precious resource. So let's raise our cups to toast the wonders of herbs with a steaming, fragrant herbal brew!

For further information on specific properties, remedies, and preparations of herbs, consult an herb book.

Cranberry Ginger Ale

A zippy and refreshing cocktail

- 1 c **Natural cranberry juice cocktail**
- 1/3 c **Lime mineral water**
- 1 tsp **Fresh ginger concentrate (see below)**
  Ice cubes

Put ice into a tumbler, fill 2/3 full with juice, add ginger concentrate and top with mineral water. Stir with a swizzle stick, and top with an orange or lime slice on the rim of a glass.

SERVES: 1

Fresh Ginger Concentrate

An easy way to have fresh ginger around. Make ahead and store in fridge. It saves preparation time.

- 1/2 c **Fresh ginger root, peeled and chopped**
- 1 c **Pure water**
- 1/4 c **Lemon juice**

Liquefy all the ingredients in a blender for a couple of minutes. Strain into a glass jar and store in the fridge. Use this in stir frys, salad dressings, soups or sauces — or add to sparkling waters or juices. You can also add 1 tsp to hot water as a beverage to increase your circulation.

Ginger

This tasty, aromatic rhizome soothes the digestive system, stimulates the circulatory system, and acts as a decongestant. To make ginger tea, pour boiling water over a bit of chopped ginger root; it will warm you up on a chilly day.

Use ginger in salad dressings, sauces, soups and baked goods. Ginger has been used for thousands of years in China and ancient India, both as a condiment to foods, and for its healing properties.

Notes:

Apricot Spritzer

A de-light-full chilled drink!
Perfect as an afternoon refreshment, or with lunch.

10 oz	Mineral water (a small bottle)
1/2 c	Frozen apricots
1 tsp	Honey

Liquefy in a blender, serve in champagne flutes or in your favorite glasses.

SERVES: 2

Strawberry Spritzer

10 oz	Mineral water
1/2 c	Strawberries, frozen

Follow directions above.

Make your own inventions according to fresh frozen fruit on hand. Try using different flavored mineral waters for unique tastes.

Fairy Tea

A creamy caffeine-free version of English tea, a delicious morning drink for all ages.

Per person:

1 teabag	French vanilla, Mu Zest, or other de-caf tea
3 Tbl	Vanilla soy milk
1 tsp	Honey

Put tea bag in a mug, pour boiling water over tea bag and let steep for 3 minutes. Remove tea bag and stir in the soy milk and honey.

Orange Banana Flips

A wonderful morning drink.

4 c	Fresh orange juice
2	Frozen bananas, chopped
	Several ice cubes

Put everything into a blender and blend until smooth. Add soya protein powder for an "Orange Julius," or bee pollen for more vitamins.

SERVES: 2

Fruity Flax Smoothie

A wonderful way to have your daily flax seeds — full of essential fatty acids.

1½ c	Pineapple juice, chilled
1 Tbl	Flax seeds
10	Frozen strawberries
1 Tbl	Soya protein powder

Blend 2 minutes in a blender; add ice as desired. Makes 2½ cups.

Banana Blueberry Shake

2 c	Cashew milk (page 15) or soy milk
2/3 c	Frozen blueberries
1½	Bananas
12	Ice cubes
1 Tbl	Soy protein powder (optional)

Put everything into a blender and grind on low for 1 minute. When ice is broken down to small pieces, turn on high to liquefy into a smooth icy shake.

SERVES: 2

Essential Fatty Acids

<u>Best Source:</u> Flax Seeds

<u>Daily Supplement:</u> 1 Tbl flax seeds (grind in food mill or soak in water before adding to foods)

<u>Other sources:</u> Walnuts, seaweeds and legumes

<u>Benefits of Essential Fatty Acids:</u> Shiny hair, smooth skin, enhances smooth muscle action, normalization of blood sugar, improved immune system, resistance to cold weather, brain and visual functions, adrenal gland function and sperm formation.

Notes:

Strawberry Nut Milk Smoothie

A nourishing blended drink.
You can substitute tofu for cashews for a less caloric drink.

1/3 c	Cashews
1¾ c	Water
1 Tbl	Lecithin granules
7	Strawberries, whole frozen
1/4 c	Blueberries, frozen
2 Tbl	Honey

Blend everything until thick and creamy.

SERVES: 2

Almond Milk

A creamy white nut beverage sweetened with raisins; easy to make.
Use like milk: over cereal, in smoothies, in baking, or just to drink.
The process of soaking almonds activates its food enzymes,
making its protein easier to digest. (If you like a
sweeter milk, add 2 tsp. maple syrup.)

3/4 c	Raw almonds
1/4 c	Raisins
5 c	Warm water

1. Put the almonds in a jar and cover them with water. Soak them for 18 hours. Put the raisins in a small bowl and soak them until soft.
2. Strain the almonds and raisins into a blender (reserve soak water for smoothies). Blend with 1 cup of water for several minutes. Add another cup of water and blend for another minute.
3. Strain the almond milk into a carafe. (Use a fine mesh strainer, the more you strain the almond milk, the finer the milk will be.) Stir in the rest of the water, then strain again. Refrigerate. Save the strained almond meal for breakfast, and top with sliced fruits.

Fresh Fig Vanilla Shake

A delicious creamy shake using fresh seasonal figs.
If using dried figs, soak overnight before using and
reduce the honey date quantity to five.

3 large	Fresh figs, chopped
1 c	"Lite" soy milk or nut milk
9	Honey dates, pitted
1/2 tsp	Vanilla extract
1/2 c	Ice cubes

Blend well in a blender. You may add 1 tablespoon each of bee pollen and soy protein powder for extra nutrition. Makes 2½ cups.

SERVES: 1 - 2

We can feed everyone!

100,000,000 people could be adequately nourished using the land, water and energy that would be freed from growing livestock feed if Americans reduced their intake of meat by 10%.

Realities for the 90's, excerpted from *Diet for a New America,* by John Robbins

Pineapple Date Shake

A sweet delight.

3/4 c	Pineapple juice, unsweetened
5	Honey dates, pitted
1	Frozen banana, chopped
	Several ice cubes

Blend well, adding ice as needed.

SERVES: 1

Mocha Date Shake

A protein-packed sweet tofu shake.

2 tsp	Pero (or coffee substitute)
1/3 c	Water
1/3 c	Honey dates, pitted
1/2 c	Silken soft tofu*
1/2 c	Crushed ice
1/2	Banana, frozen
1/2 Tbl	Roasted carob powder (or cocoa powder)

Dissolve pero and carob in water. Put everything into the blender and blend well until frothy.

*You may substitute soy milk for tofu, but use more ice to make shake thicker.

SERVES: 1

Iced Mochas

A gourmet delight on a hot day. Tastes like an iced coffee mocha. This can also be served hot, for a morning or dessert treat.

1 Tbl	Pero (or other instant grain beverage)
1 tsp	Roasted carob powder (or cocoa)
1/4 c	Hot water
1/2 tsp	Vanilla extract
1 Tbl	Honey
1 c	Lite vanilla soy milk
Dash	Cinnamon
	Ice cubes

1. Dissolve pero and carob in hot water, add honey and vanilla.
2. Fill up a large glass with ice cubes, pour in pero mixture, then top with soy milk and cinnamon. Stir and enjoy!

SERVES: 1

Classic Cashew Nut Milk

A delicious, creamy milk alternative. Pour over cereals or use as milk.

1/2 c	Raw cashew pieces, finely ground in nut mill
1 Tbl	Flax seeds, finely ground in nut mill
4 c	Water
2 Tbl	Maple syrup
2 Tbl	Lecithin granules

1. Put powdery fine ground cashews and flax seeds into a blender. Add 1 cup water and blend. Then add the rest of the ingredients and liquefy well.
2. Strain into a bowl through a fine sieve two times. Refrigerate. Keeps 3 or 4 days.

Hot 'Eggless' Nog

A creamy, sweet festive drink, very satisfying in cold weather.

4 c	Vanilla "lite" soy milk
2 Tbl	Egg replacer
1 Tbl	Lecithin granules
1 tsp each	Vanilla extract and rum extract
1/4 tsp	Almond extract
1/4 c	Honey
1/2 tsp	Cinnamon

Using a blender, blend everything until smooth and creamy. To serve hot, heat on medium in a pot, stirring often with a whisk. When foamy, pour into mugs. Top with a sprinkle of cinnamon.

NOTE: For a thicker consistency, add 1/2 tsp arrowroot before heating.
SERVES: 3

Lecithin Facts

1. High in choline — which is necessary for brain and liver functioning.
2. Is comprised of 50% essential fatty acids by weight.
3. A dissolvent — breaks down fat, emulsifies fatty substances facilitating their elimination from the body.

Add 1 Tbl of Lecithin granules to smoothies or baked goods for a smoother texture.

Breakfast Ecstasies

Cantaloupe Cleanser   19

Pink Tropic   19

Golden Mandala   19

Vibrant Oatmeal with Raw Applesauce   20

Vanilla Rice Cream with Blueberries   21

Swedish Oatmeal Pancakes   22

Universal Tofu Pancake   23

Pumpkin Walnut Pancakes   23

Matzo Scrambler   24

Breakfast Burritos   25

Blue Corn Cakes with Strawberries   26

Banana French Toast   27

Pumpkin Orange Muffins   28

Apple Spice Muffins   28

Banana Walnut Cornbread   29

Sweet Oatmeal Corn Muffins   30

Sprouted Wheat and Date Loaf   31

Fruitful Breakfasts

*These can be quickly prepared for individual meals.
Use lime or lemon juice to accent or Tofu Pineapple Creme
(page 283), Raw Apple Sauce (page 18), Apple Creme
(page 282), or Orange Sauce (page 281).*

Cantaloupe Cleanser

1/2   **Cantaloupe, seeded**
     Red grapes, seedless
     Lime wedge

Fill cantaloupe with red grape halves and serve with a wedge of lime to squeeze on top.

Pink Tropic

1/2   **Papaya, seeded**
1/4 c **Raspberries or strawberries**
     Lime wedges

Fill papaya with raspberries and squeeze lime on top, save one lime wedge for garnish.

Golden Mandala

1   **Pear, cored and cut in 8 spears**
1/2-1 **Banana, sliced**
1   **Kiwi, peeled and sliced**
1   **Strawberry**

Place pear spears radiating out vertically from the center of a circle (like bicycle spokes), leaving a small area in the center for the other fruits. Toss banana and kiwi slices, then put them in the center of the circle. Decorate top with a (whole or sliced) strawberry.

Massage

Massage promotes wellness of body, mind and spirit. It increases the circulation, enhances oxygenation of the tissues and muscles, and relaxes and rebalances the energy flow of the body.

Through massage, the lymph system becomes stimulated to cleanse the blood through its elaborate filtration process.

The benefits of massage go way beyond its physical dimension. It enriches all aspects of our daily life.

Notes:

Vibrant Oatmeal

This is a simple raw muesli and is very good for you.
By topping with raw apple sauce and some raisins or nuts,
a splendid morning meal is created.

1 c	Rolled oats
1 c	Pure water (or Almond Milk, page 12)

Raw Applesauce

2	Apples, cored (peel if you wish) and chopped
2 Tbl	Water or fruit juice
1/2 tsp	Cinnamon
1/2 Tbl	Lemon juice
	Dash of maple extract (optional)
Toppings:	Soaked raisins, chopped raw nuts of choice

1. Stir water into oats in a medium bowl. Let sit overnight to soften oats.
2. Pulse chop apples, water, cinnamon and lemon juice in a food processor until a sauce texture is created.
3. Divide the oatmeal into 4 bowls, pour apple sauce on top of each, add some nuts and raisins if desired.

SERVES: 4

Vanilla Rice Cream with Blueberries

Finely ground toasted brown rice, cooked as a hot cereal provides a very comforting and aromatic breakfast.

1 c	**Organic brown rice**
3½ c	**Water (or 2 c water and 2 c soy milk)**
2 tsp	**Vanilla**
1/2 c	**Blueberries, rinsed**
	Maple syrup or honey drizzled on top
	White Almond Milk (page 12)

1. Toast dry rice in a medium hot skillet for 2 to 3 minutes, stirring constantly until light brown. Finely grind in a blender or nut grinder until powdery.
2. Bring water (and soy milk) to a boil in a large pot, whisk in rice cream; cover and simmer for 10 to 12 minutes.
3. Stir in vanilla and sweetener of choice and top with fresh blueberries.

SERVES: 3 - 4

If everyone were to take responsibility for their own lives, we would have a completely different world.

Notes:

Swedish Oatmeal Pancakes

*A delicious wheat-free oatmeal pancake that is easy to make.
Warmly spiced with cinnamon and cardamom.*

1 c	**Rolled oats**
1 c	**Water**
3/4 c	**Vanilla soy milk**
2 Tbl	**Egg replacer**
1½ Tbl	**Baking powder**
2 tsp	**Maple syrup**
1/2 tsp	**Cinnamon**
1/4 tsp	**Cardamom**

1. Soak oats in water in a medium bowl overnight (or for
   20 minutes) to soften.
2. Put soy milk, egg replacer, baking powder, maple syrup and
   spices in a food processor and blend well. Fold blended mixture
   into oats. Heat up a skillet on medium heat for at least
   5 minutes.
3. Lightly oil the skillet and turn to low, spoon batter onto skillet to
   desired size and cook until bubbles appear, or until the liquid
   sets. Turn over and cook the other side.

Top with natural raspberry syrup, maple syrup or Apple Creme
(page 281).

SERVES: 4 (at 2 pancakes per person)

Universal Tofu Pancake

Vanilla and banana add flavor to this light pancake.
Serve with fresh berries and/or syrup of choice.

1 pack	**Silken tofu**
1/2 c	**Vanilla "lite" soy milk**
1 Tbl	**Honey**
1/2	**Ripe banana**
1 Tbl	**Vegetable oil**
1 c	**Whole wheat pastry flour**
1 Tbl	**Baking powder**

1. Preheat a griddle on medium heat for 5 minutes, then turn to low.
2. Blend the first 5 ingredients. Mix the flour and baking powder in a bowl. Whisk wet into dry. Let sit for a couple of minutes.
3. Lightly oil griddle, spoon on batter, spreading thinly to desired size. When bubbles appear, flip over. Pancakes will flip easily if griddle is sufficiently hot and if pancakes are cooked enough.

SERVES: 4

Pumpkin Walnut Pancakes

A fluffy pancake that is delicious with maple syrup.
Double this recipe for a breakfast for 4.

1/2 c	**Soy milk or White Almond Milk (page 12)**
1/2 c	**Canned pumpkin (mashed)**
2 Tbl	**Ripe banana, mashed**
2 tsp	**Egg replacer**
1/4 tsp	**Cinnamon**
1/2 c	**Whole wheat pastry flour**
1 Tbl	**Baking powder**
1/4 c	**Walnuts, chopped**

1. Preheat griddle for 5 minutes, then turn to low and lightly oil.
2. Put the first 4 items into a blender and blend well.
3. Stir together whole wheat pastry flour, baking powder and cinnamon. Using a whisk, blend the wet mixture into the dry ingredients. Stir in walnuts.
4. Let the batter sit for a couple of minutes before spooning onto griddle to the desired size. Cook each side of pancake for 2 minutes, or until they appear to have set. Serve with warm maple syrup.

SERVES: 2 (at 2 pancakes per person)

Welcome to the world of vegetarians

Nut Milks

The use of nut milks is not a new alternative to cow's milk. Up until the end of the 18th century, Europeans were making almond and walnut milk to feed their families. Almonds were introduced to Italy by the Arabs, who valued them for their high nutritional qualities. In India, they made coconut milk. China had primarily soybean milk alternatives. Native Americans made milk from pecans and hickory nuts.

Notes:

Matzo Scrambler

*A healthy take off on matzos and eggs, using tofu,
sauteed peppers and onions. Makes a filling breakfast or brunch.
Matzos are an unleavened cracker-bread.*

1/2 c	**Plain soy milk**
1/2 Tbl	**Arrowroot powder**
2	**Matzo crackers, crumbled (whole wheat)**
1 tsp	**Soy sauce**
1/2 c	**Red onion, chopped**
1/2 c	**Bell peppers, chopped (use 1/4 red, 1/4 green)**
1 large	**Garlic clove, pressed**
1 c	**Firm tofu, crumbled**
1 tsp	**Basil**
	Sea salt and cracked pepper to taste
1/3 c	**Grated soy cheese (optional)**

1. Whisk together the soy milk and arrowroot in a medium bowl, add the matzos and soy sauce. Let soak for 5 minutes.
2. Saute the onion, peppers and garlic in water for a couple of minutes. Stir in the matzo mixture, tofu and spices.
3. Let cook for 5 minutes, stirring occasionally. Serve with some salsa or chile sauce on the side. Option: grate soy cheese on top and cover the pan to melt cheese a few minutes before serving.

SERVES: 2

Breakfast Burritos

Potatoes, tofu and peppers, sauteed and rolled up in a burrito and topped with green chile or tomato sauce, makes for a hearty brunch.

	Flour tortillas
2 c	**Potatoes, cubed in 1/2" squares**
1 c	**Bell peppers, chopped small**
2 tsp	**Garlic, minced**
1 each	**Onion and tomato, chopped**
3 Tbl	**Liquid aminos**
1/2 c	**Water**
1 lb	**Tofu, mashed with:**
2 tsp	**Cumin**
1 tsp	**Oregano**
1/2 c	**Grated soy jalapeño jack cheese OR Cheezy Sauce (page 121)**
1 recipe	**Green chile (page 119) OR Fresh Tomato Coulis (Mex-Style) (page 110)**

1. Heat the tortillas on a griddle until soft. Then wrap the tortillas in foil and keep warm in a 200º oven.
2. Steam potatoes until soft. Set aside.
3. Saute the peppers, garlic and onion in a skillet with liquid aminos and water. Stir in the tofu mashed with spices, and potatoes. Cook 10 minutes until hot and all flavors meld.
4. Put about 1/2 c sauteed vegetable mixture down the center of a burrito and roll the burrito up around the vegetables, tucking the ends in while rolling. Top with a hot chile sauce.

SERVES: 4

Protein

It is almost impossible not to get enough protein when we eat an unrefined, whole natural foods diet.

It is not necessary to combine protein sources (such as rice with beans), at every meal.

The quality of complete vegetarian proteins (those containing the 8 essential amino acids), has been proven to be superior to, or at least equal to, the quality of animal proteins. They are: sunflower seeds, sesame seeds, pumpkin seeds, almonds, soybeans, peanuts, potatoes, buckwheat, all leafy greens and most fruits.

Notes:

Blue Corn Cakes with Strawberries

A very fortifying down-home favorite.

1/2 c	Blue corn meal
1/2 c	Whole wheat pastry flour
2 tsp	Baking powder
Dash	Sea salt
1 tsp	Egg replacer
1 c	Vanilla "lite" soy milk
2 Tbl	Vegetable oil
1 c	Sliced strawberries (if using frozen strawberries, let thaw on counter while making recipe)

1. Preheat a griddle on medium heat, sift blue corn meal, whole wheat pastry flour, salt, baking powder and egg replacer into a bowl.
2. Beat oil and soy milk together in another bowl.
3. Whisk together the wet mixture into the dry ingredients and let the batter stand for 5 minutes (until puffy). DO NOT REMIX!
4. Spoon the batter gently from the sides of the bowl onto a lightly oiled griddle. Make 4" cakes, turn when the edges are dry.
5. Top with strawberries and maple syrup and serve 'em hot!

SERVES: 6 cakes

Banana French Toast

A naturally sweet and delicious breakfast.
The longer the bread soaks, the more delicate the "toast."

1½ Tbl	**Egg replacer**
4 Tbl	**Water**
1/2	**Ripe banana**
1/2 c	**Vanilla "lite" soy milk**
6 slices	**Whole wheat French bread, sliced in 3/4" thick slices**

Preheat a griddle on medium-low at least 5 minutes before using.

1. Blend the egg replacer and water until frothy, using a blender or mixer. Put into a shallow container or a bowl with a flat bottom.
2. Put the banana and soy milk into the blender and whip a couple of seconds. Add to the bowl with the egg replacer mixture.
3. Put the bread slices into the liquid mixture one at a time. Let each side soak up liquid until soft. Turn griddle to low, spray with vegetable spray, then lay bread on griddle. Flip the bread slices when each side is golden.

Serve with warm maple syrup and/or a fresh fruit garnish like orange slices and strawberries.

SERVES: 2 - 3

Bananas contain one of the highest amounts of natural sugars. For this reason, they make a wonderful sugar replacement; used as a puree to sweeten desserts, or frozen and added to smoothies.

Bananas are high in magnesium, which calms the body system, and high in potassium, which is necessary for cellular electrolyte balance.

Notes:

Pumpkin Orange Muffins

Hints of orange and maple make a nice addition to this pumpkin bread, which is moistened with a prune puree.

1/2 recipe	Prune Puree (page 259)
1 c	Pumpkin, canned
3 Tbl	Pure maple syrup
1 tsp	Cinnamon
1 tsp	Grated Orange Rind (page 277)
1 Tbl	Egg replacer (mixed with 2 Tbl water)
1 c	Whole wheat pastry flour
1 Tbl	Baking powder
1/2 c	Walnuts, chopped and lightly toasted (optional)

Preheat oven to 375°.

1. Prepare prune puree in a food processor. Then add the pumpkin plus the next 4 ingredients and puree them well.
2. Sift the dry ingredients into a medium bowl, fold in the wet ingredients. When almost mixed, stir in walnuts.
3. Lightly coat muffin tins with vegetable spray or oil, and spoon the batter into them. Bake for 20-25 minutes, or until wet fork inserted comes out clean.

Apple Spice Muffins

For scrumptious muffins, follow recipe for Apple Spice Cake on page 276. Pour into lightly oiled muffin tins and bake for 40 to 45 minutes, or until toothpick inserted comes out clean.

Banana Walnut Cornbread

A coarse grain cornbread, loaded with bananas and walnuts, which keeps well in the refrigerator.

2-3 Tbl	**Honey**	
2	**Ripe bananas**	
1/4 c	**Canola oil (organic)**	
1/2 c	**Soy milk**	
2 tsp	**Vanilla**	

Sift together: 1 c	**Corn meal**	
1 c	**Whole wheat pastry flour**	
1 Tbl	**Baking powder**	
1 tsp	**Soda**	
1/2 Tsp	**Cinnamon**	

Stir in: 1½ c	**Walnuts, chopped**	
1	**Banana, sliced**	
Decorate with:	**Walnut halves**	

1. Blend in the first 5 items in a food processor until smooth.
2. Add sifted group to the food processor, pulse chop a few times until just blended.
3. Transfer to a mixing bowl. Stir in the walnuts and sliced banana.
4. Pour into a lightly oiled nonstick baking pan and decorate the top of the bread as desired.

Bake 350º for 40 to 50 minutes, until brown on top (test for doneness with a toothpick or knife).

NOTE: Makes 1 loaf

It is said that the botanical name for banana — musa sapientum, "the man who thinks"— came from a legend about wise men who sat under the shade of a banana tree, eating bananas.

The banana is actually an herb, not a tree.

Notes:

Sweet Oatmeal Corn Muffins

A light and moist muffin that can be made in a flash. This is a great basic muffin in which you can add fresh or dried fruit.

Blend:
1 lb	Soft tofu
1/2 c	Orange juice
1 tsp	Vanilla extract
1/4 c	Honey
1	Banana

Sift:
1 Tbl	Baking powder
1 tsp	Baking soda
1 c	Corn flour

Stir:
1⅓ c	Rolled oats
1 c	Softened raisins* or dried apricots (optional)

1. Blend the first 5 items in a blender until creamy and smooth.
2. Sift next group (powders and flour) into a medium bowl; stir in oats.
3. Gently add wet mixture into the dry ingredients and spoon into oiled muffin tins. Bake at 375° for 20 minutes (or until toothpick inserted comes out clean).

*Soften by soaking in warm water for 15 minutes.

SERVING SUGGESTIONS:
Serve with your favorite jam.

MAKES: 1 dozen

Sprouted Wheat and Date Loaf

An "Essene" style* bread, made from sprouted wheat kernels ground up with dates and orange juice and slowly baked to create a sweet moist loaf with a soft chewy crust. This can also be "baked" in a food dehydrator.

2 c	**Hard wheat kernels, sprouted**
1/4 c	**Orange juice**
15	**Dates, pitted (1/3 cup packed)**

1. To sprout wheat, soften kernels by covering them with water for 24 hours. Rinse and drain twice a day for 1 to 2 more days, until white sprouts appear.
2. Put wheat sprouts into a food processor or grinder and pulse chop until kernels break up, about 1 minute.
3. Add orange juice and dates and pulse together several seconds.
4. Spread onto a nonstick, small rectangular baking pan, then bake for 30 to 40 minutes at 325°.

Cut into squares when cool. Keep refrigerated.

*Essene bread is a slowly baked sprouted bread, using no flours, oils, eggs, or refined sugar; according to the *Essene Gospel of Peace.*

SERVING SUGGESTION:
Top with Homemade Apple Sauce (page 20)
for a delicious breakfast or treat.

260,000,000 acres of trees and forests have been cleared, burned, chopped and wiped out due to the American meat habit.

If we Americans adopt a meat-free diet, we would have 204,000,000 more acres of forest land.

From *Realities for the 90's,* excerpted from *Diet for a New America,* by John Robbins.

Snacks and Sandwiches

♦ Kid Stuff
  Apple Nutbutter-wich   35
  Crunchy Honey Almond Stars   35
  Elephant Spread   36
  Bee-better Butter   36
  Monkey Toast   36

♦ Mexican
  Nachoz   37
  Tostadas   38
  Sesame Eggplant Tacos   39
  Chile Tempeh Tacos   40

♦ Sandwiches
  Lentil Paté and Tomato-wich   41
  Vegetable Mousse Sandwiches   42
  Classic Tofu Sandwich   43
  Bagel and Paté Platter   44
  Tofu Salad Chapati Rollups   45
  Black Bean Chapati Burrito   45

♦ Salad Rolls
  Rice Paper Salad Rolls   46
  Seasprout Salad Rolls   47
  Seed Cheese Cabbage Rolls   48
  Seed Cheese Sushi Rolls   48
  Sprouted Sunseed Sushi   49
  Sunseed Aragula Rolls   49

Apple Nutbutter-wich

This also makes a quick and nourishing breakfast treat.

Per person
1-2 slices	**Whole wheat (poppyseed) bread**
1 Tbl	**Peanut butter**
1 Tbl	**Unsweetened fruit preserve or apple butter**
6	**Thin slices of apple**

Spread nut butter on one side of bread, arrange apple slices on top. Spread jelly on other slice and press together. If serving as an openface sandwich, put preserves over peanut butter and fan apples on top.

Crunchy Honey Almond Stars

A creative cut-out sandwich using cookie cutters. Children can make their own and eat their art piece!

1/2 c	**Banana, ripe, mashed**
2 tsp	**Honey (omit if desired)**
1/4 c	**Almond butter or tahini**
2 Tbl	**Almonds, minced**
	Whole wheat bread of choice

Whip together banana, honey and nut butter, stir in roasted almonds. Spread on a bread slice and sandwich together. Cut out shapes with cookie cutters.

Choose Wellness and Health ...

Choose happiness and joy. Find the things that make you smile, make you tingle and weave them into your daily life.

By choosing to live, eat and think in a healthy way we can re-create our world.

You really are what you think, eat, and aspire to. Being responsible for ourselves is the ultimate challenge. Let your spirit shine, choose a healthy pattern of living ... it is your choice, it is your chance.

Notes:

Try these different toast toppings using bananas. They'll give added potassium to your diet and are a nice change from jellies and jams.

Elephant Spread

1	Banana, ripe
1 Tbl	Peanut butter (substitute 2 Tbl. grated apple for a non-fat version)

Mix together and spread on rice cakes, celery sticks or toast. Sprinkle raisins on top.

SERVES: 2 - 3

Bee-better Butter

A golden yellow spread with the supercharged properties of bee pollen.

1 tsp	Bee pollen
1/2	Banana, ripe
1 tsp	Tahini or nut butter

Stir together, spread on toast of choice or on a rice cake.

SERVES: 1

Monkey Toast

1/2	Banana, sliced lengthwise

Spread on hot toasted bread of choice. Good on cinnamon raisin bread.

SERVES: 1

Live vital foods create live vital cells, which are necessary for the experience of total vibrant living.

Nachoz

Wow! All this and dairyless too! Use our sensational Jalapeño Cheezy Sauce to drizzle and bake on your no-oil tortilla chips for a fun nosh!

Traditional:

1/2 lb	Tortilla chips (or a plateful)
1 c	Jalapeño Cheezy Sauce (page 122)
1/2 c	Salsa (on top)

Baja Style add:

1 c	Black beans

Other options:

Black olives
Green Goddess Guacamole (page 126)

1. Spread chips out on a ovenproof serving platter.
2. Heat up Cheezy Sauce and drizzle all over chips. You can layer this for an even cheezy-ness effect. If you're using beans, layer in with Cheezy Sauce.
3. Broil at 400° for 15 minutes. Top with green chile or salsa. Eat warm.

Notes:

Tostadas

A crispy tortilla shell holds the Jalapeño Cheezy Sauce, beans and salad items with a flair. Easy to prepare.

1 or 2	**Flour tortillas per person**
2 c	**Sprouted Frijoles (page 206)**
***1/2 c**	**Jalapeño Cheezy Sauce (page 122)**

Salad toppings:	**Finely grated cabbage**
	Shredded beets and carrots
	Tomato slices
	Salsa
	Cilantro leaves

Optional:	**Grated soy cheese for top**

1. Preheat oven to broil. Create the crisp shells by putting tortillas inside oven-proof soup bowls (a flat bottom bowl with 1" to 2" high sides). Bake for 3 to 5 minutes until crispy but not brown. Use potholders and do not touch plates — they're *HOT!*
2. Heat beans and Jalapeño Cheezy Sauce together. (For a thicker mixture, stir in 1 tsp arrowroot powder). Spread on top of the tortilla shells.
3. Layer with salad items in the order they are given.

Eat with your hands, or with a fork or chopsticks.

*You can substitute 1/2 cup grated soy cheese and add 1/4 tsp each of cumin and red chile powder.

SERVES: 2 - 3 as a main dish (double bean amounts for 4 - 6 servings)

Sesame Eggplant Tacos

A soft taco, filled with grilled eggplant or
eggplant spread, and salad. Delish!

Corn tortillas
Grilled eggplant strips
(topped with sesame seeds)
OR
Babaganush (page 125)
Tomato slices
Alfalfa sprouts
Lemon squeeze and favorite dressing OR
Creamy Ranchero Dressing (page 93)

1. Prepare eggplant spread or grill eggplant (see side of page).
2. Heat both sides of tortilla on a hot griddle.
3. Put eggplant strips or Babaganush spread in center of tortilla,
   then top with tomatoes and sprouts. Top with Creamy
   Ranchero Dressing. Eat them hot off the griddle.

To keep tortillas hot: You can put hot tortillas in a soft towel and
wrap them up in tin foil.

Quick Grilling on a Griddle

Pre-heat a griddle on medium heat while preparing vegetables. Slice zucchini and eggplant lengthwise 3/8" thick, cut mushrooms in half, and peppers into flat rectangles. Spray griddle with a natural vegetable oil spray. Squeeze a little lemon or liquid aminos on vegetables, or if you choose, drizzle a couple of drops of olive oil on them. Lay the vegetables on the griddle and cook each side for 3 to 5 minutes. Mushrooms take 1 minute each side.

Notes:

Chile Tempeh Tacos

*A Baja style soft taco of broiled spicy tempeh,
shredded cabbage and salsa!*

1 pack	Tempeh, steamed for 5 minutes
1 Tbl each	Lemon juice and aminos (or soy sauce)

Spicy dip:	2 tsp	Chile powder
	1 tsp	Onion powder
	1 tsp	Cumin

As needed:	Cabbage, finely shredded
	Fresh tomato salsa
	Corn tortillas
	Avocado slices

Sauce:	Creamy Ranchero Dressing (page 93)

1. Cut tempeh into 1/2" thick strips. Mix together the lemon and soy sauce. Dip tempeh in sauce.
2. Shake together dry spices and dip tempeh strips into them. Broil each side of tempeh a few minutes.
3. Heat tortillas on a griddle, put broiled tempeh in center of tortilla. Fill with cabbage, salsa and sauce.

SERVES: 1 pack tempeh will serve 4

"And when
you eat,
never eat
unto fullness."

Jesus, *Essene Gospel of Peace*

Lentil Paté and Tomato Sandwich

A delicious hearty sandwich. Assemble hot from toaster oven and enjoy.

Per sandwich:

2 slices	Sprouted whole wheat bread, toasted
2 slices	Lentil Paté (page 145)
3 slices	Tomato
	Sprouts
4	Spinach leaves, washed and dried
	Eggless mayo

Assemble by putting paté on one side of toast, then layer tomato and sprouts on top. On the other slice of bread put mayo and spinach leaves. Press together the two sides and cut diagonally.

Notes:

Vegetable Mousse Sandwiches

All the vegetable mousses listed in this book make terrific sandwiches,
especially when served on toasted bread with lettuce and tomato.

Per person:
2 slices	Vegetable mousse of choice (pp. 140-144)
2 slices	Tomato
2 slices	Toasted bread

Your choice:	Spinach leaves, romaine or other lettuce
1/2 tsp	Eggless mayo or dressing

On toasted bread, put mayo on one piece and mousse slices on
other. Put tomato and lettuce over mousse and close sandwich. Slice
in half if desired.

SERVING SUGGESTIONS:
Serve with chips and veggie sticks.

SERVES: 1

Classic Tofu Sandwich

A hearty satisfying sandwich made with toasted whole grain bread, crisp vegetables and braised tofu.

Per person:

2 slices	Whole wheat bread
2 slices	Tofu (about 1 oz)
Dash of	Tamari and toasted sesame oil
1/2 Tbl	Tofu mayo
1/2 Tbl	Dijon mustard
	Dash of dill
	Cracked pepper
	Alfalfa sprouts
	Tomato slices
	Red onion, thinly sliced
Optional:	Avocado slices
	Sauerkraut

1. Toast bread, sprinkle tamari and sesame oil on tofu cutlet, broil each side until hot.
2. Spread mayo on one slice of bread, dijon mustard on the other. On top of the dijon mustard layer the tofu, tomato, spices, red onion slices and sprouts. Close sandwich and slice diagonally. Enjoy!

It takes 2,500 gallons of water to make 1 lb of meat ... the equivalent water usage of a family of four for one month. Just imagine that every time someone eats a 1/4-pound burger, they are using 625 gallons of water.

From *Realities for the 90's*, excerpted from *Diet for a New America*, by John Robbins

Notes:

Bagel and Paté Platter

For scrumptious snacking or brunches, serve 1 or 2 types of Patés from this book, along with tomatoes and toasted bagels.*

> **Bagels, sliced and toasted**
> **Tomato slices**
> **Black olives, minced**
> **Cucumber and red onions, thinly sliced**

Patés of choice: **Green Chile and Garlic (page 141)**
Tomato Red Pepper (page 140)
Spinach Mushroom (page 144)
Lentil Paté (page 145)

Arrange a platter of sliced tomatoes, cucumbers and red onion, and sliced patés. Put olives into a small bowl with a serving spoon. Keep bagel slices warm in a bread basket wrapped in a towel.

*Try sprouted whole wheat (no egg) bagels.

SERVING SUGGESTIONS:
Alfalfa sprouts go well with this, too.

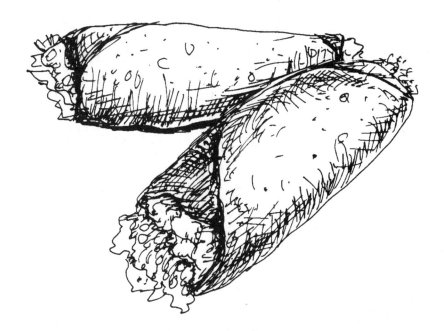

Chapati Rollup

Whole wheat chapatis make an excellent sandwich holder,
especially if heated like a tortilla.

Tofu Salad Chapatis

Per person:

1/4 c	**Tofu salad**
2 slices	**Tomato, cut in half**
	Sprouts
1	**Whole wheat chapati**

Warm both sides of a chapati on a griddle. Spread tofu salad down center, add tomato slices and sprouts (and a dab of salad dressing if desired), then roll up and enjoy!

Black Bean Chapati Burritos

1/4 c	**Instant black beans (with water added to form a thick paste)**
2 Tbl	**Salsa**
	Shredded lettuce or sprouts
1	**Chapati**

Warm up chapatis, place bean paste down center. Top with rest of ingredients and roll up.

Chapatis are an Indian soft bread, similar to flour tortillas. They are generally found as whole wheat chapatis, or made from sprouted wheat kernels. They make a wonderful sandwich holder. Heat on a griddle to warm.

Rice Paper Salad Rolls

A quick exotic and delightful meal that can be made ahead of time and kept in the fridge. Great for snacking!

6	Rice pancakes*
6	Shittake mushrooms, dried

Sauce:

1 Tbl each	Lemon juice, tamari, water
1	Garlic clove, minced
1/2 tsp	Ginger, minced

1 tsp	Honey
8 oz pack	Braised tofu (firm) cut in 1/2" strips
	Bean sprouts (or buckwheat/ sunflower greens)
Several	Cilantro sprigs
1 small pack	Bean thread noodles, rinsed and quickly boiled to soften

Dipping sauce:

2 Tbl	Rice vinegar
1 Tbl	Soy sauce

1. Rinse rice pancakes one at a time under tepid running water. Place pancakes on the counter to soften.
2. Soak mushrooms in water to soften. After 15 minutes, stem and slice. Sauté mushrooms with sauce in a small skillet, 3 to 5 minutes.
3. Assemble: put some noodles down the center of each pancake, add mushroom slices, tofu, sprouts and cilantro and roll up.

Don't pack too full or rice paper will tear (moisten edge to seal). Dip in dipping sauce if desired.

*Available at oriental grocers, rice is pounded into flat cakes and dried. They must be rehydrated before use.

SERVES: 6

Seasprout Salad Rolls

A seaweed/sprout/corn mixture deliciously tossed in a sesame dressing and stuffed inside a rice paper "burrito." Sea vegetables are rich in minerals, especially iodine, and should be a regular feature to your meals.

1/2 c	**Hiziki, dried**
1/4 c	**Dulse, dried**
1/4 c	**Salad dressing***
1 c	**Alfalfa sprouts (pull apart to separate)**
1/4 c	**Sweet white corn kernels**
1/4 c	**Cilantro leaves**
1/2	**Lime, juiced (1 Tbl)**
6	**Rice paper pancakes, moistened (or toasted Nori sheets)**

1. Put the hiziki and dulse into a glass bowl, pour water on top to barely cover, and stir and let sit until soft (approx. 20 min.). Drain, rinse, drain and set aside in a medium bowl.
2. Pour salad dressing over seaweeds. Toss in sprouts, corn, cilantro and lime.
3. Put salad mixture in center of each softened rice pancake, and roll up burrito style. Place on a platter. Slice Nori rolls in sixths if using Nori sheets (do not fold ends in).

*Use Sesame Miso or Sesame Cilantro (page 100), or Green Thai Goddess (page 103).

SERVING SUGGESTION:
Garnish with cucumber spears, tomato slices and cilantro sprigs.

SERVES: 6 rolls

Human Active B_{12} in Sea Vegetables

B_{12} MICROGRAMS

Alaria	Laver	Kelp	Dulse
15.4	5.3	3.4	2.05

From *Conscious Eating*, Gabriel Cousens, M.D.

Notes:

Seed Cheese Cabbage Rolls

Peppers, pickles and carrots accent this creamy vegetable spread.
Tightly rolled up in a cabbage leaf, these cabbage rolls
make a perfect snack at lunch.

1¼ c	Carrots, finely grated
1/3 c	Red bell pepper, minced
1	Garlic clove, pressed
2/3 c	Almond Cashew Seed Cheese (page 137)
2 Tbl	Dill pickle, minced
1 tsp each	Onion powder, dill weed, soy sauce
1/4 tsp	Grated lemon peel (optional)
6	Green cabbage leaves

Mix vegetables and spices into seed cheese. Using 2 heaping tablespoons of seed cheese mixture, tightly roll up "burrito style" in a cabbage leaf. (Parboil leaf in boiling water for 30 seconds if cabbage is tough.) Fold ends under as you roll up to prevent filling from escaping. Refrigerate. Makes 6 rolls.

Seed Cheese Sushi

Per roll:	2 Tbl	Vegetable Seed Cheese (page 139)
		Tomato slices
		Sprouts of choice
		Cilantro sprigs
	1	Toasted Nori (sushi) sheet

Lay vegetable seed cheese in center of a Nori sheet. Layer tomato, sprouts, cilantro and roll up Nori sheet. A few drops of salad dressing inside is also tasty if you like a juicy roll.

Sprouted Sunseed Sushi

This tasty carrot/sprouted sun seed and tahini dip makes a great filling for sandwich rolls.

1/2 c	**Sprouted Sun Seed Carrot Dip (page 124)**
	Sprouts
	Spinach leaves
1/2	**Tomato, sliced**
2	**Toasted Nori sheets**
1/4	**Avocado, sliced**

Spread 1/4 cup of the dip down the center of each Nori roll. Lay 2 avocado slices down center, follow with tomato, sprouts and pack down with spinach leaves. Roll up tightly (moisten edge to close). Cut in half and enjoy.

Sunseed Arugula Rolls

A light meal that is quick to prepare. Arugula has a wonderful nutty taste.

4	**Rice paper pancakes (1/4 round size)**
3/4 c	**Sprouted Sun Seed Carrot Dip (page 124)**
2	**Mushrooms, sliced**
24	**Arugula sprigs, washed, stems removed**
Optional:	**Red pepper strips, tomato slices, red onion slices**

Moisten rice paper in tepid water, let rice paper sit on counter to soften. Spread 2 Tbl of the dip in center of each rice pancake. Lay 2 mushroom slices on each, add arugula and any of the other vegetables. Roll up the rice pancake in a cone shape. Serve with a salad sauce for dipping.

SERVES: 2

May the Life Force Be with You!

The power-house foods of this planet are sprouts. Sprouted seeds, nuts, grains and grasses contain the essence of life. All essential nutrients lie within the seeds and are awakened when sprouted.

Sprouts contain essential fatty acids, vitamin E, lecithin and B vitamins, proteins, enzymes and minerals. They are full of fiber and should not be cooked, which destroys the vibrancy of their nutrients and enzymes. Eat your sprouts daily. Be a powerhouse!

Salads

♦ *Fruit Salads*

    Fresh Fruit Kabobs   53

    Honolulu Toss Salad   54

    Super "C" Salad   55

♦ *Salads with Fruit*

    Confetti Salad   56

    Orange Fennel Salad   57

    Ruby Fennel Salad   58

    Orange Palm Heart Delight   59

♦ *Appetizer Salads*

    Jicama Sticks   59

    Red Onion Pickles   60

    Daikon Carrot Salad   60

    Marinated Hiziki   61

    Edamame Beans   61

    Oyster Mushroom Shooters   62

    Eggplant Arugula Disks   63

    Chilled Endive Vinaigrette   63

    Celery Victor   64

    Marinated Cucumbers   65

    Tomato Mushroom
       Vinaigrette   65

♦ *Light Salads*

    Mainstream Romaine   66

    Wild Greens Salad   67

    Fiesta Coleslaw   68

Harvest Hiziki Salad   69

Sea "Pasta" Vegetable Salad   70

Garbanzo Nile Salad   71

Celery Root Salad   72

Chard Ribbon Salad   72

A Better Beet Salad   73

Sweet Sesame Bok Choy   74

Minted Corn Salad   74

Broccoli Eggplant Pesto Salad   75

Spicy Sprout Salad   76

Ruby Slaw   76

Grilled Eggplant, Mushroom
    and Pepper Salad   77

Japanese Eggplant Salad   78

Thai Broccoli Salad   79

String Beans with Walnut
    Vinaigrette   80

♦ *Hearty Salads*

    Spicy Tofu Mushroom Salad   81

    Imperial Salad   82

    Tuscan Tomato Rice Salad   83

    Navy Bean Salad   84

    Chinese 5-Spice Tempeh Salad   85

    Marinated Bean Salad   86

    Holy Mole Pasta Salad   87

    Grilled Vegetable Pasta Salad   88

    Pasta Fo' Y'All   89

Fresh Fruit Kabobs

Using the freshest fruit in season — springtime through summer — arrange fresh fruit in sections on a large platter. Serve on long bamboo skewers with lime wedges.

1 **Papaya, cut into spears, without skin**
2 **Mangos, chop, remove peel**
2 **Bananas, cut in half, then half lengthwise**
3 **Kiwis, skin and slice**
3 **Peaches or apricots, quartered**
2 **Oranges, cut into wedges, slice away peel**
3 **Limes, cut in wedges**
   Bamboo skewers

Arrange the fruit on a large platter. Squeeze a few lime wedges over the papaya, mango and banana, dot the remaining limes around the platter. Skewer fruit like a "kabob," alternating the colors of the fruit.

SERVING SUGGESTIONS:
*You can also create a "mandala" shape with the fruit.
Arrange in concentric circles by making outer circle first, then working inward to the center. Banana and papaya do best on the outside, while smaller fruits go in the center.*

Salt Glow

Effective salt glow skin cleansing can be done in your own bathroom. Sea salt detoxifies by facilitating the release of impurities through the pores of your skin.

Begin by taking a warm shower, lather well with an herbal soap and then rinse off. Put 1 tablespoon of sea salt into a wet wash cloth and rub the salted wash cloth on your skin. Continue the salt glow process until your whole body experiences its tingling effect. Shower to remove all the salt from your skin, finish with a cool water rinse.

While your skin is still damp, massage a sesame-almond aromatherapy oil into your skin.

You will feel renewed with softer skin. Do this once a week or as desired ... let yourself Glow!

Notes:

Honolulu Tossed Salad

A tossed fresh fruit salad that you can improvise on,
depending on what's fresh, sweet, and in season.

1 or 2*	**Papaya, halved and seeded, skinned and chopped**
2 small	**Bananas, sliced (try apple bananas)**
2 c	**Pineapple, chopped**
1	**Mango, chopped**
1/2 c	**Raisins**
1	**Apple, cored and chopped (skin if not organic)**
1	**Orange, chopped**
2 Tbl	**Lemon juice (or lime)**
1 tsp	**Honey (optional)**
1	**Kiwi, sliced — use also as a garnish**

1. Add fresh cut fruit to a large work bowl.
2. Mix honey and lemon together. Toss them into the fruit bowl with your hands. Adjust honey/lemon mixture to taste. Chill. The lemon prevents the discoloration of the freshly chopped fruit.

*Note: Use a large "sunrise" papaya or 2 smaller ones.

SERVES: 4 as a main dish/6 as a side dish

Super "C" Salad

A sweet and juicy salad high in water content and vitamin C.

3 c	Orange sections, chopped
1 basket	Strawberries, sliced
3	Kiwis, skinned and sliced
1 Tbl	Lime juice

Toss together and serve, or chill ahead of time. The longer the salad sits, the more red it becomes from the juice of the strawberries. Stir before serving, because the juice will migrate to the bottom.

SERVES: 4

Dry Brush Massage

To keep your skin soft and smooth, to increase your circulation, and to slough away dry skin, regular use of a body brush is essential.

There are three types of brushes you can use: A natural fiber body brush (which also comes in a flexible mit or sling), a loofah (a dried fibrous vine plant), and an ayate or maguey cloth (woven fibers of agave or century plant).

Because this is mildly energizing, it is best done in the morning. Rub from feet to heart area in a small circular motion. Dry brushes give a more vigorous treatment, whereas the wet cloths or loofahs have a milder effect. Your body will radiate a rosy glow from the increase of blood flow into the layers of your skin. This is nourishing and exercising to your skin tissue. It also aids in cellulite reduction.

Do daily for best results.

Confetti Salad

A refreshing tossed salad of carrots, apple, celery, and currants, enhanced by mint and orange juice.

1 c	Currants
1/2 c	Boiling water
3 c	Carrots, finely grated
1/2 c	Celery, minced
1 c	Red delicious apple (1 medium), cored and sliced into small pieces
1/3 c	Orange juice
1/2 Tbl	Fresh mint, minced

1. Put the currants into a medium glass bowl, pour water on top and cover for a few minutes to soften.
2. Add grated carrots to the bowl along with the apple and celery. Toss ingredients well.
3. Stir in the mint and orange juice. Chill.

SERVES: 4

Venus ate from the garden of Love

Fennel

All parts of the fennel plant can be used. The root or bulb has a pronounced anise taste when eaten raw, and becomes more subtle when cooked. The leaves and young stalks can be eaten like celery. The seeds can be used to make a tea that soothes the stomach and intestines. The vapors from the tea are wonderful for a cleansing facial steam. Crushed fennel seeds add an Italian flair to tempeh and tomato sauces, and are especially delicious with chile flakes.

Orange and Fennel Salad

A light and juicy salad, refreshing in spring and summer menus or with spicy fare. Easy to make and simply delicious!

1 large	Fennel bulb
5 large	Oranges
2½ Tbl	Lime juice
1/2 c	Seedless red grapes, halved
1/4 c	Pomegranate seeds (optional)

1. Trim the top and bottom off fennel bulb. Set aside several green sprigs for garnish. Quarter bulb and then slice it as thin as possible. Put into a medium size bowl.
2. Peel, seed and cut oranges into sections, then chop into smaller pieces. Add to the bowl.
3. Stir in grape halves and toss everything with lime juice. Top with pomegranate seeds and fennel.

SERVES: 4

Notes:

Roman Goddess of Harvest

Ruby Fennel Salad

This salad is so simple, yet fresh and clean tasting.
The fennel and lemon lift your taste buds and the grapes
give a nice sweetness to the otherwise "rooty" beet.

1 large	Beet, chopped coarsely
1 large	Fennel bulb, chopped coarsely (save the sprigs for garnish)
1 c	Celery, chopped coarsely
1 c	Seedless grapes, halved lengthwise
1/4 c	Lemon juice

1. Finely grate first 3 items in a food processor.
2. Transfer to a medium bowl and stir in grapes and lemon juice. Toss the ingredients well until evenly coated with lemon juice. Serve on a romaine or a wide lettuce leaf with a sprig of fennel on top.

Orange Palm Heart Delight

Colorful and simply delicious!

1 can	**Palm hearts, sliced (7.7 oz)**
2	**Oranges, skinned, sliced and seeded**
2 tsp	**Parsley, minced**
1 Tbl	**Brown rice vinegar**
1/2 tsp	**Toasted sesame oil**

Stir together, chill or serve right away.

SERVES: 2

Jicama Sticks

Refreshing, crunchy and sweet. Jicama is a root used frequently in Mexican cuisine. Served here traditional, with lime and a dash of chile pepper. Balances spicy or hot foods.

1	**Jicama, peeled**
2	**Limes, divided use**
1½ tsp	**Chile powder**
1/8 tsp	**Sea salt**

1. Slice jicama into sticks, about 1/2" thick by 2-3" long.
2. Juice 1 lime and mix into jicama in a medium bowl.
3. Mix spices together and sprinkle on a plate. Dip one end of jicama in spices and place on a platter with lime wedges. Serve chilled.

Colors

Colors enrich our daily life. They make us feel good, make us smile. Colors are light rays emitting an energy vibration which have an effect on us. The purer the frequency of the color, the more positive the energy vibration. The brighter the color, the more powerful its effect.

To increase your energy, wear clear vibrant colors which lift the spirit. And most important, color your world with love.

Notes:

Red Onion Pickles

2 c   Thinly sliced red onions
1/4 c   Lemon juice

Mix together and refrigerate overnight. Use as a condiment for sandwiches, as appetizers or serve over salads.

Daikon Carrot Salad

A daikon radish is long and white, and is used as frequently in Japanese cuisine as a potato is in the West. A light, lemony, refreshing salad.

3 c   Daikon, shredded (peel first)
2 c   Carrots, shredded
1/4 c   Lemon juice
1/4 tsp   Grated lemon zest
1 Tbl   Honey
2 Tbl   Rice vinegar
1 tsp   "Lite" soy sauce

Toss everything together in a medium bowl and refrigerate overnight before use.

YIELDS: 5 cups

Marinated Hiziki

To receive the vitamin and mineral benefits of sea vegetables, prepare this simple salad and serve it as an accompaniment to your vegetable salads, sushi rolls or oriental fare.

	1½ c	Dried hiziki seaweed
Sauce:	1 Tbl	Ginger, freshly minced
	2 Tbl	Lemon juice
	2 Tbl	Brown rice vinegar
	1 Tbl	Mirin (cooking sake)
	1/2 tsp	Chile toasted sesame oil
Garnish with		Cilantro leaves, minced green onions
	1 Tbl	Sesame seeds, toasted

1. Rinse hiziki in cool water and let soak until soft. Strain and rinse when rehydrated and put into a medium bowl.
2. Toss in sauce and chill in airtight container.

Edamame

A Japanese treat: Steamed whole green soybeans in the pod. Snap open and squeeze out the beans in your mouth. Fun to eat and good for you!

1 lb	Soybeans, generally found frozen and pre-cut in 2" lengths
6	Garlic cloves, sliced lengthwise
1 Tbl	Tamari mixed with 1/4 c steam water
	Sesame gomasio

1. Steam soybeans and garlic until tender in a steamer basket. Toss in tamari mixture.
2. Put on a plate and dust with gomasio.

Whole Soybeans

Nature made a super versatile and useful plant when the soybean was created. The bean is loaded with protein, choline, vitamin K and zinc. The Chinese have been growing soy beans for several thousand years.

Soy beans are a complete nutritional industry providing milk, curd, sauce, cheese, ice cream, cooking oil, flour and sprouts. They are extremely high in protein and low in carbohydrates.

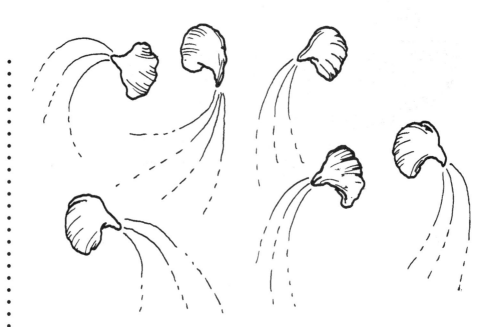

Oyster mushrooms are an excellent source of B vitamins and iron. They contain 13.62 mg iron per 3.2 oz pack, the same amount of iron as found in 1 lb. of steak, chicken or calves liver — and oyster mushrooms have trace amounts of fat (0.2 gm), no cholesterol and a low 26 calories. To get the same amount of iron from a steak, one would have to consume 1,848 calories and 157 grams of fat!

Oyster Mushroom Shooters

A most interesting and dynamic appetizer of oyster mushrooms sauteed in garlic, submerged into a spicy red cocktail sauce. Serve cold in individual shot glasses with a wedge of lemon — or lay the oyster mushrooms on a plate or on individual serving shells with sauce on the side.

1 pack 3.2 oz	Fresh oyster mushrooms
2 Tbl	Water
1 Tbl	Lime juice
1/2 Tbl	Garlic, minced
1 tsp	Aminos
1/2 tsp each	Honey and toasted sesame oil

Spicy cocktail sauce:

1/2 c	Tomato sauce
1½ Tbl	Lime juice
1/2 tsp	Hot pepper sauce (or horseradish)
1/4 tsp each	Cracked black pepper and sea salt
1/2 tsp	Sea vegetable seasoning (dulse garlic)

1. Heat up a skillet and add water, lime, aminos, honey and garlic. Saute mushrooms on low heat for 3 minutes, flipping mushrooms over from time to time. Turn off heat.
2. Stir together sauce ingredients in a small bowl. Fold mushrooms (and rest of saute) into sauce. Chill for several hours before serving.

SERVES: 2 - 3 (about 6 shooters)

Eggplant Arugula Disks

*A pleasing appetizer of grilled eggplant, topped with
sundried tomato and arugula.*

1	Eggplant, sliced into 8 rounds
8 halves	Sundried tomato (packed in olive oil)
8 stems	Arugula, washed and patted dry
	Olive oil as needed for grilling
1/2	Lemon, cut in wedges

1. Heat griddle or grill. Prepare eggplant and lightly brush with olive oil. Grill for a few minutes each side until soft. Squeeze lemon on top.
2. Sliver sundried tomatoes and place a few on each eggplant round. Lay an arugula spear on top. Arrange on a platter with olives, cucumbers or other chilled antipasto. Roll up or eat "taco style."

YIELDS: 8 eggplant disks

Chilled Endive Vinaigrette

*An attractive first course salad as a prelude
to a special main course meal.*

2	Chilled endives, halved lengthwise and cored
1 recipe	Tomato Vinaigrette (page 101)

1. Cut each endive half into 3 spears. Put on a salad plate.
2. Stir together vinaigrette sauce and spoon it over endive, equally distributing tomato pieces over each plate. Serve chilled.

SERVES: 4

Eggplant and Iron

1 cup of steamed eggplant supplies 31 mg of iron, equal to 2 lbs of beef or 10 hamburgers! Eggplant is also rich in potassium and water.

Other excellent raw sources of iron per cup are: escarole 39 mg, oats 15 mg, chick peas 6.9 mg, lentils 4.2 mg, soy beans 5.4 mg, spinach 2.2 mg, and prunes 4.86 mg.

RDA: 10 mg men, 18 mg women

Notes:

Celery Victor

Poached tender stalks of celery are tossed in a vinaigrette for a chilled accompaniment to meals.

1 bunch	**Celery, cleaned and trimmed with outer stalks removed**
2 c	**Vegetable broth (enough to cover celery)**
1/4 c	**Red pepper, marinated or fire roasted, cut into strips**
	Butter lettuce for garnish

1. Use only the tender inner ribs of celery, cut into 4" or 5" sections. Scrape off any tough outer "strings."
2. Heat vegetable broth in a skillet and add celery. Poach for 16 to 20 minutes, until tender, but not too soft.
3. Remove celery from broth. Drizzle on some vinaigrette or Italian dressing, then refrigerate. Garnish with red pepper strips and serve on butter lettuce leaves.

Marinated Cucumbers

2 c	Cucumbers, skinned and sliced thin
1	Red onion, sliced thin
1/2 c	Red Rogue Dressing (page 102)

Toss together and let chill overnight or longer.

Tomato Mushroom Vinaigrette

2 large	Tomatoes, sliced
4-6 large	Mushrooms, sliced thinly
1/2 small	Red onion, thinly sliced
1 recipe of	Raspberry Vinaigrette (page 101)
or	Red Rogue Dressing (page 102)

Arrange sliced tomatoes and mushrooms on a small platter, drizzle vinaigrette on top and garnish with freshly (or dried) chopped dill, or freshly minced parsley.

Mushrooms and Pantothenic Acid

Mushrooms are rich in niacin, pantothenic acid, potassium, zinc and phosphorus. They contain no fat and lots of water.

Pantothenic acid is a co-enzyme, assisting in the release of energy from our food and enables the body to better utilize vitamins. It stimulates the adrenals to produce cortizone for healthy nerves, keeps the digestive track healthy, and aids in promoting smooth, healthy skin.

Other sources of pantothenic acid are: broccoli, brussel sprouts, lentils, peas and soybeans.

One cup of mushrooms supplies 24 mg. pantothenic acid (RDA = 10 mg daily).

Nutrition Almanac, Nutrition Search, Inc.

Mainstream Romaine

*Crunchy romaine lettuce and marinated cucumbers
make a refreshing leafy salad to be served with hot grain dishes;
like Risotto with Asparagus and Peas (page 237).*

1	Cucumber, peeled
1/3 c	Salad dressing*
1 bunch	Romaine lettuce, outer leaves removed
2	Tomatoes, cut in wedges

Optional additions:

1/2 c	Sliced mushrooms
1/2 c	Red Onion Pickles (page 60)

1. Slice cucumber lengthwise, seed and then slice into half moons.
   Let sit in dressing for an hour or overnight.
2. Wash, dry and tear romaine leaves into a large salad bowl.
   Cut in tomatoes.
3. Toss cucumber into salad and chill — add "extras" if desired and
   serve with a carafe of salad dressing.

*Try Red Rogue Dressing on page 102.

SERVES: 4 - 6

Wild Greens Salad

The nutty, pungent and tasty flavors of arugula, radicchio and Boston bibb accent a pasta dish or heavier fare beautifully. Wild flowers in the salad are edible and delight the eyes.

1 bunch	**Arugula greens, ends trimmed off**
1 small	**Radicchio head, leaves torn**
1 small	**Boston bibb lettuce**
1/4 c	**Mustard greens, minced with their flowers**
Optional:	**Nasturtium flowers as garnish**
1/2 c	**Red pepper, julienned thinly**
1/4-1/3 c	**Red Rogue Dressing (page 102)**
	or Raspberry Vinaigrette (page 101)

Trim greens, wash and spin dry or pat with paper towels. Tear into pieces, toss together with your hands and chill.

Dress salad just before serving, careful not to overdress the delicate greens' flavors. (Start with 2 Tbl dressing, and taste before adding more.)

SERVES: 4 - 6

Wild Greens

Though often overlooked, wild greens are making a comeback in gourmet restaurants and markets.

Wild greens are full of vitamins and minerals and can be tossed into your daily salads. Mustard, turnip and dandelion greens, lambs-quarters, collards and kale are stars at providing high quantities of calcium and vitamin A.

If these greens seem too bitter for you, try finely shredding them to break up their vibrant raw tastes. The delicate, smaller and gentler plants, such as arugula and watercress are delicious whole or torn in half.

Notes:

Fiesta Coleslaw

Jicama, cucumber and fresh sweet corn off the cob enhance this "coleslaw" with a Mexican flair. An Avocado Lime Sauce tops it off.

2 c	Green cabbage, grated (approx. 1/2 head)
2 c	Small red cabbage, grated (1/2 head)
1 c packed	Carrots, finely grated (2 medium)
1 c	Sweet corn, cut off the cob (1 ear)
1 c	Jicama, sliced and diced
1 recipe	Avocado Lime Sauce (page 98)

1. If using a food processor, medium grate the cabbages; then change blade and finely grate the carrots.
2. Transfer to a large bowl and toss together with the rest of the ingredients and the Avocado Lime Sauce.
3. Garnish with tomato slices, cilantro and toasted pumpkin or sunflower seeds if desired.

SERVES: 6 - 8

Harvest Hiziki Salad

The orange and black colors make it a natural for Halloween, Thanksgiving or autumn meals. This salad is loaded with nutrients.

3/4 c	**Hiziki, dried**
1	**Carrot, finely grated**
3/4 c	**Lentil sprouts**
2 Tbl	**Lemon juice**
2 Tbl	**Brown rice vinegar**
1/3 c	**Green onions, minced**
1 Tbl	**"Lite" soy sauce**
2 tsp	**Toasted sesame oil**
1 Tbl	**Sesame seeds, brown or toasted preferred**
Dash	**Chile sesame oil or cayenne**
	Garnish with a couple of cilantro sprigs

1. Soak hiziki in water for 10 minutes to soften. Rinse and drain a couple of times with fresh water.
2. Put all ingredients except sesame seeds into a medium bowl and toss well. Chill. Garnish with sesame seeds and cilantro.

For another presentation — press into a measuring cup and invert onto serving plates.

SERVES: 2 - 4

Sea Vegetables

Raised and bathed in an ocean of minerals; sea-weeds and sea vegetables are a source of concentrated vitamins and enzymes. They are rich in calcium, magnesium, B vitamins, and vitamins A, D, E and K.

They are healing to the mucous membranes, the skin and the joints.

There are many varieties to be savored: Kombu (for soups, stews and broths) Nori (sushi rolls, crumble on salads)* Sea Palm (salads)* Wakame (highest in B_{12}, use for salads)* Hiziki (salads)* Dulse (add to all kinds of foods, eat as is) *Soak for 15 minutes, then rinse and drain before using.

Notes:

Sea "Pasta" Vegetable Salad

A wonderful salad of various sea and land vegetables. Seaweeds are super nutritious and supply you with lots of vitamin B-12 and minerals.

1/2 oz	Sea palm or wakame (alaria), dried
1 oz	Arame, dried
4	Shiitake mushrooms, dried
2 c	Cucumber, peeled, seeded and sliced
1	Bell pepper, sliced (yellow/green)
1 large	Tomato, seeded and chopped
2 Tbl	Rice vinegar
1	Garlic clove, pressed
2 tsp	Tamari or "lite" soy sauce (or to taste)
1 Tbl	Toasted golden sesame oil
Several shakes	Hot pepper sesame oil

1. Put sea vegetables and mushrooms into a large bowl. Cover with water and let soak 15 minutes.
2. Stem and slice mushrooms, set aside. Strain sea vegetables, rinse in cool water, and strain again.
3. Add vegetables, mushrooms and the rest of the ingredients to a large bowl. Toss well and refrigerate.

SERVES: 4

I speak veggie

Garbanzo Nile Salad

A quick and easy salad of garbanzo beans, carrots and cucumbers.
Spiced with Egyptian mint and garlic.

2 c	Cooked garbanzo beans (15½ oz can)
1	Cucumber, quartered and sliced
3	Carrots, finely grated
1/2 c	Fire-roasted red pepper, chopped (optional)
1/2 c packed	Green onions, chopped
1½ tsp	Garlic, chopped
2 Tbl	Virgin olive oil
3 Tbl	Herbed vinegar
1 Tbl	Mint, dried and crumbled
1/4 tsp	Sea salt
	Cracked black pepper to taste

1. Put garbanzos in a medium bowl. Add cucumber, carrots and red pepper. Toss well.
2. Put green onions into a food processor, chop in garlic and spices, oil and vinegar. Pulse chop to a thick consistency. Scrape into salad bowl and toss well. Chill.

SERVING SUGGESTIONS:
Serve with hummus or Babaganush dip (page 125) and pita triangles.

SERVES: 3 - 4

Garbanzo Beans

Garbanzo Beans have been used as a protein source for thousands of years. Also called chick peas, they contain lots of iron, folic acid, vitamins, and are especially high in the B complex vitamins.

They can be soaked overnight in water, then rinsed and drained for a few days until sprout tails appear. Sprouting greatly enhances their nutritive value.

When steamed gently, they become soft and impart a wonderful nutty taste. Blend with a bit of olive oil, garlic, tahini, parsley and lemon for a "sprouted hummus."

Celery Root Salad

A perfumed salad that goes well with a beet salad on festive occasions; crisp, bright and refreshing. This is a nice substitute for potato salad.

1 medium round	Celery root, scrubbed and coarsely chopped
1/4 c	Fresh lemon juice (1 lemon)
1/4 c	Tofu mayonnaise
2 tsp	Honey
	Cracked black pepper to taste
1/2 tsp	Celery seed
1/4 c	Celery, minced

1. Boil celery root whole in 2 cups of water in a large covered pot until tender.
2. Peel and cube, or finely shred celery root in a food processor.
3. Whisk the next five ingredients in a small glass bowl.
4. Stir in the celery root and minced celery, then refrigerate.

SERVES: 4

Chard Ribbon Salad

A deliciously healthy salad and a great way to eat vitamin-packed red chard leaves.

1½ c	Carrots, chopped and finely shredded
2 c	Red pepper, diced
2 c	Chard "Ribbons"
1/2 c	Red Rogue Dressing (page 102) (or use favorite vinaigrette)

1. Put carrots and red pepper in a large bowl.
2. Rinse and pat dry the chard leaves. Trim out stem in a "V" shape, 2" to 3" above leaf attachment. Stack 3 leaves on top of each other, then roll up tightly. From open end, slice "ribbons" off as thin as possible. Unravel into bowl.
3. Toss all together with dressing.

SERVES: 4

Notes:

Celery roots may appear fibrous and rough and quite unsavory when seen in a market — but once boiled and peeled, this succulent root with a wonderful aroma and taste quickly becomes a favorite. Pureed, it can be used as a thickener in soups or sauces. Finely grated, it makes a nice salad addition.

A Better Beet Salad

Using a fresh whole bunch of beets, this salad packs in the vitamins and minerals. The beet greens are sliced into ribbons and tossed into the creamy savory sauce.

	4 c	Beets, scrubbed and cubed (4-5 beets)
	1 c	Carrots, peeled and sliced thin
	1/2 c	Beet greens
Sauce:	2 Tbl	Lemon juice
	2 tsp	Honey
	1 tsp	Dill weed
	2 Tbl	Steam water
	2 Tbl	"Lite" eggless mayonnaise
		A dash of sea salt

1. Steam beets until tender for 10 to 15 minutes.
2. Make beet green "ribbons" by cutting out tough stems in a "v" shape. Stack up leaves and tightly roll up. Slice paper thin on exposed side to create "ribbons."
3. Whisk together sauce and toss everything together. Chill.

SERVES: 4

Water Usage

In California, it takes 33 gallons of water to produce 1 pound of carrots, 25 gallons of water for 1 pound of wheat, 815 gallons of water for 1 pound of chicken, and a whopping 5,214 gallons for 1 pound of beef. (5,200 gallons of water is 5, 5-minute showers per week for one year.)

From *Realities in the 90's*, excerpts from *Diet for a New America*, by John Robbins.

Notes:

Sweet Sesame Bok Choy

A simple salad of seasoned bok choy.

1 small bunch	**Bok choy, sliced**
2 Tbl	**Soy sauce**
1/4 c	**Mirin (cooking sake)**
1 Tbl	**Honey (or maple syrup)**
2 Tbl	**Rice Vinegar**
2 Tbl	**Sesame seeds, lightly toasted**

1. Steam bok choy lightly, until tender but crisp, 5 minutes.
2. Stir soy sauce, mirin and honey together in a small saucepan. Heat until everything dissolves.
3. Toss bok choy with rice vinegar, soy sauce, and sesame seeds. Serve warm or chilled.

SERVING SUGGESTIONS:
Serve as a side dish for an oriental meal.

SERVES: 4+

Minted Corn Salad

Simple to prepare, a healthy and refreshing salad.

16 oz	**Whole canned corn**
15½ oz can	**Garbanzo beans**
2 tsp	**Brown rice vinegar**
1	**Lemon, juiced**
1/2 c	**Grated carrot (1 or 2 carrots)**
1/4 c	**Green onions, minced**
1 Tbl	**Dried mint, crumbled or 1/4 c fresh minced**
	Dash of sea salt

Toss all together, then chill.

SERVES: 4

Broccoli Eggplant Pesto Salad

A good for you, lowfat pesto binds this pretty salad.

5 c	Broccoli, chopped (1 large stalk)
3 c	Eggplant, skinned and diced (1 medium)
1 large	Red onion, halved and sliced thick
2 Tbl	Water
1 Tbl	Lemon juice or olive oil
1/2 Tbl	Aminos or soy sauce
1/2 c	Red bell peppers, finely chopped
1/2 to 3/4 c	Basil Lime Pumpkin Seed Pesto (page 134)

1. Par boil broccoli pieces for 3 minutes, remove with slotted spoon.
2. Saute eggplant and onion in water, lemon juice or olive oil, and soy sauce until almost tender (just a few minutes).
3. Put all of the sauteed items into a bowl and toss in red peppers and pesto sauce. Marinate in fridge for a couple of hours before serving.

SERVING SUGGESTIONS:
Garnish with tomato wedges or minced red pepper—anything red!

SERVES: 6

Broccoli is high in selenium, which preserves tissue elasticity and promotes smooth healthy skin. Broccoli is also high in vitamins C, A and K, as well as calcium.

Notes:

Spicy Sprout Salad

A nourishing salad of long-stemmed sprouts.
Sunflower and buckwheat sprouts make great dining companions!

3 c (packed)	Sunflower and buckwheat sprouts (1/4 lb combined)
1/2 Tbl	Extra virgin olive oil
2 tsp	"Lite" soy sauce
2½ Tbl	Lemon juice
1/4 tsp	Hot pepper sauce (or to taste)

1. Rinse and drain sprouts and blot dry. Cut in half if desired.
2. Mix together soy sauce, lemon and pepper sauce, and toss into sprouts in a medium sized bowl. Chill.

SERVES: 2

Ruby Slaw

A definitely gorgeous ruby red colored salad,
spiked with a touch of chile and lime.

1/4 head	Red cabbage, grated
1	Beet, finely grated
1 c	Green petite peas
1/4 c	Green salsa, mild
1/2	Lime, juiced
1/2 tsp	Fresh garlic, pressed

Toss altogether and chill. Serve with lime slices.

SERVES: 3 - 4

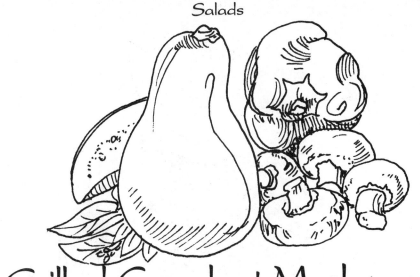

Grilled Eggplant Mushroom Pepper Salad

Grilled succulent eggplant tossed with crisp red and green peppers, sliced mushrooms and herbs. Tossed in an oil-less marinade.

1 medium	Eggplant, sliced lengthwise and cut into 3/8" thick half moons
2 c	Mushrooms, sliced
1 c each	Red and green bell pepper, julienne
*Sauce: 1 tsp each	Sweet basil and oregano
1	Garlic clove, minced
2 tsp	Dr. Bronner's Bouillon
1 Tbl	Lemon juice
2 Tbl	Red wine vinegar
	Plenty of cracked black pepper
	Cayenne to taste

1. Heat griddle on medium heat, lightly spray with vegetable oil. Trim off top and bottom of eggplant.
2. Cook eggplant for 3 minutes, flip over, sprinkle with Bronner's bouillon or a "lite" soy sauce and grill the other side 3 minutes. Put into a large bowl.
3. Add peppers and mushrooms. Stir sauce together, toss with your hands. Chill.

*You can also serve with fire-roasted Red Pepper Spa Dressing (page 95) or Red Rogue Dressing (page 102).

SERVING SUGGESTIONS:
Serve with Creamy Tomato Nut Cheese (page 137) and crackers or Cumin Rice (page 204).

SERVES: 2 - 4 (5 cups)

Over 5 billion tons of topsoil loss occurs in the United States each year. One third of our cropland is permanently unuseable due to topsoil erosion.

85% of our topsoil (cropland, pastures, and forests) is depleted from raising livestock.

It takes nature 500 years to create 1 inch of topsoil.

Realities in the 90's, excerpts from *Diet for a New America*, by John Robbins.

Japanese Eggplant Salad

Succulent sauteed eggplants are tossed with peppers, shiitake mushrooms, and tomatoes in a Ginger Vinaigrette.

5	Japanese eggplants, sliced 1/4" thick
1 Tbl	"Lite" soy sauce or aminos
1	Garlic clove, minced
3 Tbl	Water
1/2 tsp	Golden sesame oil
1 oz dried	Shiitake mushrooms, soak in water 20 minutes
1	Tomato, chopped
1	Bell pepper, julienne
1/2 c	Green onions, mince on angle

Ginger Vinaigrette:

2 Tbl	Ginger (fresh chopped)
2 Tbl	Toasted sesame oil
1/4 c	Rice vinegar
2 tsp	Peanut butter
2 Tbl	Water
1 tsp	Honey

1. Saute eggplants in soy sauce, garlic, water and sesame oil in a skillet or wok on low. Stir and cook for 3 to 5 minutes until just tender.
2. Stem soaked shiitakes, slice, then put into a bowl along with the rest of the vegetables. Add eggplant saute.
3. Blend sauce in blender, pour over salad, toss well and chill.

SERVES: 4

Thai Broccoli Salad

A terrific finely minced salad of broccoli, red pepper, cilantro and green onions, all tossed with a zesty orange-ginger-sesame Thai sauce.

3 c	**Broccoli, chopped**
1 c	**Broccoli "florettes"**
1 c	**Red pepper, finely chopped**
1/2 c	**Green onions, minced**
1/4 c	**Cilantro leaves, chopped**
1 recipe	**Royal Orange Thai Dressing (page 103)**

1. Cut away the tough outer stalk of the broccoli stem. Chop coarsely and place in a food processor. Reserve a flew clusters for "florettes." Pulse chop to a fine mince. Transfer to a large salad bowl. Add "florettes" to bowl.
2. Pulse chop red pepper and onions in food processor, or cut by hand. Toss well.
3. Prepare sauce, then toss in 1/3 cup (or to taste). Chill.

SERVES: 4

Get Your Calcium from Vegetables!

Dairy products as a source of dietary calcium contain animal protein. Dietary animal protein is known to stimulate the demineralization of our bones, in the process of which bone calcium is released into the bloodstream, and ultimately excreted out of the body in the urine. This leads to a negative calcium balance in the body.

Calcium from vegetable sources is more readily absorbed in greater quantities than dairy calcium and does not lead to a negative calcium balance. Excellent vegetable sources of calcium are:
Kale
Broccoli
Bok choy
Collard greens
Mustard greens
Turnip greens
Seaweeds

String Beans with Walnut Vinaigrette

An oil-less vinaigrette thickened by toasted walnuts and subtle hints of rosemary, melds beautifully with garden-fresh beans.

1 lb	Fresh green string beans, stemmed and cut in half
3/4 c	Walnut pieces (mixed use), toasted lightly
1 c	Tomato, seeded and chopped

Sauce:	1/2 c	Water
	1/4 c	Herbed cider vinegar
	1 Tbl	Lemon juice
	1 tsp	Tamari or soy sauce
	1 tsp	Rosemary, dried and crumbled
		Freshly cracked black pepper
	2	Garlic cloves

1. Steam green beans for about 4 to 5 minutes until crisp tender.
2. Lightly toast walnut pieces and put 1/2 cup into a blender, the rest into a medium to large bowl.
3. Blend walnuts with sauce ingredients until smooth.
4. Toss beans, walnuts, tomatoes, and sauce until coated (about 3/4 cup will do). Chill or serve warm as is.

SERVES: 4 - 6

Spicy Tofu Mushroom Salad

Steamed mushrooms, fresh ginger, scallions and spices accent firm tofu cubes. Served on a bed of various sprouts, it makes a nice main dish salad that is light, spicy and delicious. Serve with Sea Pasta Vegetable Salad (page 70) for a complete meal.

1 lb	Mushrooms, halved
12 oz	Firm tofu, cubed
2 Tbl	Ginger, freshly minced
5	Green onions, slivered
1/4 c	Sprouted sunflower seeds
1	Lime, juiced
2 tsp	Toasted sesame oil
1 Tbl	Aminos or "lite" soy sauce
1/8 tsp	Cayenne
1 Tbl	Veggie baco bits (optional)
1/2 c	Cilantro leaves, chopped (loosely packed)

1. Steam mushrooms for 5 minutes. Put into a medium bowl.
2. Toss in the rest of the ingredients, adjust seasonings as needed.
3. Serve on a bed of clover or alfalfa sprouts with larger sprouts (pea, sunflower greens, buckwheat) radiating outward. Top with cilantro sprig, sesame seeds, and a red pepper ring.

SERVES: 4

Tofu for You!

Pressed soybean curd is a versatile high-protein, lowfat food that is quite a chameleon. It can resemble chicken or scrambled eggs; makes creamy soups, sauces and desserts. Tofu's magic lies in its neutral taste. Frozen, defrosted tofu becomes a chewy, meaty addition to chile or sauces. Tofu is available in soft, regular and firm style. "Silken" packed tofu yields a creamy texture to smoothies, sauces and desserts.

Imperial Salad

Crisp bean sprouts create the backbone of this refreshing Oriental salad loaded with vegetables.

1/3 c	Hiziki (dried seaweed)
2/3 c	Warm water
3 c	Mushrooms, sliced
1/2 c	Celery, diced or sliced on angle
2	Green onions, sliced on angle
4 c	Bean sprouts, wash and spin dry
1 c	Carrots, shredded
1 c	Cabbage, grated finely
1 recipe	Ginger Cashew Sauce (page 102)
Garnish: 1/2 c	Cashew pieces, toasted lightly
1/4 c	Cilantro leaves

1. Soak hiziki in water for 10 to 15 minutes (until soft). Rinse and drain a couple of times.
2. Prepare vegetables and put into a large bowl. Toss the Ginger Cashew Sauce into vegetables until well coated.
3. Refrigerate and garnish with toasted cashews and cilantro.

Tuscan Tomato Rice Salad

*This makes a great picnic salad. Make this from leftover rice
for a real easy to prepare yet delicious salad. Accented
with dried rosemary and toasted walnuts.*

1 c	**Onions, sliced**
1/3 c	**Balsamic vinegar**
2½ c	**Roma tomatoes, chopped**
1/2 c	**Walnut pieces, toasted**
2½ c	**Cooked brown rice**
1 tsp	**Crushed dried rosemary**
2 Tbl	**Lemon juice**
1 Tbl	**Olive oil**
1 tsp	**Onion powder**
1/4 tsp	**Sea salt**
To taste	**Freshly cracked black pepper**

1. Heat up a small skillet on medium and saute onions in balsamic
   vinegar until limp.
2. Toss all ingredients together in a large bowl and refrigerate
   several hours or preferably overnight for flavors to meld.

SERVING SUGGESTION:
Use as a side dish or main lunch entree.
Surround with washed greens, and, if desired, vegetable crudites.

SERVES: 6

Flavor Your Salad with Edible Flowers

Here is a partial list of edible flowers that you can put on your foods as a garnish:

Apple (or any fruit flower), borage, chamomile, carnation, clover, hibiscus, jasmine, lavender, lilac, marigold, nasturtium, rose, rosemary flower, violet and zucchini flowers.

Try dicing them and sprinkling over your meal like colorful confetti.

Notes:

Navy Bean Salad

*A soft white bean salad with hints of raspberry, toasted walnuts
and crunchy radishes and cucumber.*

15 oz	Navy beans, cooked
2	Green onions, minced
1/2 c	Fresh cilantro, chopped
1/2 c	Cucumber, seeded, skinned and chopped
1/2 c	Radishes, halved and sliced
1 Tbl	Raspberry vinegar
1 Tbl	Lemon juice
1 medium	Tomato, seeded and chopped
1 tsp	Dried basil
1 tsp	Aminos
1/2 Tbl	Jalapeño, minced (seed if you don't like "hot" flavors)
2 Tbl	Walnuts, toasted, diced

Stir all the ingredients together in a medium bowl and refrigerate.
Garnish with a cilantro sprig and cherry tomato halves if you wish.

Option: Use Raspberry Vinaigrette (page 101) and omit items
raspberry vinegar through jalapeño.

Chinese 5-Spice Tempeh Salad

Chinese 5-spice imparts a sweetness to the succulence of sauteed tempeh and mushrooms. Added bean sprouts, red pepper, grated carrots, and cabbage round out this unusual salad.

	8 oz	Tempeh, cut into cubes
	7 large	Shiitake mushrooms (fresh are best)
Sauce:	1 Tbl	"Lite" soy sauce
	1/2 tsp	Chinese 5-spice
	1/2 Tbl	Garlic, fresh minced
	1 Tbl	Ginger, grated
	1/4 tsp	Chile sauce or hot pepper sauce
	1/2 tsp	Natural Worcestershire sauce
Salad:	1 c	Bean sprouts
	2 c (mixed)	Cabbage and carrots, grated
	1	Red bell pepper, sliced
	2 Tbl	Rice vinegar

1. Steam tempeh and mushrooms for 6 minutes until tender. Remove steamer basket from pot.
2. Pour out steam water, leaving 1/4 cup in pot. Add sauce mixture to pot and heat up. Add tempeh and mushrooms, cover, and saute on low for a few minutes.
3. Prepare salad veggies and put into a large bowl. Add sauteed tempeh and mushrooms and toss ingredients together. Chill.

SERVES: 2 - 4

Tempeh

Tempeh is a delicious meaty soybean cake that is held together by fermentation. It is a staple protein in Indonesia. There are many varieties available in natural food markets, each having a unique taste. Tempeh must be steamed or cooked before eating.

It is high in vitamin B_{12} and is cholesterol free.

Try broiling tempeh when crispy, sprinkle over a romaine salad with an Italian style dressing.

Notes:

Marinated Bean Salad

A simple bean salad studded with red peppers and green onions in a garlic vinaigrette.

2	Dried red New Mexican chiles, stemmed and seeded
2 c	Black beans, rinsed
1½ qts	Water
1½ tsp	Fresh minced ginger
3/4 c	Red peppers, chopped
1/3 c	Olive oil
1/3 c	Lemon juice
1/3 c	Brown rice vinegar
1/2 Tbl	Garlic, minced
1 bunch	Green onions, minced (trim off wilted green tops)
1/2 tsp each	Sea salt and crushed fennel seeds
1 Tbl	Dried basil

1. Bring water to a boil in a cast iron pot, add ginger, beans and chiles. Return to boil for 5 minutes, then cover and turn off heat and let sit overnight.
2. Return to boil, then simmer on low for 1 hour.
3. Transfer beans and pulp from chiles (discard skin from chiles) to a large glass (or other) bowl, stir in vegetables and seasonings and refrigerate.

SERVING SUGGESTION:
Serve on a bed of greens and radicchio leaves.

SERVES: 6

Holy Mole Pasta Salad

A pasta salad with vegetables in a creamy mole dressing.
A mole-style sauce is spiced with chile and peanuts.

6 oz	Spicy pasta, cooked al dente
1 c	Frozen peas
1/4 c	Fire-roasted red pepper, chopped
1 c	Tomato, chopped (seeded)
1 c	Cabbage, thinly shredded
1/4 c	Bell pepper, minced

Holy Mole Sauce:

2 Tbl	Mole* or Pueblo Pesto (page 135)
1 tsp	Fresh garlic, minced
1/4 c	Eggless mayonnaise
1	Lemon, juiced (1/4 c)
1/2 tsp	Cumin powder
1 tsp	Onion powder
1	Jalapeño pepper, seeded and minced

1. Cook pasta; to defrost peas, strain pasta over colander with peas inside colander. Put into a large bowl.
2. Add vegetables to bowl and toss together.
3. Stir together sauce ingredients and pour over salad, mix all together.

*Mole is a Mexican sauce made from various combinations of ground seeds, nuts, chile, spices and chocolate. Or, you can find it in stores as a condiment, or use the recipe on page 225.

Aromatherapy

Aromatherapy is the ancient healing and medicinal practice of using plant and flower essences to enhance health, beauty and well-being. Natural essential oils extracted from plants are used to stimulate and awaken the bodily functions via the olfactory sense of smell. Put a few drops of aroma-therapy oil of choice into a facial steam, body oils or creams, or apply directly to your wrists, temples or neck.

These oils are absorbed through the skin when applied, but are most effective when their vapors are inhaled.

◆ To energize: Rosemary and peppermint.

◆ To sooth: Lavender, chamomile.

◆ To decongest: Eucalyptus, fennel.

Notes:

Grilled Vegetable Pasta Salad

Quickly grilled vegetables complement this pasta salad. The specialty pasta is made from red and green chile pulp. Jalapeño pasta can also be used. If not available, add a little cayenne, chile powder or minced jalapeños to the salad.

10 oz	Hot chile pasta (cooked al dente)
3 medium	Zucchinis
3 medium	Yellow crookneck squash
3-4	Large mushrooms, cleaned and sliced
1 c	Tomato, seeded and chopped
1½ c	Garbanzo beans (15½ oz can)
1/2 tsp	Cumin seeds

Use either dressing:

1/3 c	Red Rogue Dressing (page 102) or Cilantro Pesto (page 133)

1. Cook pasta, rinse and drain and return to cooking pot or large bowl.
2. Cut zucchini and squash in half crosswise, then slice lengthwise in 1/4" thick slabs. Grill on lightly oiled hot griddle for about 3 minutes each side. Grill mushrooms 1 minute per side.
3. Slice grilled squash and zucchini into strips and add to pasta, along with rest of ingredients. Fold in pesto or salad dressing of choice.

SERVES: 4 - 6

*All life
is precious,
magical,
enchanted,
and
filled with love.*

Pasta Fo' Y'All

This makes a giant bowl of pasta salad.
Very flavorful and satisfying without being "oily."

1 lb	Rotini pasta, cooked al dente
15-oz can	Kidney beans
15-oz can	Corn kernels
1 c	Basil leaves, torn
1/3 c	Celery, minced
1	Green bell pepper, chopped
1	Red bell pepper, chopped
1/2 c	Marinated artichoke quarters
3 medium	Tomatoes, seeded and chopped
2	Garlic cloves, pressed
1/4 c	Herbed vinegar or rice vinegar
	Cracked black pepper to taste
2 Tbl	Liquid aminos (or herb salt to taste)

Toss all together in a large work bowl. (Your hands work best.)

Salad Dressings

Tahini Mint   92

Creamy Ranchero   92

Curried Sunny Dulse Dressing   93

Nutty Salad Sauce   94

Basil Beet Dressing   95

Magic Slaw Sauce   96

Fire-Roasted Red Pepper
    Spa Dressing   96

Papaya Lime   97

Avocado Lime Sauce   98

Cucumber Dressing   98

Santa Fe-an Sauce   99

Sesame Cilantro   100

Sesame Miso   100

Tomato Vinaigrette   101

Raspberry Vinaigrette   101

Red Rogue Dressing   102

Ginger Cashew Sauce   102

Royal Orange Thai Dressing   103

Green Thai Goddess   103

A Celebration of Wellness

Notes:

Da'Kine Tahini Mint Salad

1c Garbanzo
   beans, cooked

1 large carrot,
   finely grated

2c Cabbage,
   grated

1 Red bell pepper,
   julienne

Tomato wedges

Toss together with
Tahini Mint
dressing and chill.

Tahini Mint

2 Tbl	Tahini
2	Garlic cloves, pressed
1 Tbl	Dried mint
1/2 c	Pure water
1 Tbl	Lemon juice
1 tsp	White miso
1 Tbl	Vinegar

Blend in blender until smooth, chill.

MAKES: 3/4 c dressing

Creamy Ranchero

*Besides a salad dressing, use as a sauce for tacos,
on potatoes or on sandwiches.*

10 oz pack	Silken soft tofu
1/4 c	Onion, chopped (or 1 Tbl onion powder)
1	Garlic clove, pressed
1 tsp	"Lite" soy sauce or aminos
1 tsp	Cumin
1/2 tsp	Dill weed
2 Tbl	Lemon juice
2 Tbl	Eggless mayo

Blend in blender until creamy. Chill.

MAKES: About 1½ cups.

Curried Sunny Dulse Dressing

Dulse is a seaweed rich in protein, iron, chlorophyll, enzymes, and vitamins A and B. It contains more dietary fiber than oat bran! Try this spicy sauce with the delicious subtle flavor of dulse.

1/2 c	Sunflower seeds
1 c	Water
1	Lemon, peel, seed, chop flesh
1/2 c	Dulse
1 tsp	Curry paste or powder
1/2 Tbl	Dr. Bronner's Bouillon
Dash	Cayenne
1/2 tsp	Cumin powder
1 c	Tomato juice blend
1/2	Green onion, chopped

1. Soak sunflower seeds in water and cover overnight. Strain and put them into the blender with water. Blend well. (You don't have to soak the seeds to get a good dressing, however.)
2. Peel the lemon as you would an orange, add to blender along with the rest of the ingredients. Blend well. Sauce will thicken as it's blended.

MAKES: 2½ cups

Lemon

Lemons are a "Healing Hero." They stimulate, decongest, and cleanse the liver; act as a tonifier to the heart, and help to purify the blood.

Try beginning each day with a cup of warm water with 1/2 lemon juiced into it, as an aid to the digestive process.

The inside (white part) of the lemon rind can be rubbed on the back of your hands or on your face to promote healthy skin.

Notes:

Nutty Salad Sauce

Try on spinach or hearty romaine salads.

1/3 c	**Raw nuts or seeds*, toasted**
1/4 c	**Lemon juice**
1/4 c	**Brown rice vinegar**
2 Tbl	**Salsa**
1 Tbl	**Nutritional yeast**
1/2 Tbl	**Onion powder**
3/4 c	**Water**

1. Toast nuts or seeds in a toaster oven until lightly browned.
2. Blend everything in a blender until smooth and creamy.

*Use 2 Tbl sunflower seeds and 2 Tbl walnuts, or 2 Tbl pine nuts and 2 Tbl almonds.

MAKES: 1½ cups dressing.

Brush Your Vegetables

Use a natural vegetable brush to scrub away dirt from beets, carrots and potatoes.

Vegetable peelers are vitamin stealers and should be avoided on root vegetables.

Basil Beet Dressing

A nonfat vegetable dressing with a lovely red color made from pureed beets and carrots.

2 c	Beets, chopped (1 large)
1 c	Carrots, chopped (1 large)
3/4 c	Water
1/3 c	Onion, chopped
1 Tbl	Garlic, chopped
1	Jalapeño pepper, chopped
1/2 c	Rice or herbed vinegar
1 c	Fresh basil leaves, torn

1. Steam beets and carrots in water for 10-15 minutes until tender.
2. Transfer to a food processor and puree. When smooth, add all the ingredients except the basil. Pulse chop in basil until just blended.

Notes:

Magic Slaw Sauce

A simply delicious sauce over your favorite salad of grated vegetables. Try over grated cabbage, carrots and Maui onions, with chopped bell pepper and cucumber.

1	Lemon, juiced (1/4 c)
3 heaping Tbl	Eggless mayo
2 tsp	Mustard (wet)
1/2 tsp	Celery seeds
1 tsp	Honey
	OR
1 tsp	Orange, pineapple or apple juice

Blend with a fork or whisk until smooth.

Fire-Roasted Red Pepper Spa Dressing

Fragrant and alive — this sauce is a beautiful accompaniment to fresh salads. It has a rich earthy red color.

2/3 c	Fire-roasted red pepper, chopped
1 c	Green onions, chopped (green part only)
1	Garlic, chopped
1 c	Water
2 Tbl each	Vinegar and orange juice
2 Tbl packed	Basil leaves, freshly chopped

Put everything into a blender and blend well.

MAKES: 2 cups

Papaya Lime

A luscious salad sauce. Its color and texture resembles a French dressing, yet fruitier. Papayas are high in vitamin A — 7,000 IU per papaya.

1 c	Ripe papaya (1/2 papaya)
2½ Tbl	Lime juice
1 tsp	Dijon mustard
1/4 tsp	Cracked pepper
Pinch	Sea salt
2 Tbl	Pure water

1. Cut papaya in half, scoop out seeds, peel away skin and chop flesh.
2. Put all the ingredients into a blender and blend well.

SERVING SUGGESTIONS:
Serve over a butter and radicchio lettuce salad that has crumbled toasted walnuts on top and sauteed shiitake mushrooms, plus a few fresh papaya slices as a garnish.

MAKES: 1⅓ cup

Papayas contain the enzyme papain which tenderizes foods and aids in digestion. Fresh papaya soothes the stomach and intestines. Papayas are a good source of vitamin A and C and potassium. For a wonderful skin softening facial, rub the inner skin of the papaya rind on your face instead of throwing it away. Let the enzymes and juices dry on your face for 15 minutes (or longer) then rinse off with tepid water. You will be a real smoothie!

Notes:

Avocado Lime Sauce

Serve on Fiesta Salad (page 68) or other salad longing
for a creamy tart zesty sauce.

1/3 c	Avocado, mashed
2 Tbl	Herbed vinegar
1/4 c	Lime juice
2	Garlic cloves, pressed
1	Serrano chile, chopped and seeded
3 Tbl	Eggless mayo
1/2 c	Pure water
Dash	Sea salt and cracked pepper to taste

Blend in blender until smooth.

MAKES: 1½ cups

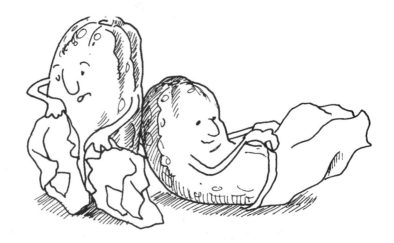

Cucumber Dressing

1/2 c	Cucumber, skinned, chopped and seeded
2 Tbl	Safflower oil
1/2 Tbl	"Lite" soy sauce
1/4 c	Tofu mayo
4	Gerkin pickles with
2 Tbl	Pickle juice
2 Tbl	Lemon juice

Put in a blender and puree until creamy.

MAKES: 1¼ cups

May you honor
the gifts
you can give
and recognize
your worthiness
as long
as you live.

Santa Fe-an Sauce

A dressing inspired by the flavors of New Mexico,
featuring green chiles.

2 Tbl	Lemon juice (or lime)
1/2 c	Fire-roasted green chiles, chopped*
1/4 c	Vinegar (herbed or rice)
1/2 c	Water
3 Tbl	Nutritional yeast
1/4 tsp	Sea salt
1/2 tsp	Cumin powder
1 Tbl	Olive oil (or canola)
1 tsp	Onion powder
2	Garlic cloves
1 tsp	Honey

Put everything in a blender and puree until smooth.

*Can substitute a 4 oz. can of fire-roasted green chiles.

MAKES: 1¼ cups

Notes:

Sesame Cilantro Dressing

A tasty, light-green colored sauce with a mellow miso backbone.

3 Tbl	Sesame tahini
1½ Tbl	Miso
1 large	Garlic clove
3/4 c	Purified water
1/4 c	Rice vinegar
approx. 1/3 c	Cilantro, fresh leaves only
Dash	Hot chile sauce
1/2 tsp	Toasted sesame oil
1 Tbl	Mirin

1. Blend first four items in a blender.
2. Add the rest of items, whirl until creamy.

MAKES: 1⅓ cups

Sesame Miso

All the Asian flavors: ginger, garlic, sesame, tahini, miso and green onion create a super salad accompaniment.

1 c	Water
1½ Tbl	Mellow white miso
1 Tbl	Tahini
2	Garlic cloves, chopped
1/2 Tbl	Ginger, freshly chopped (skinned)
1 Tbl	Lemon juice
1 tsp	Toasted sesame oil
1/2	Green onion, chopped

Blend in blender.

SERVING SUGGESTION:
Serve on spinach salads, sprout salads or even with brown rice.

MAKES: 1⅓ cups

Tomato Vinaigrette

Serve over chilled endive for a wonderful first course.
Also nice over a Wild Greens Salad (page 67).

1 tsp	Natural ketchup
1 tsp	Soy sauce
2 tsp	Olive oil
1/4 c	Rice or herbed vinegar
1/2 Tbl	Pimentos (or roasted red pepper)
1/2 tsp	Honey or fructose
1 c	Tomato, seeded and chopped fine
1 Tbl	Parsley, minced

Whisk together first 6 ingredients, stir in tomato and parsley. Chill.

MAKES: 1½ cups

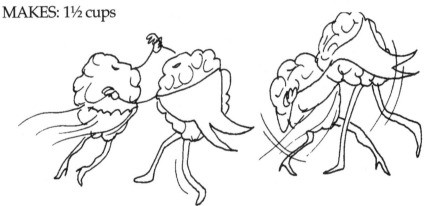

Raspberry Vinaigrette

This dressing has a luscious pink color and a pleasing
berry aroma and taste. It complements many types
of lettuce-based salads, and fruity salads.

2 Tbl	(Brown) rice vinegar
1/2 c	Raspberries
1/3 c	Water
2 Tbl	Lemon juice
2 Tbl	Olive or walnut oil
1 tsp	Garlic, chopped
1/8 tsp	Cracked black pepper (or to taste)

If you are using frozen berries, defrost berries first. Blend all the ingredients together in a blender. Strain to remove seeds. Chill.

MAKES: 1 cup

Being
a messenger
of the invisible
is an honor.

Red Rogue Dressing

A tomato-based vinaigrette, easy to prepare and delicious.
It goes well over pasta salads and leafy greens.

1 c	Fresh tomatoes, seeded and chopped
2 Tbl	Nutritional yeast flakes
3/4 c	Water
3 Tbl	Olive oil
1/2 tsp	Sea salt
1/2 tsp	Thyme
1/2 tsp	Dill weed
2 cloves	Garlic, chopped
1/4 tsp	Freshly cracked black pepper

Blend all the ingredients in a blender until smooth and creamy.
Keep leftovers in a bottle in the fridge.

MAKES: 2 cups

Ginger Cashew Sauce

Serve over Imperial Salad (page 82)
or other Asian noodle or seaweed salads.

2 Tbl	Cashew butter
3 Tbl	Fresh lemon juice
1 Tbl	Soy sauce (or tamari)
1½ Tbl	Fresh ginger, skinned and chopped
1/4 tsp	Hot pepper sauce
1/2 tsp	Toasted sesame oil
2 tsp	Honey

Blend until smooth and creamy.

MAKES: 1 cup

Royal Orange Thai Dressing

*This is a zesty sauce, good on strongly flavored salads,
like Thai Broccoli Salad (page 79). You can make this without oil for
a good nonfat dressing, but the sesame oil gives it a nice flavor.*

5 Tbl	Freshly squeezed orange juice
1 tsp	Ginger, minced (fresh)
1 tsp	Garlic, minced (fresh)
1 Tbl	"Lite" soy sauce
1 Tbl	Toasted sesame oil
1/4 c	Rice vinegar
Pinch	Cayenne pepper

Put all the ingredients into a blender and blend well. Refrigerate.

MAKES: 3/4 cup

Green Thai Goddess

Spicy and pleasing over cabbage slaws or Thai-style salads.

1½ Tbl	Peanut butter
1 Tbl	Golden miso
1 tsp	Ginger root, chopped
3/4 c	Water
1 Tbl	Rice vinegar
1 tsp	Toasted sesame oil
1/4 tsp	Red chile flakes
1/2 c	Green onions, chopped
1 tsp	Honey
3 Tbl	Lime juice

Blend in a blender until creamy. Then refrigerate.

MAKES: 1 cup

Life
is always
on the horizon,
constantly
changing.

Sauces

♦ *Saucy Ideas*   107

    Red Chile Enchilada Sauce   108

    Afro Rumba Sauce   109

    Fresh Tomato Coulis
      (Mex-Style)   110

    Carrot Garlic Red Sauce   111

    TNT Super Sauce   112

    Silken Chile Ginger Sauce   112

    Montezuma's Black Bean
      Sauce   113

    Minted Pepita Sauce   114

    Creamy Cashew Basil
      Sauce   114

    Mushroom Sauce   115

    Chunky Tomato Mushroom
      Sauce   116

    Curried Lentil Mushroom
      Sauce   117

    Chinese Brown Sauce   117

    Lemon Grass Sauce   118

    Caulipeño Sauce   118

    Green Chile Sauce   119

    Avgolemono Sauce   120
      (Greek Lemon Sauce)

    Cheezy Sauce   121

    Jalapeño Cheezy   122

Dips

Sprouted Sunseed Carrot
    Dip   124

Spicy Pinto Dip   125

Babaganush   125

Green Goddess
    Guacamole   126

Cucumber Dip   127

Pesto Dips   128

Corn Salsa   128

Condiments

♦ *Pestos:*

    Besto Pesto   129

    Sweet Chile Chutney   130

    Gingered Cashew Pesto   131

    Cilantro Walnut Pesto   131

    Spinach Pesto   132

    Pueblo Pesto   133

    Basil, Lime and Pumpkin Seed
      Pesto   134

♦ *Spreads and Seed Cheeses:*

    Spicy Peanut Spread   135

    Basic Creamy Seed
      Cheese   136

    Creamy Tomato Nut Cheese
      Sauce   137

    Garlic Seed Cheese Sauce   138

    Vegetable Seed Cheese   138

    Garlic and Herb Seed Cheese   139

    Ginger Soy Seed Cheese   139

♦ *Mousses/Patés:*

    Tomato Red Pepper Mousse   140

    Green Chile and Garlic Mousse   141

    2-Tier Fiesta Mousse   142-3

    Spinach Mushroom Mousse   144

    Lentil Paté   145

Saucy Ideas

A simple sauce will turn your vegetables and grains into a great meal. Sauces definitely give variety to simple fare. Here is a list pairing sauces with grains, pastas and vegetables; however, this is decidedly subjective territory, so don't let it limit you!

Sauces Good on Grains

Rice, millet, quinoa, bulgar and cous-cous never had it so tasty!

TNT Super Sauce

Montezuma's Black Bean Sauce

Afro Rumba Sauce

Minted Pepita Sauce

Cashew Basil Sauce

The Cheezy Sauces

Green Chile

Caulipeño Sauce

Mushroom Sauce

Lemon Grass Sauce

Sauces Good over Pasta

Mix 'em in or serve on top, whichever way it's really hot!

TNT Super Sauce

Fresh Tomato Coulis (Mex-style)

Caulipeño Sauce

All the pestos

The Cheezy Sauces

Chunky Cherry Tomato Sauce

Carrot Garlic Red Sauce

Curried Lentil Mushroom Sauce

Lemon Grass Sauce

Sauces Good with Steamed Vegetables

TNT Super Sauce

Montezuma's Black Bean Sauce

All the pestos

Silken Ginger Chile Sauce

Chinese Brown Sauce

The Cheezy Sauces

Avogolemono Sauce

Caulipeño Sauce

Minted Pepita Sauce

Cashew Basil Sauce

Lemon Grass Sauce

Notes:

Red Chile Enchilada Sauce

Roasted ancho or pasilla chiles create a great and memorable sauce. This is our own adaptation of an enchilada sauce learned directly from the Mexi-Indians in Baja.

2-3 oz pack	Pasilla chiles, dried
2¼ c	Water
1½ tsp	Oregano
2 tsp	Cumin
1 sm can	Tomato sauce
1/2 tsp	Sea salt
1	Garlic clove

1. Bake chiles lightly in a preheated 350º oven for 3 to 4 minutes, cool. (This brings out the flavor.) Remove pithy insides, stems, and seeds.
2. Put in a small pan, cover with water, bring to a boil, then simmer on low for 15 minutes. Let chiles cool, then scrape pulp away from skin, using a butter knife; discard the skin.
3. Put chile pulp into a blender along with 2¼ cups water, and blend. Add the other ingredients, continue blending until texture is smooth.

NOTE: To decrease the roasted chile flavor, just increase the tomato sauce to taste.

Besides enchiladas, you can add this sauce to rice or beans for a great flavor. Can be frozen.

YIELDS: 4 cups

Afro Rumba Sauce

A spicy tomato sauce with a hint of peanuts and saffron. Add 1 cup eggplant and 1/2 cup bell pepper for another great variation.

2½ c	**Onions, chopped**
2 Tbl	**Tamari (soy sauce)**
2 Tbl	**Broth or lemon juice**
2 c	**Tomatoes, chopped fresh**
6 oz	**Tomato paste**
2 c	**Water**
1 pinch	**Saffron**
1/4 to 1/2 tsp	**Cayenne**
2 Tbl	**Peanut butter**
3	**Garlic cloves, chopped**
1 c	**Eggplant, chopped (optional)**
1/2 c	**Bell pepper, chopped (optional)**

1. In an enamel pot, saute onions in liquids (tamari and broth or lemon juice) on low heat until tender.
2. Stir in tomatoes, tomato paste, water, saffron and cayenne (and other veggies if desired). Simmer gently.
3. Meanwhile, blend peanut butter with garlic and 1/3 cup water in a blender until smooth. Stir into sauce.

SERVING SUGGESTIONS:
Try with spaghetti squash, page 198.

Try with spaghetti squash, page 198.

A Bit of Tomato History

The tomato originally grew as a prehistoric weed in Central and South America. Through careful cultivation it thrived in maize and bean fields. It was named "tomatl" by the Aztecs.

Many varieties of tomatoes and stages of growth were utilized in the native peoples' cooking; ripe red ones were mixed with chiles as a sauce for beans, and green tomatoes were sliced into stews. Cortés discovered tomatoes in Mexico in 1519. Europe received them later that century, when first arrived as an orange-yellow fruit called "golden apple" and "love apple" because they were thought to be an aphrodisiac.

The Spanish adopted tomatoes into their cuisine first, followed by the Italians.

Notes:

*To Easily Peel Tomatoes:
Core, halve and seed tomatoes. Put them into a bowl and pour boiling water on top to cover. Let sit for 5 minutes, remove peel.

Fresh Tomato Coulis (Mex-Style)

A simple freshly chopped and simmered tomato sauce to serve over all sorts of meals: scrambled tofu, chile rell"{}os, barbecued tofu, broiled eggplant, etc.

1 c mixed	Red and green bell peppers, chopped
3	Garlic cloves, minced
2 Tbl	Broth or lemon juice
2 Tbl	Pure water
2½ c	Tomatoes, skinned, seeded and chopped*
1 tsp	Cumin powder
1/2 tsp each	Oregano and chile powder
Dash	Sea salt

1. Saute peppers and garlic in broth and water in a small pan for 5 minutes on low heat.
2. Add tomatoes and spices, stir and simmer 10 minutes. Puree only one-half of the mixture if you desire a less chunky texture.

Carrot Garlic Red Sauce

A meaty tomato sauce, sweetened with pureed carrots and textured with TVP (texturized vegetable protein).

2	Onions, coarsely chopped
6 large	Garlic cloves, minced
1/4 c	Lemon juice
2 tsp	Olive oil
1¼ c	Water (mixed use)
28 oz can	Plum tomatoes in juice, cut
1 c	Carrot, chopped
1/2 c	TVP
1 large	Tomato, chopped and seeded
1/2 to 1 tsp	Red chile flakes
2 tsp	Dried basil
1/2 tsp	Fennel seeds, ground
	Sea salt and black pepper to taste
1 Tbl	Garlic powder
Reserve: 1/4 c	Walnuts

1. Saute onions and garlic on low heat in lemon juice, olive oil, and 1/4 cup of the water in a large enamel pot for about 8 minutes, until onions become tender.
2. Add the rest of the ingredients and stir well. Let simmer for 20 minutes. You can add more water as needed.
3. Ladle out the carrots and put them into a food processor with walnuts and a bit of the sauce. Puree well, then return to pot. Season to taste and keep simmering until ready to serve.

SERVING SUGGESTIONS:
Serve over penne, rotelli or other thicker pasta,
or over Spaghetti Squash (page 198).

Carrots

Carrots contain beta-carotene, the richest source of vitamin A the body can quickly assimilate.

Carrots cleanse the liver, lymph system and skin, build blood and help digestion. They are known to increase vitality when eaten raw or juiced.

Carrots are a "Healing Hero."

TNT Super Sauce

Tahini and tofu create a delectable sauce with hints of garlic and thyme ... it's dynamite!

8 oz	Silken soft tofu
1/2 tsp	Dried (lemon) thyme
1 Tbl	Aminos
1 c	Vegetable broth
1 Tbl	Tahini
1 Tbl	Nutritional yeast flakes
1	Garlic clove, chopped
Dash	Red chile flakes

Blend in blender until smooth, then pour into a small saucepan and heat gently. Serve over grains, pasta or veggies.

How to Use the Pulp from Dried Red Chiles

Wash and dry dried red chiles. Remove stem and shake out the seeds.

Put chiles into a saucepan and cover them with water. Bring to a boil, cover and reduce heat. Let simmer until chiles are soft, about 10 minutes.

Drain water and squeeze chile pulp out from tip towards open end. Or, slice chile and lay on counter.

Scrape pulp away with a spatula or butter knife, discard skin.

Silken Chile Ginger Sauce

A creamy sauce with delicious spices.

Pulp from 4	Red chiles (see sidebar)
1/2 tsp	Cumin powder
1 Tbl	Garlic, chopped
3/4 c	Pure water
1/2 Tbl	Liquid aminos
1 Tbl	Ginger, juiced or grated
10.5 oz	Silken soft tofu
1/2 tsp	Honey
1 Tbl	Orange juice

1. Blend until creamy in blender.
2. Heat on low in a small saucepan. Pour over steamed veggies.

Montezuma's Black Bean Sauce

Pureed black beans, sauteed with slivered onions, garlic, chile and spices. Delicioso over steamed squash, tomatoes, eggplant and grilled Polenta Triangles (page 204). Serve some hot tomato salsa on the side if desired.

2 Tbl	Lemon juice (or lime juice)
3 Tbl	Water
1/2 Tbl	"Lite" soy sauce (or tamari, aminos, etc.)
2 tsp	Garlic cloves, minced
1	Chile (jalapeño or yellow wax), minced
1	Yellow onion, slivered thin
1/2 Tbl	Cumin seeds, freshly ground
1 tsp each	Basil and oregano
3 c	Black bean puree

1. Heat up liquids in a small skillet on low and saute garlic, chile and onion. Stir frequently, cook 3 to 5 minutes, then add spices. Simmer and cook until onions are transparent.
2. Meanwhile prepare the bean puree (just put homecooked black beans in a blender, add water as needed and blend until pureed), or use "instant" black beans, adding hot water to soften as instructed on container.
3. Stir black beans into vegetables, heat thoroughly before serving.

Meditation is connecting to God's frequency — the original source of energy and love in the universe.

By quieting your mind every day, you build an invisible bridge which connects God's vibration with your soul. This conscious dedication to increasing your inner well-being will fill you with peace and unspeakable joy. It is available to everyone.

Notes:

Minted Pepitas Sauce

Try over a fresh steamed yellow squash, zucchini and carrot trio. Serve with a side of pasta or cous-cous or other favorite grain to create a delicious meal.

2 Tbl	Eggless mayo
1 c	Hot water
1/4 c	Pumpkin seeds, toasted lightly
2 large	Green serrano chiles, chopped*
1/2 Tbl	Onion powder
1/2 tsp	Sea salt
2 Tbl	Mint, dried and crumbled
	Ground black pepper to taste
3	Garlic cloves, chopped

Blend well and pour over hot vegetables.

*Seed and stem the chiles.

Creamy Cashew Basil Sauce

A sublime sauce, thickened with tofu and cashews.

1/2 c	Cashew pieces
10 oz	Soft silken tofu
1/2 c	Basil leaves, chopped
1/2 Tbl	Garlic, minced
1/4 c	Minced red onions
1 Tbl	Liquid aminos
1 c	Water
	Cayenne to taste

1. Toast cashew pieces in toaster oven until light brown.
2. Put everything except water into food processor and puree.
3. Transfer to a small saucepan, add water and simmer for 10 to 15 minutes until thick.

SERVING SUGGESTIONS:
Over vegetables or grains.

MAKES: 2¾ cups

Mushroom Sauce

A savory sauce loaded with minced mushrooms that complements many dishes or grains.

4 c	**Mushrooms, chopped fine**
1/2 c	**Red onions**
1½ Tbl	**Lemon juice**
1 Tbl	**Liquid aminos**
2¼ c	**Water**
2 Tbl	**Arrowroot powder**
2	**Garlic cloves, pressed**
1 Tbl	**Tahini**
	Cracked pepper and nutmeg, freshly grated to taste

1. Saute mushrooms and onions in lemon and aminos on low heat for about 5 minutes in a wok or large skillet.
2. Blend water, arrowroot, garlic and tahini until thoroughly blended; stir into mushroom saute. Stir and heat till almost boiling, reduce heat, stirring until thick. Puree 1/2 of the sauce for a smoother consistency.

SERVING SUGGESTION:
Serve with Eggless Fu Yung (page 250) or
Asparagus Tofu Pie (page 230).

SERVES: 6 — 1/2-cup servings

Mushrooms are quite possibly the most fertile plant in the world. Sending millions of microscopic spores in the air, the spores wait for the right conditions to grow. The growing power of mushrooms is awesome — they are strong enough to push through 3 inches of asphalt.

Mushrooms come in all different colors, sizes and shapes, and are savored all over the world. Sauteed mushrooms can truly be a heavenly experience.

Some well known types of edible mushrooms are: white button, large white, brown, shiitake, oyster, enoki and porcini.

Notes:

Chunky Tomato Mushroom Sauce

When cherry tomatoes are plentiful, make this chunky sauce flavored with garlic and mushrooms. Use an instant Veggie Burger mix to make a meaty addition.

1½ dozen	Mushrooms
1/2	Yellow onion
5	Garlic cloves, minced
2 Tbl	Water
1 Tbl	Aminos
1 lb	Cherry tomatoes, halved (keep seeds in)
2 tsp	Olive oil
	Sea salt and cracked black pepper to taste
2 Tbl	Fresh oregano leaves

Optional:
1/2 c	Veggie burger mix
1/2 c	Water

1. Slice onions and mushrooms. Saute garlic in water and aminos for a couple of minutes on low heat, then add onions and mushrooms.
2. Simmer for 5 minutes, then add cherry tomatoes, oregano, oil and spices. Simmer on low for a total of 15 minutes or so.

Optional:

3. Mix veggie burger mix and water together. Let sit until absorbed. Form into 1" balls and broil each side until toasty.
4. Crumble into sauce.

SERVING SUGGESTION:
Serve over pasta or Spaghetti Squash (page 199), serve with Polenta Triangles (page 204), or Bread Sticks (page 209), and a large crisp salad, such as Mainstream Romaine (page 66).

Curried Lentil Mushroom Sauce

Baked lentils transform this tomato sauce into something quite special, and definitely more nourishing than your basic tomato sauce. Serve over linguini for a great dinner.

2 c	**Mushrooms, sliced**
1/4 c	**Broth or cooking sherry**
1 tsp	**"Lite" soy sauce**
2 c	**Tomato sauce**
1½ c	**Curried Lentils (page 205)**
1 tsp	**Garlic, pressed**

1. Saute mushrooms in broth and soy sauce for a few minutes on low heat.
2. Stir in remaining ingredients and simmer, stirring occasionally until warm throughout. Serve over pasta noodles.

SERVES: 4 — 1 cup servings. If you are a big sauce fan, this will serve 2 people.

Chinese Brown Sauce

A basic Chinese-style sauce to add to woked vegetables, noodles or rice.

1 Tbl	**Kuzu (or arrowroot powder)**
1 c	**Water**
1 tsp	**Soy sauce**
1 tsp	**Garlic, minced**
1 tsp	**Ginger, minced**
1 tsp	**Peanut butter**
1 Tbl	**Miso**

1. Put everything into a blender and blend.
2. Transfer to a small saucepan and bring to a shallow boil, then reduce to simmer, whisking all the while.

MAKES: 1 cup

Just remember ... although at times we may feel completely alone, we are not. We are one big family. Alone as ourselves, but connected to everything. What we think, say and do, ripples out into the world. Are you spreading love, joy or peace?

Whatever you send out will ripple back to you ... it is simple, since we are all connected to everything.

Lemon Grass Sauce

Use this savory sauce to provide a delicate lemon lift to Oriental fare, over grains, noodles or stronger tasting vegetables (such as broccoli or brussel sprouts).

1/3 c	**Dried lemon grass** (or 1 fresh stalk, chopped)
1¼ c	**Water**
1 Tbl	**Arrowroot powder**
2½ tsp	**Tamari**
1/4 c	**Red onion, chopped**
1 tsp	**Honey**
1/4 tsp	**Turmeric**
	Cracked pepper to taste

1. Put everything into a blender and blend well for a couple of minutes.
2. Strain into a small saucepan and whisk on low heat as sauce thickens. (Try 1 Tbl Nutritional yeast, whisked into sauce for a nice nutty flavor and increased nutritional value.)

MAKES: 1 cup sauce

Caulipeño Sauce

A spicy, healthy sauce based on pureed cauliflower and spices. Serve with vegetables, grains, or Mexican fare. Great as a topping to enchiladas.

1 medium	**Cauliflower, chopped coarsely**
1 c	**Water**
1/2 c	**Cilantro leaves, packed**
2	**Garlic cloves**
1 tsp	**Jalapeños, dried (or 1 fresh one, chopped)**
1 tsp	**Aminos**
1 c	**Water**

1. Steam cauliflower in 1 cup of water until tender, about 15 minutes, or until soft.
2. Put cauliflower into a blender or food processor, along with the remaining ingredients. Puree until creamy. Serve hot.

Green Chile Sauce

*A thick sauce of roasted green chiles, native to New Mexico.
This sauce is delicious over Pozole (page 167), burritos, enchiladas
or even over a sandwich.*

2 lbs	Green chiles (about 14 large ones) (or 2 c diced, fire roasted)
2 Tbl	Roasted garlic, minced
1/3 c	Onion, minced
1/3 c	Broth
2¾ c	Water
1 Tbl	Arrowroot powder
1 Tbl	Concentrated vegetable stock
2 tsp	Lime juice
	Sea salt to taste

1. Wash and dry chiles, roast according to side of page.
2. Roast garlics with skin on for 15 minutes at 500°, mince.
3. In a medium saucepan, saute onion in broth on low heat until soft. Dissolve arrowroot and vegetable stock concentrate in water, stir into pot on medium high heat. Add the remaining ingredients, stir together well.

Optional: Puree half of chile mixture (for a more "saucy" texture) and add back to pot.

MAKES: 4 cups

Roasting Green Chiles

Many New Mexicans couldn't live without their green chiles. They use it to spice up their basic foods. Here is a standard chile roasting procedure:

1. Wash and dry chiles, preheat oven to 500°.

2. Put chiles on top rack of oven and roast until their skin blisters evenly, about 7 minutes per side. (Turn chiles over by using their stems.)

3. Remove the chiles from the oven and put them into a plastic bag. As the chiles "sweat" to cool off, the skin will loosen away from the pulp.

4. Remove the skin, seeds and stem, and dice the chiles. You can freeze chiles for later use. Keep the stems attached if you are making "Chile Relleños" (stuffed chiles, see page 217).

Avgolemono Sauce

(Av-gó-le-mo-no)

A Greek lemony custard sauce to serve with Divine Dolmas (stuffed grape leaves, page 239), broccoli, asparagus or artichokes.

10 oz	Soft silken tofu
1/4 c	Lemon juice
1 tsp	Garlic, minced
1 Tbl	Liquid aminos
1/2 Tbl	Onion powder
1 Tbl	Arrowroot powder
1/4 c	Water
1 tsp	Honey
	Cracked black pepper to taste
	Pinch of tumeric for a nice golden yellow color
1/4 tsp	Freshly grated nutmeg

1. Blend in blender.
2. Transfer to a small pot and whisk together as it thickens at medium heat. Top with extra grated nutmeg and serve warm.

Cheezy Sauce

A delicious "cheese" sauce that goes great on all sorts of foods; from baked potatoes to macaroni and cheese. Use in any dish that calls for a savory cheesy taste. Easy to make, low fat and quite nutritious.

3 c	Water
1/4 c	Rolled oats
1/4 c	Nutritional yeast flakes
1/4 c	Tahini
1/4 c	Arrowroot powder
2 Tbl	Lemon juice
1/8 tsp	Tumeric powder
2 Tbl	Onion, minced (or 1 Tbl onion powder)
1/2 Tbl	Tamari or soy sauce
1 tsp	Basil or herb(s) of choice (oregano, thyme and dill all work well)
Dash	Cayenne
1	Garlic clove, chopped (optional)

1. Put everything into a blender and blend until very smooth.
2. Pour into a small saucepan and heat until boiling, stirring with a whisk until thick on low heat.

YIELDS: 4 cups

Wellness is a gift of life. If we cherish and shelter it with our love, our heart will blossom into meaning and fulfillment, health and happiness, and inner peace.

We wish you wellness.

Notes:

Jalapeño Cheezy

A spicy cheesy sauce that goes great on Nachos, macaroni, Mexican dishes or as a dip for veggies or chips. Keep on hand for parties, because it is super easy to whip up, and good for you, too. Jalapeño Cheezy Sauce has the texture of a soft melted cheese.

2 c	Filtered water
1/3 c	Nutritional yeast flakes
1/4 c	Tahini
1/4 c	Arrowroot powder
2 Tbl	Lemon juice
1 Tbl	Onion powder
1 tsp	Sea salt
Dash	Tumeric
1 Tbl	Jalapeño pepper, finely minced*
3 Tbl	Red bell pepper, finely minced*

1. Blend everything except the peppers in a blender.
2. Transfer to a sauce pan and whisk rapidly on high heat until mixture thickens. This should take just a few minutes.
3. Stir in peppers and pour into a small bowl or shallow dish and chill until ready to use.

*Remove seeds and pith if you don't like "hot and spicy."

DIPS!

Eureka! A zucchini stick has never tasted as good as when plunged into one of these exciting dips. Serve "party style" in a bowl, surrounded with vegetable crudites (chopped finger-sized fresh vegetables) and/or chips. For great appetizers or companions to salads, soups or entrees ... dip into one of these!

Sprouted Sunseed Carrot Dip

Babaganush

Spicy Pinto Dip

Green Goddess Guacamole

Cucumber Dip

Pesto Dips

Corn Salsa

Heat these sauces up for a cheezy-style fondue:

Jalapeño Cheezy

Cheezy Sauce

Sprouted Sunseed Carrot Dip

A nourishing stuffing from sprouted sunflower seeds, grated carrots, ginger and spices. This delightful sandwich stuffing can be whipped up in your food processor in a few minutes.

1½ c	Carrots, finely grated
1¼ c	Sunflower seeds, sprouted 2-3 days
1/4 c	Red onion, chopped
4 tsp	Lemon juice
2 Tbl	Tahini
2½ tsp	Miso
2 tsp	Ginger root, minced
1	Garlic clove
1/4 c	Pure water
1/4 tsp	Serrano pepper, minced

1. Finely grate carrots in a food processor. Transfer to a bowl.
2. Put the remaining items into the food processor and pulse chop until blended. Scrape sides as needed.
3. Add carrots, and pulse chop to a puree. Chill. Use as a filling in Nori sheets, rice paper pancakes, sandwiches, or as a dip.

Babaganush

A roasted eggplant dip, whipped with lemon, garlic and tahini.

1 large	Eggplant, slice lengthwise, trim top
2 Tbl	Lemon juice
2 Tbl	Tahini
2	Garlic cloves, minced
1/4 tsp	Sea salt
	Freshly cracked pepper and cayenne to taste

1. Prick the eggplant skin with a fork several times and bake for 30 minutes in a 450º oven.
2. Scoop out the soft roasted eggplant flesh and put it into a food processor with the remaining ingredients. Puree until creamy.

Garnish with sesame seeds, serve with pita bread triangles.

YIELDS: 1¹/₃ cups

Laughter is the voice of a smile.

Spicy Pinto Dip

A quick and nutritious snack with no-oil chips.

2½ c	Cooked pinto beans, drained
1½ Tbl	Garlic
2 tsp	Onion powder
1½ tsp	Cumin
2 tsp	Jalapeños, diced
1 tsp	Sea salt
1/3 to 1/2 c	Water
3 tsp	Brown rice vinegar
Dash	Chile powder

Put everything into a blender or a food processor and puree until smooth. Put into a small bowl and garnish with cayenne or paprika and serve with chips.

Green Goddess Guacamole

A fat-free substitute for the avocado-based condiment. None of the flavor is sacrificed, only the fat. Great with chips and crackers or Mexican fare.

1 c	Shelled green peas (fresh are best!)
1/4 c	Water
1	Jalapeño pepper, seeds and skin removed
1/2 Tbl	Fresh lime juice
1 Tbl	Fresh cilantro leaves, chopped and packed
2-3 Tbl	Onion, chopped
Dash	Cumin powder and sea salt
2	Garlic cloves, pressed

1. In a small pan of water, steam the peas for 3 minutes until tender. Strain.
2. Put the peas and 1/4 cup steam water in a food processor and puree. Add the remaining ingredients, and continue to puree until a thick, even consistency prevails. Stop occasionally to scrape down the sides.
3. Transfer to a small bowl and garnish with cilantro, cayenne, and a lime wedge.

SERVES: 2 - 4 or makes 1¼ cups as a dip

Cucumber Dip

Fresh, light and alive.

2/3 c	**Cucumber, seeded, skinned and shredded**
2	**Celery ribs**
2	**Green onions**
1	**Garlic clove**
1	**Serrano or jalapeño chile (remove seeds if you don't like "hot")**
10.5 oz	**Firm silken tofu**
1 Tbl	**Lemon juice**
1/2 tsp	**Onion powder**
1/2 tsp	**Cumin**
Dash	**Sea salt**
2 Tbl	**Cilantro leaves, minced**
	Cracked black pepper to taste

1. Prepare cucumber and set aside in a medium bowl.
2. Pulse chop celery, green onions, garlic and chile to a fine mince in a food processor. Add the tofu and pulse chop a few seconds more.
3. Transfer to the bowl with the cucumber, add the remaining spices and herbs, stir together and chill.

SERVING SUGGESTION:
Serve with crackers, toasted bagels, or with veggies.

YIELDS: 2 cups

Water Usage

An individual with a meat-based diet uses 4,000 gallons of water per day to produce their food.

To produce food for a lacto-ovo vegetarian: 1,200 gallons of water per day are used.

A pure vegetarian's water usage to produce food: 300 gallons per day.

Realities in the 90's, excerpts from *Diet for a New America*, by John Robbins.

Notes:

Pesto Dips

Turn your favorite pesto into a delicious veggie or chip dip by blending it with soft tofu. Try any one of the 7 dynamic pestos on the following pages.

1/4 c	Pesto
1 c	Silken or soft tofu

Put pesto and tofu into a blender and puree well. Refrigerate. Garnish with finely ground nuts or herbs.

Oven Baked Tortilla Chips

Make your own healthy chips by toasting corn tortillas on an oven rack at 400° for 10 minutes, or until crisp. Break tortillas apart in quarters and serve with your favorite dip.

Corn Salsa

A spicy relish for summer picnics or Southwestern foods. Use to accent salads, tacos, burritos or other vegetable dishes.

2 large	Dried red chiles (New Mexican style)*
1½ c	Cut corn (frozen works well, too)
2	Cloves garlic, pressed
2-3 Tbl	Lime or lemon juice
1/4 c	Green onions, tops trimmed, chopped
1/4 c	Cilantro, chopped
1/4 c	Red onion, chopped
1 Tbl	Jalapeño, minced (seeds and all) *or*

1. Cook chiles in a small pan, with 1 cup of water, cover. Bring to a boil, then turn to simmer for 5 minutes. Run chiles under cold water and scrape chile pulp from skin — set aside.
2. Mix the remaining ingredients together in a small container, add chile pulp, then cover and refrigerate for a couple of hours.

*Can substitute: 1/2 Tbl Red chile powder, or
1 Tbl Roasted red pepper

Besto Pesto

A fresh pesto that is delicious as a dip or as a stuffing for mushroom caps (pages 133 and 194), or celery ribs, spread on crackers or bread, or serve over pasta.

1/3 c	Pine nuts
1 Tbl	Garlic, chopped
1/3 c	Fresh cilantro, packed leaves, chopped
1/3 c	Fresh basil, packed leaves, chopped
1 Tbl	Lemon juice
1 c	Tomato, chopped
1/2 tsp	Sea salt

Put everything into a food processor, except the tomatoes, and pulse chop several times. Stop to scrape down the sides and repeat. Add the tomatoes and continue to pulse chop until just blended. Keep a texture to the pesto, it should not be a puree. Chill or serve.

Pestos

Pestos are easy to make and can be used as a dip, a sauce or a flavoring. They are concentrated and made from the freshest herbs available.

Stir into pasta, rice, or steamed vegetables; serve on top of a bowl of soup; use as a sandwich spread or just on toast. However you have them, enjoy 'em!

Notes:

Sweet Chile Chutney

Raisins, oranges and chiles create a "sweet-fire" pesto, perfect for dipping grilled fare or to complement a Southwestern menu.

5	**Dried red New Mexican chiles, stemmed and seeded**
1 c	**Orange juice**
1/4 c	**Raisins**
1/2 small	**Onion, chopped**

1. Put chiles into a small saucepan, cover with water, and bring to a boil; turn to simmer for 15 to 20 minutes.
2. Scrape chile pulp from skins and put pulp into a blender along with the orange juice, raisins and onions.
3. Blend until smooth, adding water if necessary.

NOTE: Serve hot or chilled.

Gingered Cashew Pesto

Wow! Tastes like butter, but better. A creamy green pesto with a ginger kick. Goes with vegetables, tofu kabobs and lots more!

1 c	**Cilantro leaves**
1/2 c	**Raw cashews**
3 Tbl	**Lime juice**
1/4 c	**Olive oil (or toasted sesame oil)**
1 Tbl	**Garlic, chopped**
2 tsp	**Ginger root, peeled and chopped**
	Cayenne and sea salt to taste

Puree everything in a food processor using a pulse chop motion. Scrape down the sides once while making. Put into a small bowl. Refrigerate.

A smiling heart is the caretaker of friendship's garden.

Cilantro Walnut Pesto

A nice lemony pesto that goes well over grilled corn on the cob or as a sauce for pasta and vegetables.

1 c	**Cilantro leaves**
1/2 c	**Walnuts, lightly toasted**
1/4 c	**Olive oil**
2 Tbl	**Fresh lemon juice**
1 Tbl	**Garlic, chopped (3 cloves)**
1/2 tsp	**Sea salt**
Dash	**Cayenne**
3 Tbl	**Purified water**
1/4 c	**Soy parmesan cheese (optional)**

Blend everything except soy cheese in a food processor until smooth. Transfer to a small bowl and stir in the soy cheese by hand. Refrigerate or freeze.

Spinach Pesto

A rich green pesto. Stir into steamed vegetables,
serve with a baked potato, bread or pasta.

1/2 c	Walnut pieces
1 bunch	Spinach, rinsed and coarsely chopped
1	Jalapeño pepper, chopped
1 tsp	Olive oil
2	Garlic cloves
2 Tbl	Lemon juice
	Cracked black pepper
1 Tbl	Aminos (or 1/2 Tbl "Lite" soy sauce)

1. Toast walnuts in toaster oven until they are light brown.
2. Steam cook spinach in a pot with a scant bit of water, just a few minutes until it wilts.
3. Put walnuts and the remaining ingredients into the food processor and pulse chop until a creamy-chunky consistency prevails.

SERVES: 4

Notes:

Pueblo Pesto

A red-adobe colored sauce, thickened with California chile pulp.
A perfect accent to grilled foods, Mexican or Southwestern dishes,
pastas or pizza crusts (see Pueblo Pizza, page 255). This pesto has a
memorable flavor that you'll want to use again and again.

3 oz bag	Dried California red chiles
	(makes 1/2 c chile pulp)
1/2 c	Red onion, chopped
1½ Tbl	Garlic, chopped
2 Tbl	Peanut butter
1 Tbl	Lemon juice
1 c	Tomato, seeded and chopped
1 Tbl	Raisins
1 tsp each	Cumin and oregano
1/2 tsp	Sea salt
	Cayenne to taste

1. Wash, seed and stem the chiles. Put in a medium saucepan, add water to cover and bring it to a boil. Cover and turn to low heat for 20 minutes. Turn off heat and let steam 10 minutes.
2. Using a spatula, scrape the chile pulp away from its skin. Put chile pulp and the remaining seasonings into a food processor and pulse chop, then puree. Stop and scrape down the sides and blend again.

MAKES: 2 cups

Presto Pesto Caps

Broiled pesto-filled mushroom caps are great appetizers!

Clean several large mushrooms, turn cap-side down and remove stem by wiggling it out. Put 1/2 tsp pesto of your choice into each mushroom cap. Place on broiling tray and broil a few minutes. Serve hot.

Notes:

Basil, Lime and Pumpkin Seed Pesto

*Fresh and delightful. No need for oil in this fragrant
and versatile sauce with a citrus bite.*

1 c	**Fresh basil leaves, packed full (1 bunch)**
1/2 c	**Fresh squeezed lime juice (about 4 limes)**
1/2 c	**Pumpkin seeds, lightly toasted**
1 Tbl	**Garlic, chopped**
1/2 tsp	**Sea salt**

1. Tear basil leaves and measure.
2. Lightly toast pumpkin seeds (until they pop), put seeds into a
   blender and grind 30 seconds.
3. Add the remaining ingredients, blend until smooth. You might
   have to stop blender to scrape down the sides.

SERVING SUGGESTION:
Spread on baguette or toast, or toss into pasta.
See Broccoli Eggplant Salad (page 75).

MAKES: 1½ cups

Spicy Peanut Spread

Dynamically delicious! Use on toast or add to pasta or vegetables.
Thin with a bit of water for a sauce.

1 c	Roasted peanuts (unsalted)
2 Tbl	Ginger, fresh chopped
1 Tbl	Garlic, chopped
1/2 c	Onion, chopped
1/2 c	Peeled tomatoes, chopped
1/3 c	Fresh cilantro leaves, packed
1/4 c	Lime or lemon juice
1 Tbl each	Tamari and ketchup
1 tsp each	Cumin and chile powder
	Cayenne to taste

1. Pulse chop peanuts, ginger, garlic and onion in a food processor. Stop and scrape down the sides.
2. Add the remaining ingredients and puree.

MAKES: 2 cups

Cayenne Pepper

Cayenne increases the circulation. It is one of the highest sources of vitamins C and A, and makes an excellent health tonic and internal disinfectant when added to warm water and lemon juice.

Use as a spicy flavoring to foods.

Basic Creamy Seed Cheese

An easy recipe to create a creamy seed cheese that is fermented a bit in a bottle or jar. The fermentation renders lots of friendly bacteria and enzymes, which also make the nuts easy to digest. There are many delicious combinations of seeds and nuts that may be blended to create interesting textures and tastes. Cashews or macadamia nuts are very rich and creamy and are great when blended with almond or sunflower seeds.

> 2 c   **Seeds or nuts***
> 3 c   **Pure water**

Combos to Try

> #1   **1 c Sunflower seeds with 1 c Cashews**
> #2   **1 c Almond with 1/2 c each Pumpkin seeds
>   and Macadamia nuts**
> #3   **1 c Almond with 1/2 c Sun seeds and
>   1/2 c Walnuts**

1. Grind seeds powdery fine in a coffee/seed mill. Transfer to a blender. Add 1 cup water to blender and liquefy. Add the remaining water and puree well.
2. Pour into a glass jar and cover the jar with a paper towel. Wrap a kitchen towel around the jar and keep in a warm place for 8 hours or so; until separation of "cheese" and liquid occurs from fermentation. (The "cheese" will be at the top and the liquid will be at the bottom.) Spoon out cheese and season as desired.

NOTE: You can also add herbs and spices to seed cheese before fermentation, or forgo fermentation altogether and use as a dip (use less water in this case).

MAKES: 2 cups

Notes:

Each of us has our own being, and our own way ... to live, to celebrate, to sing and to dance in the ecstasy of Life.

Creamy Tomato Nut Cheese Sauce

A fermented seed cheese sauce, blended with fresh tomatoes and herbs.

1/3 c	Seed Cheese (Cashew Almond, page 136)
1¼ c	Tomatoes, seeded and chopped (3 tomatoes)
1 Tbl	Parsley, trim off stems
1	Garlic clove
1 tsp	Natural Worcestershire sauce (or aminos)
Dash	Cayenne
2 Tbl	Soy parmesan cheese (optional)

Blend everything in a food processor until creamy, about 2 minutes.

SERVING SUGGESTIONS:
Serve in a sauce bowl or toss into steamed zucchini squash.
Or use as a salad dressing.

Notes:

Garlic Seed Cheese Sauce

1/2 c	Seed Cheese (page 137)
1½ c	Vegetable broth
1 Tbl	Arrowroot or kuzu powder
1 Tbl	Onion powder
2 Tbl	Garlic, roasted or pureed
Twist of	Lemon
1/2 tsp	Basil, crushed

1. Whisk together broth and arrowroot powder, mix in spices and heat up in a small saucepan on low heat, stirring until thick.
2. Stir in the seed cheese and serve over rice, pasta or other grains or steamed squash.

YIELDS: 2 cups

Vegetable Seed Cheese

Mix seed cheese with the pulp from making vegetable juices.
A healthy combo.

1/2 c	Seed Cheese (page 137)
1/2 c	Carrot or beet pulp
1 tsp each	Lemon juice, aminos
1 tsp each	Ginger and garlic, minced

Stir together. Use as a sandwich filling, on crackers or in sushi rolls — enzyme packed!

Garlic and Herb Seed Cheese

A tasty spread for crackers, toast, celery ribs or mushroom caps.

1 c	Seed Cheese (see recipe, page 137)
2	Garlic cloves, crushed
1/2 tsp	Dill weed (or 1/2 Tbl fresh minced)
1 tsp	Onion powder
1/2 tsp	Basil (or 1/2 Tbl fresh minced)
1 tsp	Lemon juice
1/2 Tbl	Finely minced parsley
	Cracked pepper and sea salt to taste

Mix everything together in a small bowl. Enjoy now, or let sit overnight to bring out all the flavors.

Ginger Soy Seed Cheese

1 c	Seed Cheese (see page 137)
1 tsp	Fresh ginger, minced
1/2 tsp	Sesame oil, toasted
1 tsp	"Lite" soy sauce
1	Garlic clove, pressed
1 Tbl	Green onions, finely minced (reserve a few for garnish)

Stir all the ingredients together in a small bowl. Let sit overnight in fridge before serving for maximum enjoyment and flavor!

Seed Cheese Pesto Caps

- 6 large Mushrooms, cleaned and stemmed
- 1/2 c Seed Cheese
- 2 Tbl Fresh minced basil
- 1 clove Garlic, pressed
- Olive oil and aminos

Place mushrooms (round caps down) on a lightly oiled baking tray. Put a dash of aminos in each cavity. Bake for 5 minutes at 400°. Mix together Seed Cheese, basil and garlic. Stuff each cap and broil again for 5 minutes more.

SERVES: 2

Notes:

You can slice a
paté or mousse
and use it as a
filling for lasagne
or enchiladas.
Also, place a slice
of mousse on
cooked lasagna
noodles and roll up
pinwheel style.
Cover with a
sauce and bake
30 minutes at 350°.

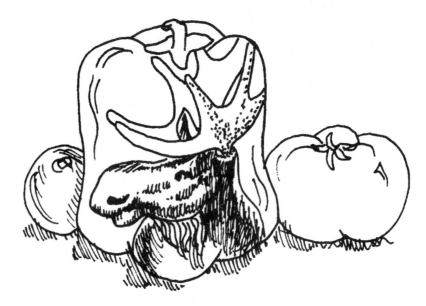

Tomato Red Pepper Mousse

A tasty cheese-like mousse to serve at parties or home gatherings.

2 c	Water
1/2 c	Agar flakes
1/2 c	Tahini
6 oz	Tomato paste
1/4 c	Nutritional yeast flakes
2½ Tbl	Lemon juice
1 Tbl	Onion powder
1 tsp	Garlic powder (or 2 cloves garlic)
1 tsp	Sea salt
Dash	Cayenne pepper
1/3 c	Roasted red pepper, minced

1. Whisk together water and agar flakes in a medium saucepan. Bring to a boil, then reduce heat to medium low, stirring now and then for a few minutes more.
2. Put all the ingredients into a blender (except red pepper), and blend well. Stir red pepper into the mixture by hand.
3. Put mixture into a lightly oiled mold and chill for 2 hours until set. Unmold before serving.

SERVING SUGGESTIONS:
Serve with crackers, and vegetable crudites.

Green Chile and Garlic Mousse

A sensational and spicy mousse, light green in color.
Especially good as an appetizer if served with toasted whole wheat
sourdough slices or crackers.

1/2 c	**Vegetable broth or white wine**
1/4 c	**Garlic cloves, crushed**
1¾ c	**Water**
1/3 c	**Agar flakes**
1/2 c	**Tahini**
1 tsp	**Sea salt**
1/2 Tbl	**Onion powder**
1/3 c	**Cilantro leaves, chopped**
1/3 c	**Nutritional yeast flakes**
1/2 tsp	**Garlic powder**
1/8 tsp	**Cayenne**
1/2 c	**Roasted green chiles, chopped (4 oz can)**

1. Bring the vegetable broth and garlic to boil in a small cast iron skillet. Reduce heat and simmer for 8 minutes. Add a bit of water if pan begins to brown slightly.
2. Whisk together water and agar flakes in a medium pot and bring to a boil. Reduce heat to low and let the mixture cook for a couple of minutes more.
3. Put all the other ingredients (except green chile) into a blender and blend until creamy. Stir in green chile with a spoon.
4. Pour into a lightly oiled mold — something with an interesting pattern or shape is best. Refrigerate 2 hours before unmolding.

NOTE: For a greener mousse, add 1 tsp. Spirulina powder to blended ingredients.

SERVING SUGGESTIONS:
For a light meal, serve with toasted bread
and a large grated salad.

SERVES: 4 - 8

Garlic

Garlic is definitely one of humanity's "Healing Heroes." It has been said to act as a tonic for purifying the circulatory system.

This ancient bulb has been praised for its medicinal properties by the ancient Egyptians and Chinese.

Since garlic's medicinal properties are unstable in heat, use it raw as much as possible.

2-Tier Fiesta Mousse

A red/orange colored salsa mousse rests on a green Spinach Jalapeño Mousse. A stunning presentation and an exceptionally good taste combination. Decorate the top for a beautiful finale. Great for parties.

Salsa Mousse

1½ c	Water
5 Tbl	Agar flakes
1/3 c	Sesame Tahini (see page 143)
1 c	Salsa (mild, medium or hot to suit taste)
2 Tbl	Nutritional yeast flakes
1 Tbl	Onion powder
2 Tbl	Lemon juice
1/2 Tbl	Dried New Mexican red chile powder
1/2 Tbl	Garlic, chopped
1/4 tsp	Sea salt

Spinach Jalapeño Mousse

(or use Green Chile Garlic Mousse)

1½ c	Water
1/4 c	Agar flakes
1 c	Steamed spinach leaves
1/4 c	Sesame Tahini
3 Tbl	Lemon juice
1/2 c	Walnuts, toasted gently
1 tsp	Jalapeño, minced (fresh or dried)
1/2 Tbl	Garlic, chopped
1	Green onion, chopped (or 1 Tbl onion powder)
1/4 c	Fresh basil leaves, chopped (optional)
1 tsp	Spirulina powder
1/2 tsp	Sea salt

2-Tier Fiesta Mousse
(continued)

Begin with the Salsa Mousse (bottom layer):
1. Whisk agar flakes and water together in a medium saucepan and bring to a boil. Let boil a few minutes on medium heat.
2. Meanwhile, put the remaining ingredients into a blender and pour agar mixture on top. Blend until creamy. Pour into a mold that has been lightly sprayed with vegetable spray. Refrigerate.

Top Layer:
1. Prepare Spinach Mousse by whisking agar flakes and water together in the same saucepan for Salsa Mousse. Follow the same procedure: Put the remaining ingredients into the blender, add agar mixture on top and blend until well mixed and creamy.
2. Test Salsa Mousse for firmness before pouring spinach mixture on top. Pour spinach mixture in up to the rim of the mold and let it firm up in the fridge for at least 1½ hours.
3. Unmold on a bed of shredded greens (kale or chard) decorated with carrot shavings. Roasted red pepper strips, olives, and avocado slices can be used for a top garnish.

SERVING SUGGESTIONS:
Serve with a serving knife, chips, and crackers.

Sesame Tahini

Tahini (sesame butter) has been used for over 3,000 years by the Egyptians and other cultures in the Middle East. Sesame butter thickens soups, dressings, mousses, patés, dips and sauces. Tahini is a natural complement to rice and tofu.

Sesame seeds are rich in protein, the B complex vitamins, calcium, iron, vitamins D and E, phosphorus, magnesium, zinc and fatty acids.

Spinach Mushroom Mousse

A tasty, healthy mousse to serve at a party as an hors d'oeuvre. It even makes a delicious sandwich on toasted whole wheat sourdough bread.

1	Garlic clove
1 c	Onions, chopped
1/2 lb	Mushrooms, cleaned and chopped
1/4 c	Broth (or white wine)
1¼ c	Spinach, cooked
	(or 10 oz frozen pack steamed)
1/4 c	Agar flakes
1½ c	Water
1/2 c	Tahini
1 tsp	Sea salt
1/4 c	Nutritional yeast flakes
3 Tbl	Lemon juice
1/8 tsp	Cayenne pepper
1/2 tsp	Dill weed

1. Saute on low heat the first three items in broth until soft.
2. Steam spinach until wilted.
3. Whisk agar flakes into water in a small pan, bring to a boil on high for a couple of minutes.
4. Put everything into a blender and puree until creamy (stop and scrape the sides of the blender). Pour into a lightly oiled mold and chill 1 to 2 hours until set. Invert on large platter decorated with lettuce or chard leaves.

SERVING SUGGESTION:
Garnish with dill sprigs and lemon twists.

MAKES: Approx. 4 cups, enough for an average mold.

Lentil Paté

Soft, satisfying and easy to slice — a yummy grain paté that is good for you and a great regular for your family.

2 Tbl	"Lite" soy sauce
1 Tbl	Olive oil
1 Tbl	Lemon juice
1¼ c	Onions, finely minced
1½ c	Lentils, dry (organic)
3½ c	Water
3 Tbl	Nutritional yeast flakes
1½ tsp	Basil
1/4 tsp	Sage*
1 tsp each	Curry and cumin powder
1 tsp	Garlic, minced
1/4 tsp	Freshly ground black pepper

1. Put the first 3 liquids into a medium saucepan and saute onions a couple of minutes on low heat.
2. Finely grind the lentils in a food mill 1/2 cup at a time until powdery, then add to the onions. Add spices and stir in water 1 cup at a time, using a whisk to prevent lumps. Boil a few minutes on low, then cover and simmer for about 45 minutes (it will resemble a thick porridge). Be careful not to scorch the bottom of the pan.
3. Transfer to a lightly oiled bread pan and chill to set overnight or 3 hours. Unmold by inverting on a plate. Garnish with parsley or tomato slices.

*Can substitute asofetida with good results.

SERVING SUGGESTIONS:
Makes great sandwiches and appetizers.

When we are ready to listen with our heart, we are transformed ...

Soups

♦ **Live Energy Soups**
*(*live and uncooked, a liquid salad,
    the revitalizers!)*

Garden Ginger Soup   149

Euphoria Soup   150

Gazpacho   151

Chilled Papaya Mint
    Bisque   152

♦ **Cleansing Soups**
(nonfat, oil-free, vegetables only)

Gentle Stew   152

Garden Stew   153

Bok Choy Bliss   154

Cauliflower Okra Stew   155

♦ **Cleansing Purees**

Mexican Cauliflower   156

Green Supreme Puree   157

Spiced Vegetable   158

Spiked Cabbage   158

Careflower Bisque   159

Asparagus Puree   160

Kale Mushroom Leek   161

Golden Squash Bisque   162

Purple Cabbage Puree   162

Basil Broccoli California   163

Carrot Flower Puree   164

♦ **Fortifying Soups**
(with grains, nuts, tofu or soy milk)

Southwest Corn Stew   165

Homestyle Split Pea   166

Native Pozole   167

Pozole and Squash Stew   168

Holy Mole Pozole   168

Creamy Green Chile Potato   169

Creamy Cauliflower Cashew   170

Sunset Cashew Bisque   171

Fennel Asparagus Bisque   172

Creamy Grilled Eggplant Soup   173

Yellow Tomato Nut Bisque   174

Green Corn Chowder   174

Creamy Tomato Chilé   175

Creamy Corn and Red Pepper
    Chowder   176

Thai Navy Bean Soup   177

African Eggplant Peanut Stew   178

Riso Verde Stew   179

Braised Onion Soup   180

Tomato Garden Minestrone   181

Fresh Herb Zitistrone   182

Egyptian Red Stew   183

Miso Soup with Mushrooms
    and Peas   184

Soup'r Fresh Parsley Vegetable   185

Garden Ginger Energy Soup

Live, uncooked foods contain the maximum vitamins and life force; if you tire of chewing pounds of veggies, try blending them into a delicious refreshing soup.

1½ c	Cucumber, skin, seed and chop
1 bunch	Spinach leaves, rinsed and torn in half
1 c	Filtered water
1/2 c	Avocado, mashed
1 Tbl	Ginger, peeled and minced
2½ Tbl	Lemon juice
2 tsp	"Lite" soy sauce (or aminos)
Dash	Cayenne pepper
1 c	Zucchini, finely grated
1 c	Corn kernels, cut off of cob (1 ear)

1. Put the first 3 items into a food processor and pulse chop, then blend in the avocado and spices. Puree until smooth. Scrape into a medium-size bowl.
2. Stir in corn and zucchini and season to taste. Chill until ready to serve.

SERVES: 4

Exercise

Cellular Rejuvenation occurs when there is sufficient oxygen to the body. Exercise is one of the best ways of providing oxygenation.

Swimming, running, biking and walking are among the top ways to get a consistent source of fresh oxygen, while expelling carbon dioxide, your body's natural biological waste product.

Deep rhythmic breathing is essential in achieving the benefits of exercise. The muscles contract and expand, pumping blood throughout the body, which carries oxygen to the heart, brain, tissues, muscles and other organs. This increase of circulation during exercise promotes vitality, improves concentration, revitalizes the tissues, and helps to maintain a healthy heart and body.

Euphoria Soup

A live, uncooked pretty pink-colored soup,
loaded with alive enzymes, minerals and vitamins! Delicious!
Use organically grown produce if you can.

2 medium	Beets, trimmed
2 medium	Carrots, trimmed
1/2 large	Cucumber, skinned
1/2 c	Avocado, mashed
1/3 c	Cilantro leaves, loosely packed
3 c	Water
2 Tbl	Natural (mild) rice vinegar
1 Tbl	"Lite" soy sauce or tamari
1	Garlic clove, crushed
1	Serrano chile, stemmed, seeded
1 tsp	Onion powder
1/2 tsp	Cumin
1 c	Corn, freshly cut off of cob

1. Finely grate the first 3 ingredients in a food processor. Transfer into a large bowl and toss.
2. Return 3 cups of veggies back into the processor (or blender) with work blade attached. Puree until smooth with everything except the corn.
3. Pour into bowl of grated veggies, add corn, stir and serve or chill.

SERVING SUGGESTION:
Garnish with cilantro leaves and lemon wedge.

SERVES: A meal for 2, or can serve 4.

a garden kiss

Gazpacho

A tomato garden soup, refreshing and energizing.
Plan to make this the night before or in the morning so there
is enough time to serve it well chilled.

2 c	Tomatoes, chopped
1/2 c	Red onion, chopped
1 c	Cucumber, peeled, seeded and chopped
1 large	Garlic clove, halved
1/2 c	Green pepper, chopped
1½ c	Tomato juice (or vegetable blend)
1/2 c each	Bell pepper (green and red or yellow), minced
1/3 c	Red onion, minced
1 c	Cucumber, peeled, seeded, diced small
1½ c	Pure water
1 tsp	Basil or dill
1/4 c	Green onions, minced (save some for garnish)
Dash	Sea salt and cayenne or paprika

1. Put the first 5 ingredients into a food processor and puree. Transfer to a large bowl.
2. Stir in remaining ingredients and then chill for several hours before serving.

MAKES: 4 - 5 bowls

Filtered Water

Pure water is important for eliminating bodily wastes and hydrating your skin. It helps maintain a healthy skin and muscle tone, promotes healthy bowel functions, and acts as a natural appetite suppressant.

Have 8 (8 oz.) glasses of a good quality filtered water each day. Invest in a carbon filter for your sink tap, or get a portable filtration device.

A Gentle Stew

Ideal for cleansing diets, or for a simple sauce with pasta.

2 small	**Red onions, chopped**
2	**Carrots, quartered, chopped**
8 large	**Plum tomatoes, chopped**
4	**Garlic cloves, pressed**
1 tsp	**Lemon juice**
Dash	**Dill weed**

1. Put the carrots and onions in a small saucepan, add 1/2 cup water and cover. Bring to a boil, then turn down to simmer for 8 to 10 minutes.
2. Stir in the tomatoes and garlic. Cover and cook for a few minutes more, until soft. Stir in lemon and serve in bowls with dill as a garnish.

MAKES: 1 to 2 portions

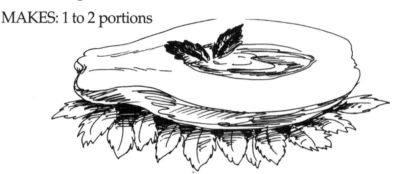

Chilled Papaya Mint Bisque

An exotic and delicious appetizing first course. The papaya, mint and lime create a delightful combination.

1/4 c	**Fresh mint leaves, torn**
2½ medium	**Chilled Hawaiian papayas, seeded**
1/2-2/3 c	**Water**
2	**Limes, juiced**
2 Tbl	**Frozen pineapple juice concentrate**

Pulse chop the mint in a food processor. Scrape papaya flesh from its skin into the food processor and pulse chop. Add the remaining ingredients and puree well. Spoon into 4 goblets and top with a tablespoon of Tofu Pineapple Creme (page 283), a mint leaf and 1/2 a red grape for a stunning presentation.

SERVES: 4

A Garden Stew

An all-vegetable stew spiced with oregano, fennel, red chile flakes and orange peel.

1	Yellow onion, chopped
1 lb	Young green beans (frozen okay), cut into 1" pieces
1 c	Potatoes, diced
4	Garlic cloves, pressed
1/4 c	Broth (or wine)
2 Tbl	Dr. Bronner's Bouillon (or 1 Tbl "Lite" soy sauce)
28 oz can	Chunky tomato sauce
28 oz	Purified water (fill up tomato can)
1 tsp	Basil, dried, or 1/4 c minced fresh
2 tsp	Oregano, dried
1/4 tsp each	Dried grated orange peel, ground fennel seeds, and red chile flakes Cracked black pepper to taste

1. Saute the onions, green beans, potatoes, garlic, and Dr. Bronner's in a heavy cast-iron pot for 5 to 10 minutes or so, stirring often.
2. Stir in everything else and simmer for 1/2 hour.

MAKES: About 5 bowls

Caring for Potatoes

Keep potatoes covered up in a brown bag in a cool, dark place until ready for use. They keep best in the same condition as which they grew ... underground away from light.

Scrub potatoes well before using. Peel only if not organically grown.

Notes:

Bok Choy Bliss

Delicate shiitake mushrooms float in this garlic miso broth, enhanced with lemon and chile slices. Bok choy will supply you with lots of readily assimilated calcium.

2¾ qt	Pure water
1	Kombu seaweed strip
3 c	Yukon gold potatoes, diced
1 bunch	Bok choy, sliced
1½ Tbl	Garlic, minced
1 c	Fresh shiitake mushrooms,* sliced and stemmed
1	Onion, halved and sliced
1	Jalapeño or serrano chile, sliced thin
1/3 c	White miso
1/4	Lemon skin, finely slivered (yellow part only)

1. Bring water to a boil in a large pot. Add kombu strip and cook 10 minutes. Add the potatoes, return to boil on medium flame, stir often.
2. Add the remaining ingredients. Dissolve the miso into a cup of the hot stock and stir back into the pot. Simmer on low for 15 to 20 minutes, covered.
3. Add lemon slivers into the soup, or as a garnish on each serving. (Freeze leftovers.)

*If you only have access to dried shiitakes, rehydrate in water before using.

SERVES: 6 - 8

Cauliflower Okra Stew

1½ c	Cauliflower, chopped (1/2 head)
12-15	Okras, stemmed and sliced
1	Yellow onion, chopped
1/4 c	Filtered water
1 Tbl	"Lite" Soy sauce
1 tsp	Garlic, minced (approx. 3 cloves)
2 c	Mushrooms, quartered
1 c	Celery, inner ribs chopped
1	Bell pepper, diced
6 c	Water
28 oz	Pureed yellow tomatoes
1 tsp	Cumin
1 Tbl	Dried mint, crumbled
1 c	Cilantro leaves
1/4 tsp	Cayenne
	Sea salt and pepper to taste
1 c	Tomatoes, chopped

1. Saute the cauliflower, okra and onion in 1/4 cup water and soy sauce on low heat.
2. Add the garlic, mushrooms, celery and pepper after a couple of minutes.
3. Cover with water, stir in the tomato puree and spices. Cover the pot and simmer about 20 minutes. Stir in tomatoes before serving.

Okra is one of the soul foods of the south. Cook it whole as a vegetable or use chopped as a thickener for gumbos, soups and stews.

When sliced, its sticky viscid insides encase small edible seeds. Okra liquid thickens a broth or vegetable medley wonderfully.

Mexican Cauliflower Puree

A zesty puree, rich in flavor — delicious!

1	Cauliflower, chopped
2	Carrots, chopped
2	Fire-roasted Anaheim green chiles (6" long), skin, stem, seed and chop
1	Dried red chile, cook to soften, (6" long), skin, stem, seed and chop
2	Garlic cloves
1 tsp each	Chile powder and oregano
2 tsp	Cumin seeds
Dash	Clove powder
1 tsp	Aminos (or to taste)

1. Steam the cauliflower and carrots in a medium pot with 1 cup water until tender.
2. Add the green chile pulp to a food processor, add the steamed veggies, and spices. Puree (in batches if necessary), then return to pot.
3. Stir in water as needed, simmer before serving.

Green Supreme Puree

*A green delight of pureed spinach and cabbage
with garlic and a hint of nutmeg.*

2 c	Water
1 large bunch	Spinach leaves
1/2 head	Cabbage, chopped coarsely
1	Jerusalem artichoke
5	Garlic cloves
1 Tbl	Liquid aminos (or Dr. Bronner's Bouillon)
1 tsp	Marjoram, dried
1/2 Tbl	Arrowroot powder, mixed with
2 Tbl	Cool water
Dash each of	Cayenne pepper and freshly grated nutmeg

1. Bring water to a boil in a soup pot, add the veggies and steam covered on low heat until tender. Add the garlic cloves after 5 minutes.
2. Puree in a food processor, along with 1 garlic clove.
3. Transfer to the pot and add the spices and arrowroot mixture. Stir and simmer several minutes more, until it thickens.

We choose how we want to feel. It is a choice, our choice. We choose to search for the meaning of life. Does the sea water search for the ocean? When we attain our highest ecstasies, our ultimate magical fulfillments, are we searching then or are we far from thought, afloat and free in a timeless moment?

May your life become a timeless moment for you.

Notes:

Spiked Cabbage

1 head	Cabbage, coarsely chopped
1	Bell pepper, chopped
1	Onion, quartered
2 c	Water
1 Tbl	"Spike" seasoning mix*
	Cayenne to taste

1. Steam the veggies in 1 cup water in a large pot until tender.
2. Transfer to a food processor; puree and add seasoning.
3. Return to pot, add water to thin to desired consistency.

*You can use an onion powder, dill, basil mixture with a dash of sea salt to substitute — or a vegetable salt-free seasoning.

Spiced Vegetable

5	Carrots, chopped
1	Onion, chopped
1/2	Apple, cored and chopped
1/2	Broccoli stalk, chopped
1/2	Celery stalk, chopped
2 c	Water
2	Garlic cloves, pressed
2 tsp	Aminos or Dr. Bronner's Bouillon
1/2 Tbl	Lemon juice
Dash each of	Cayenne, chile powder, clove, curry, oregano and maple syrup to taste

Steam the veggies in water until tender. Puree in a food processor, add spices and transfer back to pot. Simmer until hot.

Careflower Bisque

A cauliflower-based puree spiked with caraway seeds.

6	Celery stocks, chopped
1 large head	Cauliflower, chopped
1	Onion, chopped
1 small	Carrot, chopped
2 c	Water
1	Garlic clove
1/2 Tbl	Caraway seeds
1/2 Tbl	Dill weed
1 Tbl	Liquid aminos
1 Tbl	Lemon juice
	Cracked pepper and cayenne to taste

1. Bring water to a boil, steam the veggies until tender.
2. Puree veggies with some steam water in a food processor or blender, adding spices.
3. Transfer back to pot and add water as needed. Add seasonings to taste.

Notes:

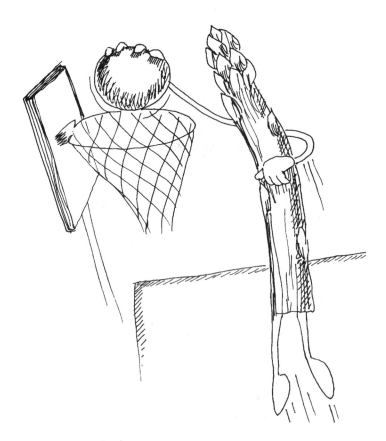

Asparagus Puree

Simple, light lemony flavors enhance the subtle asparagus.

3 bunches	Asparagus, chopped, tough ends removed
2 bunches	Green onions, chopped coarsely
2 tsp	Lemon grass
1	Garlic clove, pressed
2 tsp	Lemon juice
To taste	Cracked black pepper, cayenne and sea salt or vegetable salt.

1. Steam asparagus for 10 to 15 minutes until tender.
2. Put green onions on top of asparagus and let steam another minute.
3. Put veggies in a food processor with some steam water and the remaining spices and puree until smooth (you may have to do this in batches).
4. Transfer back to pot, add water as needed, heating gently until ready to serve.

SERVING SUGGESTION:
Garnish with a fresh dill sprig or thin lemon slice "butterfly."

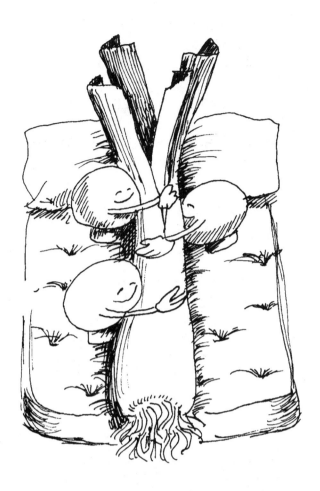

Kale and Mushroom Leek

A hearty puree, high in vitamins and calcium.

1 lb	Mushrooms, cut in half
1 bunch	Kale, stems trimmed, leaves chopped
2	Leeks, chopped
3	Garlic cloves
2 Tbl	Dr. Bronner's Bouillon or aminos
1/2 Tbl	Lemon juice
1/4 tsp each	Sage and oregano
1/2 tsp	Basil
Pinch	Cayenne pepper

1. Steam mushrooms, kale and leek until tender in 2 cups of water.
2. Puree veggies in a food processor with some steam water, then transfer back to a cooking pot. Stir in spices and some steam water. Simmer before serving. Add water if you want a thinner consistency.

Dr. Bronner's Bouillon is a concentrated soya liquid broth seasoning. It has a natural sodium-potassium-chloride balance with vitamin C, papaya enzymes, dulse, vege-amino-acid protein, and gives a hearty flavor to soups, stews and sautes.

For a light meal, put 1/2 Tbl in a cup of hot water. Flavor with 2 Tbl nutritional yeast, a small clove of pressed garlic, and a dash of lemon juice and cayenne.

Golden Squash Bisque

1½ c	Onion, chopped (1 medium)
1/4 c	Broth
1 Tbl	Garlic, minced
1 Tbl	Liquid aminos
1 tsp	Oregano
Dash	Sage
4 c	Zucchini, chopped
1½ c	Cooked, squash (butternut, acorn, Tahitian, pumpkin, etc.)

1. Saute onion in broth for a few minutes on medium low.
2. Add garlic and aminos. When golden, add spices and set aside.
3. Cook or steam zucchinis and puree them in a food processor. Add saute mixture to the processor, pulse chop until evenly distributed. Return to pot, keep warm until ready to serve.

SERVING SUGGESTION:
Garnish with a few fresh herbs (thyme, basil or parsley).

SERVES: 2 - 4

Purple Cabbage Puree

A very cleansing puree.

1 small	Red cabbage, chopped
2	Carrots chopped
2 tsp	Onion powder
1 Tbl	Liquid aminos
1/2 tsp	Dill weed
1 Tbl	Lemon juice
	Water as needed
	Garnish with dill or a small yellow flower, such as mustard.

1. Steam cabbage and carrots until tender.
2. Put into a food processor and puree. Add the remaining ingredients and water as needed. You can do this in batches.
3. Return puree to soup pan, add water till desired consistency. Heat before serving.

SERVING SUGGESTION:
Put a dollop of plain soy yogurt on top of each serving.

Basil Broccoli California

A delicious green puree of broccoli, carrots, bell pepper and herbs which gives it the flavor of a West Coast pizza.

1 bunch	**Broccoli**
2	**Carrots**
1	**Red or yellow bell pepper**
2	**Celery ribs**
3 c	**Water**
1	**Fire-roasted Anaheim chile*** **(or 2 Tbl canned)**
4	**Garlic cloves, pressed**
1 Tbl	**Basil, dried (or 1/4 c fresh leaves)**
1/2	**Lemon, juiced** **Sea salt and cayenne to taste**

1. Chop the first 4 veggies, and steam for 10 minutes or until tender. Puree in batches in a food processor using the water as needed. Transfer back to pot.
2. *Toast Anaheim chile in the oven until skin blisters (3 to 5 minutes). Remove and skin, stem and seed. Chop flesh. Add to pot.
3. Stir in spices, garlic, and rest of water. Simmer gently.

Broccoli

Broccoli is high in fiber, selenium, calcium, vitamin C and beta-carotene.

One cup of broccoli has more vitamin C than an orange.

Welcome to the world of vegetables

Notes:

Carrot Flower Puree

A cauliflower and carrot puree, warmly spiced with cardamom,
cinnamon and orange with a hint of jalapeño chile.

2 c	Pure water
2 c	Carrots, coarsely chopped
1 head	Cauliflower, coarsely chopped
1/2	Jalapeño chile, seeded and minced
1 tsp	Cardamon, ground
1 tsp	Honey or maple syrup
1/4 c	Fresh squeezed orange juice
Dash	Cinnamon (no more than 1/4 tsp)
	Sea salt or liquid aminos to taste

1. Put water, carrots and cauliflower into a large pot. Cover and bring to a boil. Turn to simmer and cook until tender, about 8 to 10 minutes.
2. Transfer veggies into a food processor with a large spoon; pulse chop, then puree until smooth. This may require 2 batches. Return to cooking pot.
3. Stir in the remaining ingredients. Simmer gently.

SERVING SUGGESTION:
Float a cilantro leaf, dill sprig or lemon garnish atop each bowl.

SERVES: 2 - 4

corn maiden

Southwest Corn Stew

A fantastic spicy corn stew featuring fresh sweet white corn and yellow wax chiles in a fragrant corn-meal thickened broth.

1	Dried red chile
2½ qts	Water
1/2 c	Yellow corn meal
2 ears	Sweet white corn, cut off of cob (2 c)
2	Yellow onions, chopped (approx. 2 c)
9	Small yellow wax chiles, chopped, seeded (approx. 1 c)
4	Zucchini (approx. 5" long x 1" thick), sliced
1 Tbl	Garlic, fresh minced (approx. 4 cloves)
2 tsp each	Oregano, cumin and coriander powder
1/4 tsp	Crushed fennel seeds
2 Tbl	Aminos
Dash	Clove powder and cinnamon
Small pinch	Saffron threads
1/4 c	Cilantro

1. Bring water to boil in a large pot, add red chile and boil 10 minutes, strain out and set aside. Skin, seed and reserve chile pulp for later.

2. Stir in the corn meal using a whisk, cook 5 to 7 minutes. Add the corn, onions, yellow chiles and zucchini and return to boil, then turn down to simmer.

3. Add spices and garlic and chile pulp, cover and cook 30 minutes on low. Stir in cilantro before serving, with salsa garnish.

SERVING SUGGESTION:
Garnish with 1 Tbl salsa fresca (or chopped tomatoes) and chopped cilantro leaves per bowl.

Spicy Foods Burn Up Calories

Hot foods like chiles, garlic, cayenne, mustard or horseradish, boost our metabolic rate an additional 25%, thus burning more calories.

According to researchers at Oxford Polytechnic in England.

Welcome to the world of vegetables

Notes:

Homestyle Split Pea

A gentle nourishing soup.

5½ c	Purified water
1½ c	Split peas, rinsed
1 Tbl	Concentrated vegetable stock
1/2 Tbl	Onion powder
1/2 tsp	Dill (or 1 Tbl fresh minced)
Dash	Cayenne
1/2 c	Green pepper, chopped
1/2 c	Carrots, minced
1/2 c	Carrots, quartered and sliced thin

1. Bring water to boil in a large pot, add peas. Stir and cover, cook on low for 1 hour.
2. Add the remaining spices and vegetables, simmer covered another 20 to 25 minutes. You may wish to add more water as needed.

SERVES: 6 — 1 cup servings

Native Pozole

Top with red or green chile, add beans or vegetables to taste.
A hearty and satisfying soup for colder weather.

2½ c	Pozole, soaked overnight
1	Kombu strip (optional)
9 c	Water
1 c	Onion, chopped
2 Tbl	Garlic, minced
2 tsp	Oregano
1 Tbl	Onion powder
2 Tbl	Liquid aminos (or 1 Tbl "Lite" soy sauce)
1 tsp	Sea salt
1	Garlic bulb, roasted (see page 189)
2	Dried small red chiles, minced
1 recipe	Green Chile Sauce (page 119)

1. Rinse Pozole in warm water in a strainer. Sort through to pick out any stones. Bring large pot of water to boil and add pozole and Kombu. Return to boil, cover and simmer.
2. Add onions and garlic after about 1 hour and cook about 4 hours until kernels open and are soft.
3. Stir in the additional spices and minced roasted garlic, add 1 to 2 cups of water as desired. Simmer another 10 minutes before serving. Ladle green chile on top of each bowl.

*For a richer chile taste, add 2 Tbl red chile powder and 1 tsp cumin to broth.

SERVING SUGGESTIONS:
Garnish with fresh chopped tomatoes, cilantro and/or avocado
slices. Serve with hot tortillas, kept warm on the side.

SERVES: 6

Pozole is cooked dried corn, or hominy. It is the whole kernel, and is available as blue or white corn. Blue corn has more protein, less fat and has a nuttier taste.

It takes 4 to 5 hours to cook, unless you use a pressure cooker.

Pozole is a hearty meal in itself and a staple food to the Indians and other peoples of the Southwest.

Notes:

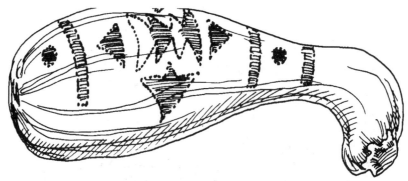

Pozole and Squash Stew

Cooked dried "hominy" corn forms the base to this
cold weather treat. Very nourishing.

1 recipe	**Native Pozole (page 167)**
3 cups	**Yellow crook-neck squash**
3 cups	**Zucchini**
3 large	**Tomatoes, seeded and chopped**
2-4 c	**Water or broth, as needed**
1/2 c	**Cilantro leaves, chopped**
1/4 c	**Soy cheese to taste (optional)**

1. Cook Pozole according to recipe. Quarter and slice squash.
2. When Pozole is almost completely soft, add vegetables and water.   Cover and simmer 20 to 25 minutes.
3. Garnish with fresh tomatoes and cilantro and grated soy cheese.

Holy Mole Pozole

A very hearty dish for a cold night.

1 recipe	**Native Pozole, page 167**
1 recipe	**Mole Sauce, page 226**

1. Prepare Pozole and Mole Sauce separately, according to recipes.
2. When Pozole is soft, stir in Mole Sauce.

SERVING SUGGESTION:
Serve with hot tortillas and a salad.

Creamy Green Chile Potato

A potato-based vegetable soup made creamy by pureeing half of it, and thickened with arrowroot. Green chile puts a touch of Southwest into this sizzling soup.

10 c	Filtered water (about 2 qts)
1	Bell pepper, chopped
1	Celery rib and leaves, chopped
1½ Tbl	Garlic, minced
1	Serrano chile, minced (seeds removed if you don't like "hot")
1 small	Cauliflower head, cut into "flowerettes"
2 c	Yukon or yellow finn potatoes, cut into 1/2" cubes (approx. 5)
1½ tsp	Dill weed, or to taste
2 Tbl	Liquid aminos
1 c	Fire-roasted green chile, diced (or Green Chile Sauce, page 119)
1 tsp	Cumin
1 Tbl	Arrowroot powder, mixed with 1/4 c water
1 c	Soy milk (optional)

1. Bring water to boil, add next 8 items, cover and simmer for 20 minutes.
2. Stir in the remaining ingredients. Ladle half of the vegetables into a food processor and puree. Return to soup pot. (The more veggies you puree, the creamier the soup.) Serve hot.

What is truly significant is never seen by the eye: The invisible golden thread of light that is woven into the fabric of all life.

Notes:

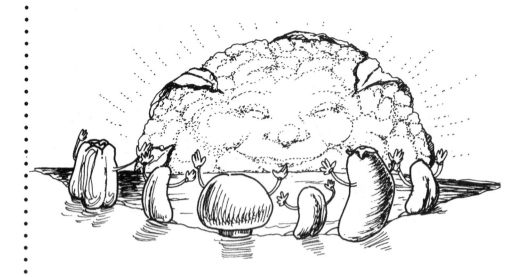

Creamy Cauliflower Cashew

A spicy, creamy and wonderful puree!

1 qt	Pure water
1 large	Carrot, chopped
2	Jalapeño chiles, seeded if desired
1	Celery heart (inner ribs and leaves only)
1/2	Eggplant, skinned and chopped
6-8	Mushrooms, quartered
1 large	Cauliflower, chopped
1	Dried red chile, seeded and stemmed
1/2 c	Cashew pieces
2-3 Tbl	Liquid aminos
1	Garlic clove, pressed
	Slivered green onions as garnish

1. Bring water to a boil in a large soup pot. Add chopped veggies and both whole chiles, cover and return to boil. Simmer for about 10 minutes, until veggies are tender.
2. Remove chiles, scrape pulp from skin and return chile pulp to soup pot. Transfer (in batches) to a food processor, add cashews and remaining ingredients. Puree well until smooth and creamy. (If you want texture —reserve a few cauliflower pieces.)
3. Return to pot and heat gently, garnish with green onions.

SERVES: 6

Sunset Cashew Bisque

*Naturally sweet and creamy, loaded with beta carotene
and easy to make!*

2 c	**Pure water**
4 c	**Butternut squash (yellow flesh), peeled and chopped coarsely**
2 large	**Carrots, chopped**
1 large	**Yellow onion, quartered**
2/3 c	**Raw cashew pieces**
1/2 Tbl	**Fresh ginger, peeled and minced or pressed through a garlic press**
1 small	**Serrano green chile (remove seeds if you are sensitive to hot foods)**
1/2 tsp	**Sea salt**

1. Put water in medium pot; bring to boil, covered. Add squash and cover. Cook for 5 minutes on low. Add carrots and onions, cover and cook until tender (approx. 10 minutes), set aside.
2. Grind cashews in a food processor until fine; then add cooked veggies, ginger, serrano chile and salt. Puree until smooth, adding water as needed.
3. Transfer puree to pot, heat until warm, add water to desired consistency.

SERVING SUGGESTION:
Garnish with fresh minced herbs (mint, cilantro or parsley work well).

SERVES: 4 - 6

We see the wonder of life through the eyes of eternity when we move our focus from the visible to the invisible.

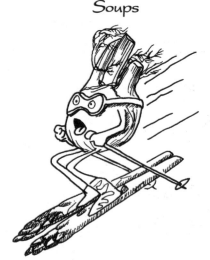

Fennel Asparagus Bisque

This soup is as delicate and fresh as springtime.

4 c	Water
1 large	Carrot
1	Fennel bulb, trim bottom, chop
1 bunch	Green onions
2 c	Asparagus, cut into 1/2" pieces
1 c	Parsley, minced
1 tsp	Fresh grated lemon peel (organically grown!)
1 Tbl	Dill, fresh minced

Cream Sauce:

3 Tbl	Arrowroot powder
10 oz	Soft silken tofu
2-3	Garlic cloves
1/2 tsp	Sea salt (or to taste)
1 Tbl	Lemon juice
1/4 c	Stock from vegetable broth
	Fresh cracked pepper to taste

1. Bring water to boil in a large pot. Coarse chop carrots in a food processor, then add onions and fennel stalk, pulsing to an even "mince."
2. Add minced vegetables to pot, return to boil, then cover and simmer for 10 to 15 minutes. Then add lemon peel, dill and pepper to soup.
3. Put cream sauce ingredients into blender and puree until smooth. Add 1½ cups of soup to blender and puree all together. Whisk this mixture back into soup pot. Simmer until it thickens. Add water as needed.

SERVES: 2 - 4

Creamy Grilled Eggplant Soup

A sublime and nutritious blend of grilled veggies and many spices.
The creamy tofu-soy milk base is high in protein and low in fat.

1 large	Eggplant, skinned if desired and sliced into 1/2" rounds
1	Onion, sliced into 1/2" rounds
1	Pulp of dried red chile, cooked to soften, seeded and skinned (page 119)
1/2 Tbl	Garlic cloves, chopped
2 c	Water
2 c	Soy milk or Almond Milk (page 12) blended with
1/2 c	Soft tofu
2 Tbl	Liquid aminos
1 tsp	Fresh grated ginger
1 tsp	Dried basil
1/8 tsp	Fresh grated nutmeg
1/8 tsp	Cayenne
1/4 tsp	Curry powder

1. Heat griddle on high, spray with a bit of natural vegetable spray, and grill eggplant and onion on medium flame on each side. Flip them over as they become golden brown.
2. Chop eggplant and onion and put into the food processor.
3. Puree vegetables and chile pulp, adding garlic and water. Return to a soup pot and add soy milk, tofu and spices.
4. If you desire a thicker soup, add 1 tsp arrowroot powder mixed with a little water.

SERVING SUGGESTION:
A fresh, light, organic baby leaf salad goes well.

SERVES: 2 as a main dish

Onions were worshiped by some Egyptians and they even swore oaths on them. They were almost sacred, especially because they were used in various healing ceremonies, according to the Codex Ebers of medical papyrus of 1550 B.C.

Even today, we are discovering more qualities about onions that seem to elevate their status as a respected health food.

Notes:

Yellow Tomato Nut Bisque

Very quick to make and delicious.
Yellow tomatoes have less acidity than red tomatoes.

28 oz can	Yellow tomato puree
3	Garlic cloves, pressed
1 Tbl	Peanut butter, dissolved in
1/4 c	Hot water
1 tsp	Onion powder
1 sprig	Basil, use leaves as garnish

Stir all the ingredients together in a medium pot until hot. Garnish with crumbled dried basil or fresh basil leaf.

SERVES: 2 - 4

Green Corn Chowder

This soup is green from the green onion blended into the creamy tofu base. Whips up in minutes for a light delicate soup.

15½ oz can	Corn kernels
2	Garlic cloves
10.5 oz pack	Soft silken tofu
1 Tbl	Arrowroot powder
1/2 Tbl	Aminos
1½ c	Water
1/2 tsp	Cumin powder
Dash	Cayenne
1/3 c	Green onion, chopped

1. Heat corn in medium pot on low heat.
2. Blend the remaining ingredients together in a blender until creamy, then pour over corn in pot.
3. Heat a few minutes on low, stirring as it thickens. Garnish with cilantro sprig or paprika.

MAKES: 4 — 1 cup servings

Peace on Earth begins with peace in our heart.

Creamy Tomato Chilé

A cream of tomato soup Santa Fe style; with black beans, corn, garlic and chile — super! The creaminess is from a tofu base.

2 c	**Water**
28 oz can	**Yellow tomato puree**
1/4 c	**Cooked black beans**
1 c	**Corn kernels**
1½ Tbl	**Red chile powder**
1 tsp	**Basil**
1 Tbl	**Onion powder**
1 Tbl	**Garlic, minced**
10.5 oz	**Silken soft tofu**
1½ Tbl	**Tahini**
1 Tbl	**Liquid aminos (or 1 tsp sea salt)**

1. Bring water, tomato puree, beans and corn to a near boil in a soup pot.
2. Put spices, tofu and tahini in a food processor and blend until creamy. Scrape down the sides of the food processor and blend again.
3. Stir creamy mixture into soup pot. Simmer a few minutes before serving.

SERVING SUGGESTION:
Garnish with cilantro or chives.

Creamy Corn and Red Pepper Chowder

A scrumptious chowder. Use 1 cup tofu instead of cashews for a less rich version.

1 c	Cashew pieces (or tofu)
3 c	Water
2 Tbl	Arrowroot powder
1 Tbl	Onion powder
1 tsp	Garlic powder
1/2 tsp	Sea salt
1/3 tsp	Thyme
2	Garlic cloves
1/4 c	Broth
1 Tbl	Aminos
2 c	Onions, diced
1 c	Red pepper, diced small
3 c	Corn kernels
1½ to 2 c	Water (as needed)

1. Put cashews into a blender and grind. Then add the next 7 ingredients and blend until creamy.
2. Put broth and aminos into a saucepan and saute onions on low for a few minutes. Add red pepper and corn and saute on low for a few minutes more.
3. Stir in creamy cashew mixture. Add water until desired thickness is attained.

SERVES: 4

Thai Navy Bean Soup

A savory coconut milk broth flavored with ginger and peanuts creates a very unusual navy bean soup. Prepare in 4 easy steps.

4 c	**Cooked navy beans***
1	**Onion, chopped**
3	**Garlic cloves, minced**
1/4 c	**Broth**
2 Tbl each	**Lemon juice and aminos**
Vegetables: 1	**Carrot, chopped coarse**
4	**Celery ribs, chopped coarse**
1	**Bunch spinach (or chard), sliced, stems removed**
1/2 c	**Parsley, packed and trimmed**
Spicy Puree: 2 Tbl	**Curry paste condiment**
1 tsp	**Curry powder**
1 Tbl	**Onion powder**
1/2 c	**Coconut milk**
2 Tbl	**Peanut butter**
1 Tbl	**Honey**
1	**Serrano chile, chopped, seeded**
1/4 tsp	**Cayenne or red chile flakes**
16 oz	**Peeled chopped tomatoes**

*Start with 1½ cups dried navy beans: Soak in water overnight. Rinse and drain, then fill a soup pot with water, covering beans by 2". Bring to a boil, reduce to simmer for 1½ to 2 hours, until beans are slightly soft.

1. Saute onion and garlic in liquids until onions are transparent. Add to the bean pot.
2. Pulse chop vegetables, shredding spinach leaves by hand. Add these to the bean pot.
3. Put spicy puree ingredients into the food processor and pulse chop. Add a ladle full of soup stock from bean pot and continue chopping. Stop and scrape down sides, then puree. Add this to the soup pot. Stir in tomatoes and simmer 10 minutes more for flavors to meld. Top each bowl of soup with green onion slivers.

We weave the fabric of our lives with the invisible golden thread of love.

Notes:

African Eggplant Peanut Stew

This eggplant and tomato stew yields a lovely coral color, heavenly scented with garlic and peanuts for quite a wonderful meal. Serve it with a leafy green salad of organic baby greens and either Basmati rice or cous-cous studded with green peas.

1/2 Tbl	"Lite" soy sauce or tamari
1/4 c	Fresh lemon juice
1 med	Eggplant, diced (unpeeled)
2 small	Brown onions, chopped
1 Tbl	Fresh fennel sprig, minced
1½ c	Leeks, thinly sliced
28 oz can	Peeled pear tomatoes in juice
3 c	Filtered water
1 Tbl	Garlic, chopped
1/3 c	Peanut paste* (or peanut butter with no oil added)

1. In a soup pot, heat the liquids at medium heat. Add eggplant, onion and fennel, saute 10 minutes on low heat, stir well to coat evenly.
2. Add leeks, then stir in tomatoes and their juice (cut them into the soup pot) and add 2 cups of water.
3. Put the remaining water, peanut paste and garlic into a blender and liquefy several seconds. Stir gently back into soup pot. Simmer 30 minutes on low before serving.

*Try roasted unsalted peanuts and blend them in the food processor, adding a bit of water to create a paste. This is a less fat version of peanut "butter."

SERVES: 6

Riso Verde Stew

A creamy soup with nice hints of basil and fennel, using riso (rice-shaped pasta) and assorted vegetables.

1½ qts	Water
2	Zucchinis, chopped
1	Onion, sliced
1 c	Cabbage and/or beet greens, shredded
3-4	Carrots, sliced in half-moons
2	Anaheim chiles, roasted, skinned, seeded and diced (page 119)
2 Tbl	Fresh basil leaves, torn
2 Tbl	Fresh parsley, minced
1/3 c	Riso (rice pasta)
1/4 c	Elbow pasta
2 tsp each	Fennel seeds and chile flakes
1 Tbl each	Oregano, onion powder and coriander
2 Tbl	Tamari
2	Garlic cloves, chopped
Dash	Fresh grated nutmeg
2 c	Soy milk mixed with 2 Tbl arrowroot powder

1. Bring water to boil in a large soup pot. Add veggies and pasta, stir and return to boil, turn down to medium-low heat. After 5 to 8 minutes, add spices.
2. Puree half of soup after it has cooked 15 minutes, pour puree back into soup pot.
3. Add soy milk, mix and stir into pot, heat gently for 10 more minutes.

SERVES: 6

The path of our own ecstasy, of our own freedom, of our own fulfillment is found within our own heart.

Notes:

Braised Onion Soup

A rich broth with the flavor of "French Onion Soup."
Use elephant garlic for a mellow garlic taste.

4-5	Onions
1	Daikon radish
1	Celery heart (inner ribs)
1/3 c	Garlic, minced
1/3 c	Pure water
2 Tbl each	Lemon juice and "Lite" soy sauce
1 Tbl	Olive oil (optional)
2 Tbl	Dr. Bronner's Bouillon
2 tsp	Natural Worcestershire sauce
2 Tbl	Hot salsa
3 tsp	Honey

Topping: 6 1/2" Thick slices of a baguette
(one per serving)
Extra virgin pure olive oil
Oregano and soy cheese
Minced chives and parsley

1. Shred onion, daikon and celery in a food processor. Stir in garlic.
2. Heat water with lemon, olive oil and soy sauce in a large cast-iron pot. Stir in shredded vegetables, cook 5 to 10 minutes on medium heat. Add hot water to 3/4 full, cover and simmer for 20 minutes stirring occasionally.
3. Add the remaining seasonings to pot. Simmer while assembling topping: Sprinkle olive oil on bread slices, top with oregano and soy cheese. Broil at 450° until toasted. Put one toast on bottom of each soup plate, cover with soup, top soup with soy cheese, chives and parsley.

SERVES: 6

Tomato Garden Minestrone

A minestrone without beans or pasta, but loaded with high-energy vegetables and greens (which are high in calcium).

1 Tbl	Garlic, minced
2 c	Onion, chopped finely
1/2 c	Mushrooms, chopped
1 tsp	Olive oil
1/4 c	Water
1 Tbl	"Lite" soy sauce
3 c	Carrots, minced (3 carrots)
1/2 head	Cauliflower, finely chopped
4 ribs	Celery, minced (use leafy part, too)
2 c packed	Field greens (dandelion, mustard, lambs quarters, or kale)
2 c	Plum tomatoes, cut (with juice)
6 c	Boiling water
1 Tbl	Concentrated vegetable stock
1 tsp	Rosemary, dried and crumbled

1. Saute garlic, onions, mushrooms in olive oil, water and soy sauce in a large pot on low heat. Stir to evenly coat veggies. Cook for 5 to 8 minutes on medium heat.
2. Continue to add remaining ingredients, stirring after each addition. Cover and simmer another 15 to 25 minutes.

SERVING SUGGESTION:
Serve with crusty warm bread or Polenta Triangles (page 204).

SERVES: 4 - 6

What is soup?
... Water and anything you love.

Fresh Herb Zitistrone

*A fantastic blend of fresh garden herbs, vegetables,
and ziti noodles. Improvise with whatever fresh vegetables
you have on hand. An especially satisfying soup.*

4¼ qts	**Pure water**
6 oz	**Ziti pasta**
2 Tbl	**Olive oil**
1 each	**Onion and carrot, chopped**
4	**Celery stalks, sliced**
2	**Zucchini, quartered and sliced**
1	**Red pepper, seeded and diced**
1 Tbl	**Concentrated vegetable broth**
1/3 c	**Nutritional yeast flakes**
2 Tbl	**Liquid aminos (or to taste)**
3 Tbl each	**Fresh basil and rosemary, minced**
1 Tbl	**Fresh thyme leaves**
1 c	**Fresh tomatoes, chopped and seeded**
15 oz can	**Garbanzo beans**
1/2 tsp	**Fennel seeds**
1/4 tsp each	**Red chile flakes and cracked pepper**
6	**Garlic cloves, chopped**
1 c	**Parsley, minced**
6 oz	**Soy mozzarella cheese, grated (optional)**

1. Bring large pot of water to boil, add ziti and return to boil. Add olive oil and cook about 8 minutes on medium low.

2. Add the next four vegetables; cook another 5 minutes. Add herbs and seasonings (next 5 ingredients); cook another 10 minutes on low heat.

3. Stir in the remaining ingredients, saving soy cheese for top. Simmer about 5 minutes before serving.

SERVING SUGGESTION:
Serve with Focaccia (page 208) or Bread Sticks (page 209)
for a nice meal.

MAKES: About 10 servings

Notes:

Egyptian Red Stew

Fragrant, enchanting and satisfying.
A perfect accompaniment to that mystical evening.

1/2 c	Water
1/2 Tbl	Olive oil
1	Red pepper, coarsely chopped
1	Onion, chopped
1	Eggplant, peeled and chopped
2	Green chiles (or jalapeños), sliced
1/2 Head	Cauliflower, coarsely chopped
1/2 Tbl each	Coriander and cardamom powder
1 Tbl	Onion powder
1/2 tsp	Curry powder
2 tsp	Sweet basil
	A few threads of saffron
28 oz can	Plum tomatoes, cut
5	Tomatoes, chopped
1 can	Garbanzo beans
2 c	Water (fresh and pure)
2	Garlic cloves, pressed

1. Saute first 5 vegetables in water/oil mixture in a large cast-iron or stainless steel soup pot, stirring for 5 minutes or so.
2. Add spices, stir to coat evenly, then add remaining ingredients except garlic. Simmer covered for 15 minutes.
3. Stir in garlic. Simmer a few minutes longer before serving.

May your life be an awakening and may you see each choice as the dawning of a new you.

The mushrooming of Enlightenment

Miso Soup with Mushrooms and Peas

Our quick and easy favorite miso soup with a rich savory broth.

2 Tbl	White miso
1½ tsp	Peanut butter
1 Tbl	Tahini
1 large	Garlic, chopped
1 c	Water
1 tsp	Arrowroot powder
3 c	Water
1/2 c	Green onions
5 oz	Firm tofu (marinated), diced
3/4 tsp	Ginger root, grated
3 large	Mushrooms, halved and sliced
1 c	Green peas, frozen

1. Put first 6 items into a blender and blend well. Transfer contents into a medium pot, heat on low.
2. Add the remaining ingredients and stir well, cook on medium-low heat for 10 to 15 minutes.

SERVES: 3 - 4

Soup'r Fresh Parsley Vegetable

A delicious vegetable soup loaded with garlic, fresh parsley and dill in a savory mock chicken style broth. The parsley is added last to retain the vitamins (calcium, A, and C).

1	Maui onion
2	Carrots
1	Celery stock (outer ribs removed)
2 Tbl	Virgin olive oil
1/3 c	Cooking sherry (or broth)
2 Tbl	Tahini
2 Tbl	Arrowroot powder
1/4 c	Golden miso
5 qts	Pure hot water (mixed use)
2 Tbl	Garlic (1 bulb) chopped
1/2 Tbl	Concentrated vegetable stock
2	Yellow zucchinis, sliced
1 c	Cabbage, chopped
2 c packed	Parsley, finely minced
1 bunch	Dill, fresh minced

1. Mince onion, carrots, and celery in a food processor. Put oil and sherry in a large pot and saute veggies on medium high. Stir often for about 8 minutes.
2. Quickly blend tahini, arrowroot and miso with 1 cup water in a blender. Stir in garlic, aminos and vegetable stock, and blend again. Pour into soup pot.
3. Add water, squash and cabbage. Bring to boil, then turn down to simmer. Stir in parsley and dill. Simmer gently 5 minutes before serving.

SERVES: 8 - 10

Parsley
Loaded with vitamin C, it is a wonderful addition to soups, salads and fresh vegetable juices.

It contains A and B vitamins, calcium and iron.

Parsley aids in digestion, and is high in chlorophyll, which makes it useful as a natural breath freshener.

Hot Side Dishes

♦ Vegetable

Roasting Garlic   189

Grilled Garlic and
    Vegetables   189

Garlic Roasted Corn   189

Oven Roasted Potatoes with
    Garlic and Herbs   190

Tamari Spicy Fries   190

Southwest Steamers   191

Braised Carrots with
    Apricots   192

Orange Blossom Carrots   192

Indian Cauliflower   193

Mushrooms La Jolla   194

Garden Steamers   195

Woked Chard and
    Mushrooms   195

Desert Cauliflower   196

Butternut Maple Bake   197

Ratatouille   198

Spaghetti Squash   199

Green Beans Almandine   200

♦ Other Side Dishes

Garlicky Soba Noodles   200

Anasazi Beans with Roasted
    Garlic   201

Twice as Wild Rice   202

Wild Tofu Jasmine Rice   203

Sprouted Millet   203

Polenta Triangles   204

Cumin Rice   204

Curried Lentils with
    Tomatoes   205

Sprouted Frijoles   206

Sprouted Peas and Minted
    Peppers   206

Whole Wheat Pizza Dough   207

Focaccia   208

Panne con Pomodore   209

Bread Sticks   209

Garlic Roasted Corn

A deliciously different way to enjoy corn! The husk keeps the juices in, rather than its nutrients escaping in the boiling water bath. Per person:

1 ear	**White corn, with husk on**
2	**Garlic cloves, sliced**
1	**Lime wedge**

Preheat oven to 500°.

1. Soak corn in water (with husk on) for 15 to 20 minutes.
2. Peel back husk of corn, remove all corn silk, and wash corn cob. Rub corn with garlic, pull husk up around corn and place garlic slices inside. Tie husks with string.
3. Place in oven and roast for 30 minutes, unhusk before serving. Squeeze lime over corn before eating.

This can also be cooked in a barbecue or grill if desired.

Grilled Garlic and Vegetables

3	**Garlic bulbs, roasted (see sidebar)**
1 each	**Green and red peppers, seeded and ribbed**
4	**Green onions, tops and bottoms trimmed**
1 sm	**Eggplant, sliced thinly lengthwise**
	Extra-virgin olive oil
	Lemon juice
	Cracked pepper
1 tsp each	**Oregano or basil and sea salt to taste**

Preheat oven at 550°.

1. Slice off bottom and top of peppers, then cut peppers into 3 slabs vertically.
2. Brush vegetables lightly with olive oil and lemon, place on a ventilated rack for oven broil or on a grill. Broil at 450° for approximately 5 minutes, until softened. Put roasted whole garlics and vegetables on a platter. Sprinkle with herbs.

SERVING SUGGESTION:
Arrange on a platter as a side dish; especially good with pasta.

SERVES: 2 - 4

Roasting Garlic

1. Preheat oven to 450°.
2. Cut top off garlic bulb so all cloves are exposed. Be sure to use a fresh hard garlic bulb.
3. Drizzle top with olive oil, put garlic on a baking sheet.
4. Roast close to heat about 15 to 20 minutes, until skin is crusty and light brown and cloves are soft. Squeeze out cloves and enjoy as is or use in recipes.

USES: sauces, salads, pizzas, soups, condiments

Notes:

Oven Roast Potatoes with Garlic and Herbs

Savory potatoes, with garlic and basil.

4 medium	Yellow potatoes, scrubbed
1 Tbl	Garlic, minced
2 Tbl	Red wine (or broth)
1 Tbl	Liquid aminos (or 1 tsp sea salt)
1 tsp	Basil
2 tsp	Onion powder (or 1/2 onion, sliced)
1/4 c	Walnut pieces, lightly toasted (optional)

Preheat oven to 450°.

1. Halve potatoes lengthwise, then turn and slice into 3/8" long strips.
2. Lightly oil a glass baking dish, then add all ingredients, toss well so everything is evenly coated.
3. Cover with foil and bake at 400° for 20 minutes, then uncover and bake for another 5 minutes.

SERVES: 2 - 3

Tamari Spicy Fries

No-fry crispy potato spears.

5	Potatoes, scrubbed and sliced into spears
1/4 c	Tamari ("Lite" soy sauce)
1/4 tsp	Cayenne
1/2 tsp each	Curry, cumin, basil

Toss potatoes in a large pot with tamari and spices, toss well using your hands. Spread onto a baking sheet (lightly oiled with vegetable spray). Roast at 500° for 10 to 15 minutes until brown, turn over and repeat. Serve hot.

NOTE: Do not cover with a towel to keep warm, for they will loose crispiness due to condensation of heat turning to moisture.

SERVING SUGGESTIONS:
Serve with catsup and tofu burgers or sandwiches,
or just to complement a salad.

Southwest Steamers

*A quick and easy way to dress your vegetables
right out of the steamer basket.*

4	**Zucchini, crisp young firm ones**
4	**Yellow crookneck squash, firm ones**
1 large	**Tomato, chop coarsely**
1/4 c	**Cilantro leaves, packed**
1/2 Tbl	**Onion powder**
1/2 tsp	**Cumin powder**
1 Tbl	**Liquid aminos**
1/2 to 1 Tbl	**Lemon juice**

1. Slice zucchini and squash, then steam until crisp tender.
2. Put tomatoes into a large bowl, add steamed vegetables and spices and toss well. Adjust seasoning to your liking.
3. Transfer to a platter or keep warm until ready to serve.

SERVES: 2 - 4

With all the land in the United States, it's amazing that only 2% of it is used to produce fruits and vegetables — the most health promoting forms of human nutrition available.

And yet, 64% of our cropland is used to raise livestock feed — to produce meat, the least health promoting form of nutrition available.

Realities in the 90's, excerpted from *Diet for a New America*, by John Robbins.

Braised Carrots with Apricots

2 large	Carrots, cut lengthwise
1/3 c	Water
7	Dried apricots, cut in half
2 Tbl	Lemon juice
1 tsp	Honey
Pinch of	Chinese 5-Spice

1. Cut carrots in half-moons 1/8" thick. Put them into a small saucepan, add lemon juice and water and bring to a boil. Cover, then reduce to simmer for 5 minutes.
2. Add the remaining ingredients, tossing all together. Cover and let cook another 10 minutes or until carrots are tender.

Orange Blossom Carrots

A carrot puree, fragrant with orange yet not too sweet.

4	Carrots, chopped
2	Onions, chopped
1/3 c	Orange juice
1/2 tsp	Grated orange zest
1/2 tsp	Coriander powder

1. Par boil carrots and onions for 10 minutes.
2. Transfer to a food processor, puree with the remaining ingredients until smooth.
3. Spoon into an oven-proof casserole and heat or keep warm until ready to serve.

SERVES: 4 - 6 as a side dish

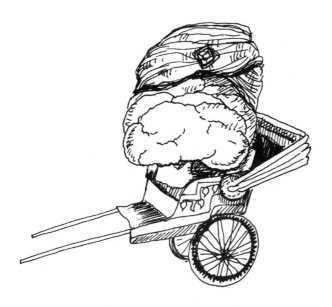

Indian Cauliflower

Tender spicy cauliflower in a tomato-onion sauce.

1 med to large	Cauliflower, trim into "florettes"
1	Onion, chopped
2 tsp	Coriander powder
1/2 tsp	Sea salt
1/2 tsp	Cayenne
1 tsp	Garlic, chopped
1 c	Whole pear tomatoes, canned
3/4 c	Tomato juice (from canned tomatoes)
1/4 tsp	Cardamom powder
1/2 tsp	Chinese 5-Spice
1/2 tsp	Caraway seeds

Preheat oven at 375°.

1. Steam cauliflower lightly (about 8 to 10 minutes), remove steamer basket from pot. Cauliflower should be firm — not mushy.
2. Put everything (except cauliflower) in a food processor and puree. Transfer to a cooking pot and heat up on medium-low for 12 minutes, covered.
3. Stir in cauliflower, and then put everything into a baking dish or casserole, cover and bake for 15 minutes.

SERVING SUGGESTION:
Serve with cous-cous or basmati rice, and small bowls of soaked raisins (1/2 cup), toasted cashews (1/2 cup) and coconut (1/4 cup).

Onions

Alexander the Great fed his army onions to give them strength, and perhaps to maintain their health, because onions contain the same health promoting properties as garlic, yet in smaller amounts.

Onions have been found to lower blood pressure and help keep the arteries clear.

Mushrooms La Jolla

A broiled succulent mushroom, stuffed with fresh herbs,
garlic, pine nuts and tomato. A delicious appetizer
or side dish that is easy to make.

1 recipe	**Besto Pesto (page 130)**
1½ lbs	**Large mushrooms (the bigger the better)**
	Extra-virgin olive oil as needed

Preheat oven to broil.

1. Wash and set aside mushrooms, stems up. Hold the cap firmly and wiggle the stem until it comes out. Pour a bit of extra-virgin olive oil into cavity and use fingers to spread it around on top of mushroom.
2. Put 1 Tbl of Besto Pesto inside cavity and arrange mushrooms in a baking pan. Broil for 15 minutes. Put on a plate and garnish with tomato wedges or fresh sprigs of fennel, parsley or basil.

YIELDS: Approx. 12-15 large mushrooms

Garden Steamers

3 small	Zucchinis
2 c	Carrots, sliced
1 small	Red onion, coarse chopped
4 small	Red potatoes, scrubbed and cubed
1 large	Green bell pepper, coarse chopped
1 recipe	Creamy Cashew Basil Sauce (page 114)

1. Steam vegetables; putting potatoes in first for 3 to 5 minutes, then carrots, peppers, zucchinis, and onions. Steam another 8 or so minutes. Test for doneness: veggies should be crisp, yet tender.
2. Pour Creamy Cashew Basil Sauce on top before serving.

Woked Chard and Mushrooms

1 bunch	Swiss chard
8 large	Mushrooms, sliced
2 Tbl	"Lite" soy sauce or tamari
1/3 c	Rice vinegar
2 cloves	Garlic, pressed
1 tsp	Toasted sesame oil
1/3 c	Water (as needed)

1. Remove the tough stems of the chard by cutting out an inverted "V" shape into the leaf, then slice.
2. Heat wok and add tamari, vinegar, water and garlic. Stir and add mushrooms and chard. Cook quickly in a hot wok. Drizzle on sesame oil, toss quickly and serve.

Swiss chard grows like a celery stock with long graceful leaves. It contains lots of calcium, iron, magnesium, and vitamin A.

It makes a delicate side dish steamed, or shred finely and add to stir frys or soups.

Like all green leafy vegetables, don't overlook them for your salads. They love the company of other vegetables and will provide you with much more nutrition than lettuce.

Notes:

Desert Cauliflower

A spicy stewed cauliflower with a Southwest kick.

1 c	Broth
1 tsp	Lemon juice
1 tsp each	Cumin and basil
1 Tbl	Dried red chile powder
1 Tbl	Garlic, minced
1 large head	Cauliflower, wash and cut into florettes
1/2 c	Red peppers, fire-roasted and chopped
1/4 c	Cilantro leaves

1. Saute broth and spices in a medium skillet.
2. Stir in cauliflower. Cover and bring to a boil, then turn to low heat and cook for 10 to 13 minutes more.
3. Stir in peppers and garnish with cilantro before serving.

SERVES: 2 - 4

Butternut Maple Bake

Once the squash is baked, this is a snap to put together. Loaded with vitamin A, this complements a light vegetable or salad meal. Especially pleasing in colder weather. Equally delicious as a dessert.

1 small	**Butternut squash**
1 c	**Soaked raisins**
4 Tbl	**Maple syrup**
4 Tbl	**Toasted walnut pieces**
	Grated orange zest garnish on top

1. Preheat oven to 450°. Slice the squash in half lengthwise. Scoop out seeds and place squash face down on a baking tray. Fill the tray with water up to 1/2" high. Prick squash with a fork a couple of times. Cover with foil and bake at 425° for 30 minutes (or until tender). Chop squash when cool enough to handle.
2. Soak the raisins in hot water to soften. (Keep a jar of raisins in the fridge covered with water to use when needed.)
3. Per person: Put 1 cup cubed squash in bowl, drizzle on 1 Tbl of maple syrup and top with 1/4 cup of raisins, 1 Tbl walnuts and orange zest.

SERVES: 4

Squash is high in vitamin A, and is an excellent source of complex carbohydrates. They can be used to replace desserts at the end of a light meal.

Pureed squash is very versatile. Try adding soups and sauces to thicken and impart a rich savory taste.

Welcome to the world of vegetarian

Ratatouille

A Mediterranean classic of slowly simmered vegetables with garlic and basil and a touch of fruity virgin olive oil. Delicioso hot or cold.

1 large	Onion, chopped
3 Tbl	Lemon juice
3 Tbl	Extra-virgin olive oil
1 large	Eggplant, skinned, and chopped
3-4	Zucchinis, sliced
1	Yellow bell pepper, cut in half, seed, de-rib, cut in strips
1	Green bell pepper, cut in half, seed, de-rib, cut in strips
2 c	Mushrooms, quartered
2 Tbl	Garlic, chopped
1/4 c packed	Fresh basil leaves, torn
8 oz	Tomato sauce
1/4 tsp each	Sea salt and cracked black pepper)
2 c	Tomato flesh*, peeled, seeded and chopped (8-12)

1. Saute onion in olive oil and lemon juice in a large enamel pot with the lid on for 8 minutes on low heat.
2. Add eggplant, zucchinis, peppers, mushrooms, tomato sauce and spices.
3. *To skin tomatoes effortlessly: Bring a small pot of water to boil, add tomatoes and poach for 1 minute, until skins crack. Transfer to colander with a slotted spoon, rinse under cold water. Peel.
4. Add tomato flesh to ratatouille. Stir well, cover and cook on low for 45 minutes.

SERVING SUGGESTIONS:
Serve over pasta, or serve cold as a salad on bibb lettuce leaves.

Notes:

Spaghetti Squash

This squash makes a hearty side dish and is very versatile.
For a smashing main dish, try topping with Carrot Garlic Red Sauce
(page 111) or Afro Rumba Sauce (page 109).

1		**Spaghetti squash, sliced in half lengthwise**
	1 tsp	**Basil, crumbled**
	1/4 tsp each	**Sea salt and cracked black pepper**
	2 tsp	**Olive oil**
	1	**Garlic clove, pressed (optional)**
Optional:	**1 Tbl**	**Nutritional yeast flakes (adds a nice nutty flavor)**

Preheat oven to 375°.

1. Scoop seeds out of squash and place squash face down on a baking sheet. Pour 1/4" of water in pan and bake squash for 45 minutes, until tender.
2. Fork the flesh of the squash away from its skin into "pasta." Season with spices and drizzle a bit of olive oil into it. (Press a clove of garlic into it if you like.)
3. Return squash to the oven to keep warm until ready to serve.

SERVING SUGGESTIONS:
Pour a sauce on top, or serve as a side dish as is.

16 pounds of grain and soy are needed to produce 1 pound of edible food from a cow. Yet 90% of the protein, 99% of the carbohydrates and 100% of the fiber in soy and grains is wasted in recycling grains to feed livestock.

Seven people can be fed for a whole year from the grains and soy needed to produce the meat, poultry and dairy products eaten by the average American.

Diet for a New America, by John Robbins

Notes:

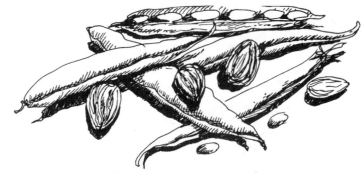

Green Beans Almandine

A quick fresh side dish speckled with carrot, tomato and almonds.

1 lb	Green beans, trimmed
1/3 c	Red onions, sliced thin
1	Tomato, seeded and chopped small
1	Carrot, sliced
2 Tbl	Dry roasted almonds*, chopped fine
1/2 Tbl	Lemon juice
1/2 Tbl	Aminos
	Cracked pepper to taste

1. Steam green beans and carrot until tender, yet crisp (5 minutes).
2. Put red onions into a bowl, add steamed veggies on top. Put tomatoes over veggies, add the remaining ingredients and toss. Serve warm, or room temperature.

*Put almonds into a toaster oven and gently brown.

SERVES: 4

Garlicky Soba Noodles

An easy side dish for 2.

1/2 pack	Soba (buckwheat noodles)
1 packet	Miso-cup instant soup mix
2 Tbl	Green onions, slivered
1 large	Garlic clove, finely minced
1 Tbl	Sesame seeds, toasted slightly
	Water as needed

Cook noodles al dente. Strain, return to pot. Add soup packet and the remaining ingredients to noodles. Stir together.

SERVING SUGGESTION:
Top with steamed and/or seasoned veggies.

SERVES: 2

Anasazi Beans with Roasted Garlic

The "better" bean, cultivated from ancient Anasazi burial chambers. They cook faster, are non-gaseous, have more protein and a sweeter taste.

3 c	**Anasazi beans, soaked overnight, or for 24 hours**
6 c	**Pure water**
3	**Dried red chiles (New Mexican), rinsed, stemmed and seeds shaken out**
1	**Onion, chopped**
2 Tbl	**Liquid aminos**
1 Tbl	**Lemon juice**
1	**Garlic bulb, roasted and minced (page 189)**

1. Rinse and sort soaked beans. Bring water to a boil, then add the beans and red chiles. Return to a boil, then cover and simmer for an hour.
2. Remove the chiles, and scrape chile pulp back into the beans — discard skin.
3. Saute onion in aminos and lemon until light brown, add garlic and pour into bean pot. Cook another 45 minutes or so until beans are soft.

SERVING SUGGESTIONS:
Put green chile on top, serve with flour tortillas, or as a side dish to Mexican dishes or burritos.

A rainbow is a miracle whispering peace across the universe.

Notes:

Twice as Wild Rice

Nutty wild rice is topped with sauteed wild mushrooms and garlic.

1¹/₃ c	**Wild rice, rinsed**
1/2 tsp	**Sea salt**
4 c	**Boiling water**
6 oz	**Wild or oyster mushrooms**
1 Tbl	**Lemon juice**
2 large	**Garlic cloves, pressed**
2 tsp	**"Lite" soy sauce or aminos**
1 tsp each	**Honey and toasted sesame oil**
Dash	**Cayenne**
1	**Zucchini, sliced**
1 tsp each	**Paprika and aminos (or "lite" soy sauce)**

1. Stir the rice into boiling salted water. Cover and simmer 40 minutes.
2. Saute mushrooms in lemon juice, garlic, soy, honey and sesame oil. After a few minutes set aside.
3. During the last 5 minutes of cooking the rice, put zucchini on top, replace lid and let the steam cook the zucchini. Stir in paprika, soy or aminos, and zucchini.

Serve on a platter and lay sauteed mushrooms on top. Garnish with parsley.

SERVES: 4 as a side dish

Wild Tofu Jasmine Rice

A savory blend of wild rice and jasmine rice with spicy tofu cubes.
Makes a nice side dish for woked veggies.

3 c	Filtered water
1/2 c	Wild rice, rinsed
1 c	Jasmine rice, rinsed
1/2 tsp	Sea salt
1 tsp	Sesame oil
	Freshly cracked black pepper to taste
3/4 c	"Teriyaki" tofu, cubed*
1 tsp	"Lite" soy sauce if needed
	Scallions or green onions as garnish

1. Bring water to boil, add wild rice and return to boil, then cover and simmer for 20 minutes.
2. Stir in jasmine rice, salt, pepper and sesame oil, return to a boil, then cover and simmer for 15 minutes (or until jasmine rice is cooked).
3. Fork in tofu cubes, being careful not to mash the rice. Simmer uncovered another 5 minutes.

*Teriyaki tofu is firm tofu marinated in a thick soy-based sauce. You can find it packaged in the fridge in health food stores.

Sprouted Millet

Millet is an excellent grain for transitional diets.
It is non-mucous forming and alkaline in nature. This is a delicious and nutritious way to eat millet.

1 c	Millet, sprouted
1¾ c	Water
1/2	Lemon, juiced
1 tsp	Tamari
Dash	Chile sesame oil

1. Put 1 cup of millet in a jar and cover with water, let it soak for about 15 hours. Rinse and drain millet, two times daily, for another day or two until small sprouts appear.
2. Bring 1¾ cups of water to boil, add millet, then cover and simmer for 13 minutes on low.
3. Stir in seasoning and fluff with a fork.

Eat It Wild!

Wild rice has two times the amount of protein, four times the phosphorus, eight times the thiamine and 20 times the riboflavin as white rice.

Whole brown rice (long and short grain), contains a generous amount of B vitamins, calcium, phosphorus and iron.*

Try mixing wild rice into brown rice dishes for a nuttier flavor. Just make sure you begin cooking wild rice 15 minutes prior to adding the brown rice, for wild rice needs 45 minutes as compared to 30 minutes cooking time for brown rice.

*From *Nutrition Almanac*, Nutrition Search, Inc.

Polenta Triangles

*Grilled polenta studded with roasted red pepper
makes a nice menu addition.*

3¼ c	Water
1 tsp	Sea salt
1 c	Coarse grain corn meal (Polenta)
1/2 c	Roasted red pepper, chopped fine

1. Bring water to a boil, add salt, then pour in polenta in a thin stream, whisking it together so no lumps appear. Let thicken on low until polenta does not stick to the sides when stirred, 10 to 20 minutes.
2. Stir in red pepper and pour into a small, lightly oil bread pan. Let cool completely, then unmold*. Slice into 3/8" sections, then cut on diagonal to create triangles.
3. Grill on a hot, lightly oiled griddle for a few minutes on each side. Serve with a basil sprig to garnish, or with some slivered sun-dried tomatoes packed in olive oil.

*You may wish to refrigerate this until it sets firm, before slicing and grilling.

MAKES: About 14 slices

Cumin Rice

A simple, tasty brown rice.

4	Water
2 c	Brown, long-grain basmati rice, rinsed
1/2 tsp	Sea salt
1 tsp	Cumin seeds, lightly toasted
1 tsp	Toasted sesame oil

Bring water to a boil in a medium pot. Stir in rice and other ingredients, cover and cook 30 minutes on low.

Curried Lentils with Tomatoes

This dish is delicious as a side dish, or featured as a main dish with some rice or cous-cous. You can also turn it into a great sauce by adding tomato sauce and sauteed mushrooms. Delicate and light.

1/4 c	Water
2 Tbl	Lemon juice
2 c	Red onions, chopped
3	Garlic cloves, minced
2 c	Lentils, washed
2 tsp	Curry powder
1 tsp	Cumin powder
1/2 tsp	Cinnamon
1 tsp	"Lite" soy sauce or aminos
2 c	Boiling water
1¼ c	Cheezy Sauce (see recipe page 121)
3 c	Tomatoes, seeded and chopped

1. Heat up water and lemon juice in a large cast-iron skillet and saute onions for a couple of minutes. Add garlic and lentils and simmer 8 minutes. Stir in the spices. Preheat oven to 400°.
2. Add boiling water to skillet, stir and cover. Return to a boil, then turn to low and simmer 25 minutes. Meanwhile prepare Cheezy Sauce and cut tomatoes.
3. Stir Cheezy Sauce into lentils, then fold in tomatoes. Cover and bake at 375° for 20 to 30 minutes, until lentils are soft and everything is hot.

SERVES: 5 - 6

Sprout Your Lentils!

Lentils are rich in protein, the B complex vitamins, choline, potassium and pantothenic acid. This ancient legume is delicious sprouted. To easily do so, soak overnight in a bowl of water. Rinse and drain twice daily for 2 to 3 days, until sprout tails appear. They make a nutritious salad and can be added to all sorts of foods. Try a <u>Sprout Drink</u>, adding lentil sprouts to a blender of vegetable juice or water, a bit of garlic, miso and lemon: Blend to perfection.

Sprouted Frijoles

*Known as "gasless" beans, since the sprouting converts
the sugars, proteins and carbohydrates into a more nutritious food;
they also cook in a quarter of the time.*

2 c	Pinto beans
	Water to cover
3 Tbl	Red chile powder
1	Onion, chopped
2	Garlic cloves, minced
1 tsp	Oregano
2 tsp	Cumin
1 Tbl	Aminos or 1/2 tsp sea salt

1. Soak pintos for 24 hours. Rinse and drain two times daily, until sprout tails appear, approximately 2 days.
2. Cover with water in a pot, bring to a boil, then reduce to simmer for 10 minutes. Add onions and spices and cook another 10 to 15 minutes (or until soft).

SERVES: 6

Sprouted Peas and Minted Peppers

A delicious and fortifying side dish

2 c	Sprouted peas*
1 large	Yellow bell pepper, chopped coarsely
2	Garlic cloves, minced
2 tsp	Olive oil
2 Tbl	Water
2 Tbl	Dried mint, crumbled
	Sea salt and cayenne to taste

1. Steam peas in steamer basket 5 minutes to soften.
2. In a medium skillet, saute peppers and garlic in olive oil and water. Stir in mint, peas, and season to taste.

*Sprout dried green peas by first soaking in water overnight. Rinse and drain 2 times daily for 3 days, until sprout tails appear.

Notes:

Basic Wheat Pizza Dough

*Whole wheat "pastry" flour makes a better crust,
it is more pliable and not as heavy as whole wheat flour.
This recipe is easy to make and can be used in Focaccia (page 208),
Bread Sticks and Panne con Pomodore (page 209).*

3 c	Whole wheat pastry flour
1 tsp	Sea or vegetable salt
1 pack	Active dry yeast
1 tsp	Honey
1 c	Water (warm to wrist)
2 Tbl	Extra-virgin olive oil or sesame oil

1. Put flour and salt into a food processor and mix quickly. Stir yeast, water, and honey in a small bowl and let sit until foamy (about 5 minutes).
2. Turn on the processor, pour in the yeast mixture, mix in olive oil and let the processor knead it for a minute.
3. Put the pizza dough on a kneading surface and knead for 5 minutes or more until soft. Place dough in an oiled bowl, cover with a towel and set in a warm place for 1 hour to double dough in size. Crank up your oven to 550º.
4. Divide dough into 6 balls and roll them out, making an 8" circle. Spread olive oil on crust and top with your favorite ingredients (see recipes following). Broil for 8 minutes.

Save unused crusts by stacking them in between layers of waxed paper with an outer covering of foil (pinched tightly around edges to seal). Keep in fridge up to 2 days.

Today is God's gift to us ...

that is why it is called the "present."

Focaccia

Using Whole Wheat Pizza Dough, your favorite fresh herbs, garlic, olive oil and perhaps some soy cheese, a scrumptious appetizer is born.

1 recipe	**Whole Wheat Pizza Dough (page 207)**
1 Tbl	**Dried Onion granules (or minced)**
2 Tbl	**Virgin olive oil**
2 Tbl	**Garlic, minced**
1/4 c	**Parsley, fresh minced**
1/4 c	**Basil, fresh minced (or 1 Tbl dried)**
Several sprigs	**Fresh rosemary, oregano or thyme, crumbled**
6 oz	**Soy mozzarella, grated (optional)**

Preheat oven to 500º.

1. Prepare pizza dough according to recipe, and work in onion. Roll out into 6 thin crusts.
2. Spread each crust with some olive oil and prebake 8 minutes. Add rest of garlic and herbs and soy cheese and bake 5 to 8 minutes longer. Cut in wedges and serve.

NOTE: You can try adding the herbs into the dough before you roll it out.

MAKES: 3 pizzas

Panne con Pomodore

Fresh tomatoes and basil top a thin, crispy pizza rectangle.
It makes a delicious appetizer or accompaniment to pasta.

1 recipe	Whole Wheat Pizza Dough (page 207)
1/2 c	Onion, finely minced
1½ Tbl	Olive oil
2 c	Fresh tomatoes, chopped and seeded
1/2 c	Fresh basil, shredded
	Sea salt and cracked pepper

Preheat oven to 450º.

1. After dough rises, knead in onions. Separate into 4 balls and roll each one into thin rectangles. Brush some oil on top and bake for 10 to 12 minutes.
2. Put tomatoes on top of each pizza dough, add basil, drizzle on olive oil and spices and bake for 8 minutes more.

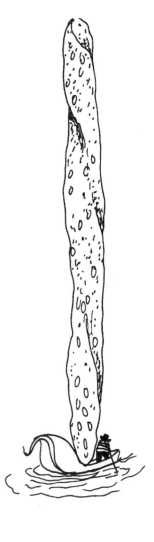

Bread Sticks

Make 'em plain or super seedy. Store in airtight bag for freshness
when they are cool. Serve in a vase or interesting glass.

1 recipe	Whole Wheat Pizza Dough (page 207)
1 tsp	Egg replacer
2 Tbl	Water

Your choice topping:

> Dehydrated onion and garlic, dill weed, sesame seeds, poppy seeds

1. After dough rises, roll out sticks into desired lengths.
2. Mix egg replacer with water and brush over bread sticks.
3. Immediately roll onto seasonings and bake for 10 to 15 minutes in a hot 450º oven. For fatter sticks, it may take 20 minutes. Turn once while cooking on baking sheet. Bread Sticks should be crispy.

Entrees

Entree Introduction 213

Quick Meal Ideas 215

◆ Vegetables in the Spotlight

Golden Nugget Squash Pockets 216

Corn Souffle Stuffed Chiles 217

Eggplant Tomato Boats 218

Cheezy Broccoli Stuffed Potatoes 219

A Grilled Affair 220

Pesto Kabobs 221

◆ Meals in a Skillet

Mushroom Seitan Stroganoff 222

Green Bean Curry 223

Spicy Asparagus and Black Beans 224

Italian Peppers and Links 225

Tofu Mole 226

Chinese Woked Vegetables 227

◆ Casseroles, Quiches and Pies

Wild 'n' Cheezy Casserole 228

Pronto Enchilada Casserole 229

Asparagus Tofu Pie 230

Green Chile Quiche 231

Tamale Pie 232

Cheezy Corn and Zucchini Enchiladas 233

Southwestern Cornbread Quiche 234

Tempeh Cauliflower Quiche 235

◆ Dishes with Grains

Oyster Mushroom Saute 236

Risotto with Asparagus and Peas 237

Stuffed Acorn Squash Americana 238

Divine Dolmas 239

Kasha Nut Loaf 241

◆ Pasta Dishes

Fettucine "Faux" Fredo 240

Cheezy Noodle Bake 240

Spicy Sesame Noodles with Chard 242

Garlicky Zucchini with Bean Thread Noodles 243

Pasta Fagiole 244

Vegetable Lo Mein 245

Hong Kong Pasta 246

Glass Noodle Shiitake Surprise 247

Fusilli Primavera 248

Broccoli Bean Thread Saute 249

◆ Other Delights

Vegetable Eggless Fu Young 250

Spinach Spring Rolls 251

Pizza! 252

Viva Spinizza 253

California Pizza 254

Pueblo Pizza 255

Pacific Rim Pizza 255

What is an Entree?

An entree is the main dish of the meal, the center of a mandala from which other foods are served.

Entrees are flexible and diverse. They can be a cooked extravaganza, or a large salad filled with all your favorite sprouts and vegetables. An entree can even be a hearty soup or breakfast burritos, or as simple as salad rolls with a hot side dish of grains to accompany them. As you can see, most categories of this book can be turned into a main dish, it's just a matter of how you serve it.

Your creativity creates a main dish. Select a theme; a vegetable, grain, pasta or a sauce to revolve your meal around. Use the Quick Meal Ideas on the following page for inspiration.

The main dishes listed here are meals we've enjoyed preparing and eating. Through innovative pies, pizzas, quiches, casseroles, pastas, and stir frys, we feature various vegetables, grains, legumes, tofu and tempeh products. Some are traditional take-offs, others are cosmic blast-offs!

Bon Appetite!

Quick Meal Ideas

Combining recipes from the Sauces, Dips and Condiment section with basic foods such as pastas, grains, tortillas and potatoes leads to delicious variations and a perfect diversion from ho hum food ruts. Here are a few combinations worth trying:

Besto Pesto — over whole wheat or vegetable linguini, on a baked potato, broiled mushrooms, as a lasagne filling, or with scrambled tofu.

Pueblo Pesto — Melt over steamed squash and serve over rice or pasta, as saute for tofu cutlets, or stir into pureed vegetables.

Tomato Red Pepper Mousse — As ravioli stuffing, inside lasagne or enchiladas with zucchini, as a sandwich filling, or in salads.

Cheezy Sauces — Over baked potato and choice of steamed vegetable, mixed into vegetable soups, baked with cooked grains casserole style.

Lentil Paté — To stuff lasagne and raviolis, put a slice on top of rice balls and tie up with a 1/2" ribbon of Nori (Japanese style sandwich).

Chunky Tomato Mushroom Sauce — Over angel hair pasta, spaghetti squash, baked potato, or polenta.

Notes:

Golden Nugget Squash Pockets

A healthful and simple to prepare meal that looks "gorgeous."
All differently colored vegetables spill out of the cavity of a cooked
squash, laced with a savory creamy sauce.

1	**Golden nugget squash**
1½ c	**Cauliflower pieces**
1	**Bell pepper, coarsely chopped**
1	**Red bell pepper, coarsely chopped**
1/2 c	**Corn, cut**
2 c	**Mushrooms, quartered**
1/3 c	**Vegetable broth**
1/2 Tbl	**Liquid aminos**
1 recipe	**Silken Chile Ginger Sauce (page 112)**

1. Cook the whole squash in a large pot of boiling water until tender, about 30 minutes. (Water should be at least 3" deep in pot.) When tender, let cool, cut in half and remove seeds. Set aside.
2. Saute the other veggies in the broth and aminos for 10 to 15 minutes until crisp yet tender.
3. Put half of the squash on each plate. Fill with steamed veggies, to resemble an abundant cornucopia. Top with sauce.

SERVES: 2

Corn Souffle Stuffed Chiles

An onion and potato puree binds corn in this elegant spa-style chile relleño, which is baked on a bed of Mexican-style tomato coulis. A stunning nonfat meal!

1 large	Potato, chopped
1 large	Onion, chopped
1 c	Water
1/4 tsp	Sea salt
1/2 tsp each	Cumin and basil
	Black pepper to taste
1 Tbl	Kuzu (or arrowroot powder) thinned with
2 Tbl	Steam water
1½ c	Corn kernels, cut from cob
6 large	Green chiles*, roasted
1 recipe	Tomato Coulis (page 110)

Preheat oven to 375º.

1. Bring the potato, onion and water to a boil in a covered pot. Turn down to simmer 10 to 12 minutes, or until soft. Strain out water and set aside. Put veggies in a food processor and puree with the spices.
2. Return potato puree to pot, stir in kuzu thickener thinned with water; stir in corn. Cover and cook 5 minutes on low, then set aside.
3. Make a slit in the roasted chiles, remove seeds, then stuff with potato puree. Put 2 chiles in individual baking dishes, put some Tomato Coulis around the sides. Bake 15 minutes at 400º.

*See how to roast a chile, page 119.

SERVES: 3

Be a non-overeater and enjoy more vitality in your life!

Eggplant Tomato Boats

A delectable creation of broiled eggplant halves, imbedded with garlic, and topped with a simmering fresh Tomato Coulis. Simple to prepare.

2	Eggplants, sliced lengthwise in half
12	Garlic cloves, sliced in half lengthwise (or more for garlic lovers)
2 tsp	Virgin olive oil
1/2 c	Soy cheese, grated (optional)
5 c	Tomatoes, peeled, seeded and chopped
1 large	Onion, chopped
1 tsp	Liquid aminos
1/4 c	Basil leaves, slivered

Preheat oven to broil.

1. Make 3 lengthwise slits on eggplant halves (careful not to pierce the skin) and stuff grooves with garlic slices. Rub a bit of olive oil on top. Put on a baking tray and bake at 450º until tender (20 to 25 minutes). If you like, after 15 minutes baking, sprinkle eggplants with 1/4 cup soy cheese, return to oven and bake until tender (5 to 10 minutes more).
2. While eggplants are cooking, simmer tomatoes and onions with aminos in a medium pot for 20 minutes, or until tender.
3. Assemble boats: Ladle sauce on top of each eggplant half and sprinkle a little basil on top. Serve hot.

SERVES: 4

Cheezy Broccoli Stuffed Potatoes

A satisfying healthy meal using a hot baked potato.

2 large	**Russet potatoes**
2 c	**Broccoli flowerettes and trimmed stems**
1/2 c	**Cheezy Sauce (page 121)**
Garnish	**Veggie baco-bits**

Preheat oven to 375º.

1. Scrub the potatoes, prick them a few times with a fork and bake in oven for 35 to 45 minutes.
2. Steam the broccoli for a few minutes; don't overcook.
3. When potatoes are ready, slice down the center lengthwise, 1" deep. Squeeze the ends together to push center open. Stir potato flesh with a fork to fluff it up. You may wish to sprinkle in some vegetable salt. Top with broccoli and cover with hot Cheezy Sauce.

SERVING SUGGESTIONS:
Garnish and serve with a leafy sprout salad.

SERVES: 2

Foods with potassium and calcium help lower the blood pressure.

People with potassium-rich diets, vegetarians in particular — have been found to have lower blood pressure. High levels of both potassium and calcium are found in broccoli, soy beans, navy beans and almonds.

<u>Potassium rich foods are:</u> Bananas, potatoes, avocados, raisins, apricots, dates, orange juice, cantaloupe, endive and peanuts.

Notes:

A Grilled Affair

Succulent, mouth-watering eggplant and accompanying garden entourage cooks on a barbecue grill or pancake griddle. Bon appetite!

2 medium	Eggplants, sliced lengthwise in 1/2" slabs
1 each	Green and red bell pepper, sliced lengthwise into 2" wide rectangles
1	Radicchio, quartered
1	Zucchini, sliced 1/4" lengthwise
12	Mushrooms, halved
1	Lemon, cut in wedges

Basting sauce:

1/4 c	Olive oil
1 tsp	Garlic, minced
1/2 c	Fresh basil "ribbons," sliced finely Cracked black pepper, liquid aminos or sea salt to taste
1	Crusty baquette, heated (keep warm by wrapping with a towel in a basket)

1. Prepare vegetables, and heat a nonstick griddle on high.
2. Spray skillet with vegetable spray and turn down to medium heat. Cover skillet with vegetables, turning veggies over when golden brown or as they soften.
3. Brush turned side with a bit of lemon, aminos and olive oil. Sprinkle with cracked pepper and transfer them to a platter when they are done. Put basil ribbons on top. Serve hot with bread and arrange the lemon slices around the sides.

SERVING SUGGESTION:
Serve with a large spinach, tomato, cucumber salad and your favorite vinaigrette. Place grilled veggies on a wedge of hot bread for an informal openface sandwich, or serve with grilled Polenta Triangles (page 204).

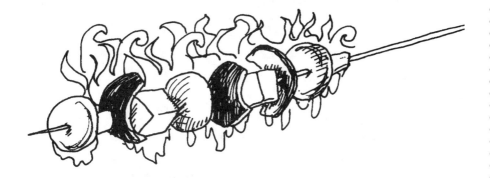

Pesto Kabobs

This is a quick dish to prepare using wooden skewers, a pesto sauce and fresh vegetables. Simply skewer your favorite veggies, spread pesto on top and broil. Perfect for summer entertaining. We suggest Cilantro Walnut Pesto, Pueblo Pesto, or Gingered Cashew Pesto.

1	Bell pepper, veined and coarsely chopped
1	Red onion, halved and sliced into 4 sections
10	Mushrooms, cleaned, stem ends trimmed
8 oz	Firm tofu, cubed
2 tsp	"Lite" soy sauce
1/3 c	Pesto (see pesto section, pages 132-135)

1. Preheat oven to broil (or crank up your barbecue for grilling). Soak wooden skewers in cold water and marinate tofu in soy sauce while preparing vegetables.
2. Alternately skewer vegetables and tofu, cover with pesto sauce on all sides with a brush or with your fingers.
3. Place on a baking sheet and broil on top rack for 15 minutes, turn kabobs over once while cooking.

SERVING SUGGESTION:
Serve with a crispy salad and side of rice if desired.

SERVES: 2 (makes 4-6 skewers)

Alternate layers of colors and textures in these interesting kabobs

Hawaiian Kabobs

Pineapple chunks
Maui onion wedges
Red bell peppers
Tomato wedges
Tempeh cubes
(steam and marinate)

Italian Kabobs

Eggplant cubes
Radicchio quarters
Zucchini rounds
Other additions:
Palm hearts,
Steamed potatoes
or yams

Notes:

Mushroom
Seitan Stroganoff

A creamy, slightly tart mushroom sauce with strips of seitan (wheat gluten). Serve over noodles for a typical stroganoff, or over steamed broccoli or cauliflower or baked potato for a lighter version. Quick to make!

1/4 c	Lemon juice
1/4 c	Cooking sherry (or broth)
2	Garlic cloves, pressed
1½ c	Red onion, chopped
1/2 lb	Mushrooms, sliced
1 c	Marinated seitan, sliced into strips
1 Tbl	"Lite" soy sauce
1/2 c	Green peas

Sauce:
1 Tbl	Arrowroot powder
1 c	Water
2 Tbl	Tahini
1/4 c	Nutritional yeast flakes
	Freshly cracked black pepper and grated nutmeg

1. Saute the lemon juice and broth with the garlic and onion in a large skillet for a couple of minutes. Stir in the mushrooms and simmer 10 minutes more. Add the seitan and soy sauce.
2. In a blender, blend together the sauce ingredients until creamy, then pour the sauce into a skillet. Heat at medium low, stirring until thick and thoroughly heated.
3. Stir in the green peas and simmer for a couple of minutes more. Sprinkle 2 Tbl toasted walnuts or pine nuts on top and 2 Tbl minced parsley or chives. Serve over a half pound of cooked fettucine noodles.

SERVES: 2 - 3

Green Bean Curry

Light and alive, pungent yet delicate.
This is a very nice curry served with or without rice.
Serve on a platter surrounded by small bowls of condiments.

1/4 c	Water or broth
1 Tbl	Lemon juice
1 lb	Green beans, trimmed and cut in half
2	Red or green bell peppers, chopped
1/2	Red onion, chopped coarse
3	Yellow tomatoes, wedged
3	Garlic cloves, pressed
1½ c	Water mixed with
1 Tbl	Kuzu or arrowroot powder
1/2 Tbl	Concentrated vegetable broth
1/2 tsp each	Coriander and onion powders
1/4 tsp each	Cardamom and curry powder
1 small	Jalapeño chile, minced (remove seeds if you don't like "hot")

Condiments:

1/2 c each	Cashews, toasted and raisins

1. Heat the water and lemon in a wok or skillet on high. Add the beans, onions and peppers, stirring quickly at medium flame for several minutes.
2. Add the remaining ingredients, stirring well. Cover and simmer on low for a few minutes more until the veggies are tender but not too soft.

SERVING SUGGESTIONS:
Serve with cilantro (or another herb) on top — surround with small bowls of condiments. A long-grain brown basmati rice goes nicely with this curry, or try Cumin Rice, page 204.

Encouragement is the voice of friendship's spirit.

Notes:

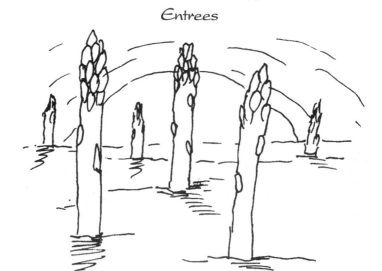

Spicy Asparagus and Black Beans

This is a quick and easy meal to make with dehydrated black beans. By sprinkling beans on top of the spicy sauteed vegetables, it "thickens," creating a nice sauce with South American flavors. You can also serve this with rice.

1/4 c	Water
1 Tbl	"Lite" soy sauce or aminos
1 c	Asparagus, chopped
2	Onions, coarsely chopped
12	Baby carrots (frozen okay)
1/2 tsp	Cumin seeds

Sauce:	1/4 c	Pueblo Pesto (page 133)
	1 c	Water
	1 c	Black beans, dehydrated

	1/2 c	Red bell peppers, chopped
Garnish:	1	Tomato, sliced
		Fresh cilantro sprigs

1. Put the water and soy sauce in a skillet and heat on low. Stir in the asparagus and onions on medium heat. Cover, turn to low and cook for 8 to 10 minutes. Add the carrots and cumin seeds.
2. Stir sauce ingredients together, then stir into the asparagus. Add water as needed, until an even sauce forms. Sprinkle red peppers on top. Cover for a few more minutes.
3. When bean mixture softens and thickens, put it on a platter or a bowl with the garnish. Serve with warm tortillas, salsa and a shredded salad — such as Fiesta Cole Slaw, page 68.

Italian Peppers and Links

A spicy saute of peppers and Italian soy sausage.
Serve with your favorite hot bread or over pasta.

4	Italian "lean-links" tofu sausages
3	Multi-colored bell peppers, chopped coarse
1	Red onion, chopped coarse
2	Garlic cloves, minced
2 c	Mushrooms, halved
1/3 c	Red wine
1 Tbl	Liquid aminos
up to 1/4 c	Water (as needed)
1 tsp	Basil
1 tsp	Oregano
1/2 tsp each	Ground fennel seeds and crushed red chiles
2	Tomatoes, chopped
1 tsp	Olive oil

1. Spray a cookie sheet with vegetable spray and make a few vertical slits on the soy sausages. Broil sausages in a toaster oven or on the top rack of the oven until brown on all sides. Set aside to cool, then slice 1" thick.
2. In a large skillet, saute peppers on medium flame in a bit of vegetable spray. Add the onion, garlic, mushrooms, wine and a bit of water. Stir often.
3. Add the remaining spices, olive oil, tomatoes and soy sausage. Adjust seasonings to taste. Serve hot.

SERVES: 2 - 4

Protein from soy beans saves fossil fuels!

78 calories of fossil fuel are expended to produce 1 calorie of protein from beef.

2 calories of fossil fuel are expended to produce 1 calorie of protein from soy beans.

Realities for the 90's, excerpted from *Diet for a New America*, by John Robbins

Mole is a thick rich sauce of chiles, peanuts, chocolate, sesame seeds, tomatoes and spices. Created over 2 centuries ago by Mexican nuns using everything they had in the kitchen. It has been a favorite national sauce of the Mexican people ever since.

This is our version, served over Cumin Rice.

Tofu Mole

Mole Sauce:	5-6	Dried mild red chiles (page 112)
	1 c	Onions, chopped
	1 Tbl	Liquid aminos (or 1 tsp "Lite" soy sauce and 2 tsp water)
	28 oz can	Pear tomatoes, cut
	1/4 c each	Raisins and peanut butter
	1 Tbl each	Garlic, chopped & Cocoa powder (or carob)
	1/4 tsp each	Ground cloves and coriander
	1/2 tsp each	Cumin and cinnamon
	2 Tbl	Sesame seeds, lightly toasted
	3 Tbl	Chile powder

Tofu Saute:	1	Onion, sliced
	1/4 c	Water
	2 tsp	Soy sauce
	1 lb	Firm tofu, cubed in 1/2" squares

1. To begin the sauce, see page 112 on how to soften the pulp from dried chiles. Put the chile pulp into a blender.
2. Saute onions in aminos on low in a small skillet. When soft, put them into the blender. Then add the rest of the sauce ingredients to blender and whirl for 3 minutes until smooth and creamy. Set sauce aside and prepare Tofu Saute.
3. Braise onion in water and soy sauce in a large heavy skillet for a few minutes until soft. Add tofu and turn up the heat to medium. Use a spatula to turn tofu.
4. Pour 2 to 3 cups of mole sauce into tofu, add 1/2 cup water and simmer for 15 minutes. Serve over hot Cumin Rice, page 204.

SERVES: 4 - 6

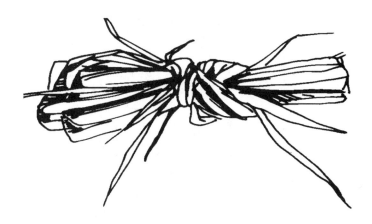

Chinese Woked Vegetables

A quick classic — woked vegetables, oyster mushrooms and tofu is an easy yet delicious meal to prepare.

Tofu marinade:

6 oz	**Firm tofu, cubed**
2 Tbl	**"Lite" soy sauce, mixed use**
1 tsp	**Toasted sesame oil**
2 Tbl	**Lemon juice**
1/3 c	**Mirin cooking sake (or a sweet broth)**
1 large	**Carrot, sliced in thin rounds**
4 ribs	**Celery, sliced on angle (use leaves, too)**
3.2 oz pack	**Oyster mushrooms (leave whole)**
1 c	**Bean sprouts**
6 large	**Mushrooms, sliced**
1 can	**Water chestnuts, quartered**
1-2 Tbl	**Garlic, minced**

1. Stir tofu cubes together with 1 Tbl "Lite" soy sauce and sesame oil. Set aside while preparing vegetables.
2. Heat up wok to high. Add lemon juice and mirin, stir in carrots, celery and 1 Tbl soy sauce. Stir constantly until crisp-tender.
3. Add mushrooms, bean sprouts, water chestnuts and garlic. Stir for a couple of minutes, then toss in tofu marinade and green onions. Stir until thoroughly heated. Turn off heat, toss in cilantro and serve. This woked dish is best when vegetables are crisp and alive — do not overcook.

SERVING SUGGESTION:
Serve as is, or with steamed long or short grain brown rice.

The message of love, is the voice of our heart telling its story.

Notes:

Wild 'n' Cheezy Casserole

Cheezy wild rice and sauteed kale combine to create a sumptuous baked casserole loaded with vitamins and calcium.

Rice:	4 c	Water
	1 c	Wild rice, rinsed
	1 tsp	Concentrated vegetable broth
	1 c	Long grain brown rice, rinsed
Sauce:	2 c	Cheezy Sauce (page 121)

Vegetable Saute:

1 Tbl	Lemon juice
1/4 c	Broth (or wine)
1/2 Tbl	"Lite" soy sauce
1 large	Garlic clove
1 c	Red onion, sliced
3 c	Mushrooms, sliced
5 c	Kale, shredded
1/2 c	Water
1	Carrot, shredded coarsely
	Cracked pepper to taste

Preheat oven to 400º.

1. To prepare rice: Bring water to a boil in a medium pot, add wild rice and vegetable broth concentrate and a dash of sea salt. Cover and cook on low for 10 minutes. Add brown rice, stir, cover and cook for another 30 minutes. Turn off heat, keep lid on until ready to serve.

2. Prepare Cheezy Sauce and fold into rice. Spread cheezy rice mixture on the bottom of a glass baking dish.

3. Put liquids in skillet, saute garlic, onion and mushrooms. After a couple of minutes add kale, water, carrots and cracked pepper. Stir to coat. Spoon veggies over rice in the baking dish. Cover with foil and bake for 20 minutes. Uncover and broil for 5 minutes.

SERVES: 4 - 5

Pronto Enchilada Casserole

This enchilada is layered like lasagne, using corn tortillas for the noodles. Sweet corn, tofu, mushrooms, and enchilada sauce fill the layers with soy jalapeño cheese on top. Very easy and quick to make.

10 oz	Enchilada Sauce (page 108)
6	Corn tortillas
1 lb	Tofu, sliced into 1/2" thick cutlets
1/2 tsp each	Onion powder, oregano, basil and cumin
Dash	Sea salt
4 large	Mushrooms, sliced
1 ear	Sweet white corn (1 cup)

Garnish:	1 c	Soy jalapeño cheese, grated
	1/2 c	Black olives, sliced
	2	Jalapeños, sliced
	2	Green onions, minced

1. Preheat oven to 400º. Put a bit of the Enchilada Sauce on the bottom of a rectangular baking pan (11" x 7"). Place 3 corn tortillas on the bottom (cut tortillas to fit into corners). Place tofu cutlets on top of tortillas and season with spices.
2. Put a layer of mushrooms and corn over the tofu, then add the remaining tortillas and Enchilada Sauce.
3. Garnish, cover with foil and bake for 35 minutes at 375º. Uncover the last 10 minutes.

SERVES: 4 - 6

We are responsible for our own fulfillment.

Life is what we make of it.

Notes:

Asparagus Tofu Pie

A delicate custard-style pie without a crust, topped with a savory mushroom sauce. This makes a nice light meal for spring or summer.

1 c	Asparagus pieces (1"-2" long)
6 small	Asparagus (whole spears) for top of pie

Tofu custard:

2½ c	Tofu
1 Tbl	Garlic, chopped
1/2 c	Asparagus broth (from steaming)
1/2 Tbl	Lemon juice
1/8 tsp each	Grated nutmeg, cracked black pepper and lemon peel
1/2 tsp	"Lite" soy sauce
1 Tbl each	Lemon juice and aminos
1 medium	Onion, sliced
1/4 c	Soy cheese, grated (optional)
1 recipe	Savory Mushroom Sauce (page 115)

1. Trim and steam asparagus for 15 minutes (or until soft). Puree tofu custard ingredients in a blender or a food processor.
2. Heat up the lemon juice and aminos in a small skillet and saute the onion for about 5 minutes. Fold onion and asparagus pieces into the tofu custard. Pour into a lightly oiled pyrex baking dish, sprinkle soy cheese on top.
3. Bake 350º in preheated oven for 25 minutes. Put the asparagus spears on top like the spokes of a wheel, and serve with Savory Mushroom Sauce.

SERVING SUGGESTIONS:
A tomato/mushroom/cucumber vinaigrette or
green salad goes nicely also.

SERVES: 6

Green Chile Quiche

A Southwest version of the classic quiche, made lighter without a crust. Sauteed red peppers, onions and garlic accent this roasted green chile quiche. Decorate the top with red pepper shapes for a very stunning visual presentation.

Tofu Custard:

1 lb	Soft tofu
10.5 oz	Silken tofu
1 Tbl	Kuzu (or arrowroot powder)
1/2 c	Vegetable broth
1/4 c	Whole wheat pastry flour
1 Tbl	Baking powder
1/4 tsp	Sea salt
2 tsp each	Cumin and onion powder

Vegetable filling:

1/2 c	Red bell peppers, chopped
1/2 c	Onions, chopped
1 tsp	Garlic, minced
1 Tbl each	Liquid aminos and lemon juice
2 Tbl	Water or broth
1/2 c	Grated (jalapeño) soy cheese
1 c	Green chile, roasted, peeled and chopped

To decorate top: Red pepper shapes and bell pepper rings

1. Preheat oven at 400°. Put the tofu custard ingredients into a food processor and puree. Scrape into a medium bowl.
2. Saute peppers, onions and garlic in aminos, lemon juice and broth until softened. Stir into the tofu custard mixture along with the soy cheese and green chiles.
3. Pour into a large, lightly oiled quiche pan, or pyrex pie dish. Lay shapes of cut peppers on top. Bake for 35 minutes.

How to Make an Easy Veggie Broth

Put 1/2 Tbl of concentrated vegetable broth or aminos in 1/2 cup water — stir. This broth may also be used (instead of fat or oil) to sauté your vegetables.

Tamale Pie

*A quick and easy favorite. Yields a large pan of savory
Southwest flavors, hearty and delicious.*

4 c	Filtered water
1¼ c	Coarse corn meal (polenta)
1 tsp	Onion powder
1/2 tsp each	Cumin and sea salt
1/8 tsp	Cinnamon

Vegetable filling:

5 c	Zucchini,* quartered and chopped
1 each	Onion and bell pepper, chopped
1 Tbl	Aminos
1/4 c	Water
1 tsp each	Cumin seeds, toasted lightly, and oregano
2 tsp	Chile powder
1/4 tsp	Cinnamon
1 c	Cut corn kernels
3	Tomatoes, seed and chop
2 c	Cooked beans (Anasazi Beans, page 201, or Sprouted Frijoles, page 206)
2 Tbl	Tomato paste

1. Preheat oven to 450º. Bring water to a rolling boil in a medium pot. Slowly shake in corn meal while you quickly whisk it. Lower heat and continue whisking for 5 minutes. Add spices and stir occasionally as mixture thickens for another 5 minutes.
2. Saute zucchini, onion and pepper in aminos and water for 10 minutes on low. Stir in spices, tomatoes, corn, beans and enough tomato paste to hold it together.
3. To assemble pie: Put veggies on bottom of large baking dish, spread corn meal crust on top evenly. Cover with foil, prick foil for steam to escape, and bake 25 minutes. Remove foil and bake 5 minutes more. Let cool before cutting into squares. Garnish with cilantro.

*Use green and gold zucchini or other summer squash.

SERVES: 6

Notes:

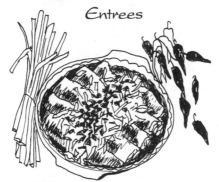

Cheezy Corn and Zucchini Enchiladas

A delicious cheezy enchilada filled with sauteed vegetables.
You can freeze them for later use. They also make a
scrumptuous brunch or lunch.

Stuffing:	1½ c	**Corn (cut from 2 ears)**
	3 c	**Zucchini, chopped**
	1 c	**Onion, chopped**
	1/4 c	**Water (or broth)**
	1 Tbl each	**Aminos and lime juice**
	1 tsp	**Cumin powder**
	1/4 tsp	**Freshly grated nutmeg**
	1 lb	**Firm tofu, mashed**
	1 c	**Cheezy Sauce (page 121)**
	1 pack	**Corn tortillas**
Toppings:	8 oz	**Soy cheddar cheese, grated**
	1/4 c	**Green onions, minced**
	1/3 c	**Black olives, minced**
	1 recipe	**Red Chile Sauce (page 108)**

1. Saute corn, zucchinis and onion in water, aminos, lime juice and spices, for 10 minutes on medium heat in a skillet.
2. Stir tofu into Cheezy Sauce and stir into veggie mixture in skillet, turn off heat. Put 1/2 cup of Enchilada Sauce on bottom of baking pan. Now prepare the tortillas.
3. Heat tortillas until soft (both sides), one at a time on a griddle, then dip tortillas into warmed Red Chile Sauce. Put a heaping spoonful of stuffing down the center of the tortilla and roll up. Place in a rectangular baking pan, against one side. Fill up pan, packing in enchiladas tightly.
4. Drizzle more Red Chile Sauce on top. Cover with grated soy cheese, green onions and olives. Bake 40 minutes in preheated 350º oven.

SERVING SUGGESTION:
Serve with roasted pepper and eggplant salad.
Garnish with radishes, jicama and tomatoes.

MAKES: 22 enchiladas (2½ pans)

We see
the invisible
with
our heart.

Notes:

Southwestern Cornbread Quiche

A spicy cornbread crust nestles sauteed vegetables in a creamy tofu custard. Great way to use up your favorite day-old sliced corn bread.

	Sliced corn bread,* 1/4" thick, to fit pie dish
2 Tbl	Lemon juice
1/4 c	White wine or broth
3 c	Zucchini, sliced
1/2 c each	Bell pepper, minced, and onion, chopped
2	Garlic cloves
1 small	Dried red chile, crumbled in

Tofu custard: 1 c	Tofu, mashed
1¼ c	Soy milk
1 Tbl	Arrowroot powder
1 tsp each	Garlic and cumin powder
1 Tbl	Egg replacer mixed with
1/4 c	Water
1/4 c	Salsa, chunky type

1. Preheat oven to 350º. Treat a glass quiche dish with vegetable spray. Line with cornbread slices (make sure they are dry), cutting smaller pieces for around the rim and sides. (Toast cornbread if it is soft.)
2. Put lemon juice and wine in a large skillet. Heat and add veggies, saute for 8 minutes on medium low.
3. Put tofu custard ingredients together in a blender and blend until smooth and creamy. Stir in salsa by hand.
4. To assemble: Put veggies over crust, then pour tofu custard on top. Bake 350º for 45 minutes (or until firm).

*Use a dense bread rather than the cake style cornbread.

Tempeh Cauliflower Quiche

Sauteed tempeh, onions, cauliflower and peas
punctuate the interior custard filling of this nouveau tofu pie.

	1	Pie crust
Filling:	1/4 c each	Lemon juice and broth
	8 oz	Tempeh, cubed in small pieces
	1	Onion, sliced
	3 whole	Garlic cloves (with jackets on)
	3 c	Cauliflower, cut into florettes
	1 Tbl	"Lite" soy sauce (or aminos)
	1/4 c	Water
	1 tsp each	Dried rosemary, minced garlic, basil
	1½ c	Petite green peas
Tofu custard:	2 c	Almond Milk (page 12) or soy milk
	1 c	Tofu, mashed
	2 Tbl each	Arrowroot powder and egg replacer
	1 Tbl	Onion powder
	1/2 tsp	Thyme
	1/4 tsp	Black pepper

1. In a wok, put in lemon juice and broth, then heat. Stir in tempeh, onion, garlic and cauliflower. Saute for 5 minutes, quickly stirring. Add soy sauce, water, herbs and peas. Turn off heat and remove garlics. Lay veggies over the pie crust with a slotted spoon.
3. Blend tofu custard in blender until smooth. Squeeze in garlics from their jackets, continue blending. Pour over the veggies.
4. Bake for 35 minutes in a preheated 350º oven. Slice a tomato and lay it on top; sprinkle a bit of dill over the dish. Bake another 5 to 10 minutes.

SERVES: 6

Soybeans and Soy Products

are a great source of protein, potassium, calcium, B vitamins and fiber.

Soybeans are a good source of choline, which aids in the metabolism and transportation of fats, choline normalizes nerve transmission and regulates the liver and gall bladder functions.

Notes:

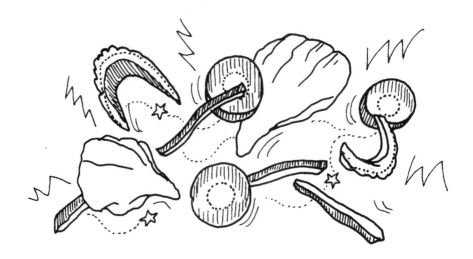

Oyster Mushroom Saute
with Lemon Grass Sauce

You can prepare the lemon grass sauce ahead of time and keep it in a saucepan. Begin cooking your rice 30 minutes before making the recipe, so vegetables don't have to wait around. Lemon grass compliments the delicate oyster mushroom beautifully.

1	Celery heart (1 stock, outer ribs removed)
1	Bell pepper, chopped
1	Carrot, sliced in rounds
1	Zucchini, julienne
2 Tbl	Mirin (cooking sake)
1/2 Tbl	"Lite" soy sauce
1 Tbl	Water
2 c	Fresh oyster mushrooms
1 tsp	Chile sesame oil
1 recipe	Lemon Grass Sauce (page 118)
1 recipe	Wild Tofu Jasmine Rice (page 201)
	Cilantro sprigs as garnish

1. Slice the celery at an angle. Put liquids in a hot wok and saute the first 4 vegetables.
2. Add the oyster mushrooms, stir to coat, then stir in lemon grass sauce and sesame oil. Simmer on low before serving.

SERVING SUGGESTIONS:
Have hot rice prepared and serve garnished with a cilantro sprig.

SERVES: 2

"Do you, Asparagus, take the lovely Jasmine Rice to have and to hold, ..."

Risotto with Asparagus and Peas

Risotto is a classic creamy Italian way to cook rice. One stirs hot broth into the rice a little at a time, allowing the rice to absorb the liquid slowly. The key to delicious risotto is in the stirring, so as to form a creamy union of flavors. This version adds asparagus and peas.

3 c	**Vegetable broth**
1 bunch	**Asparagus, cut in 1½" pieces**
1/2 c	**Petite green peas**
1/2 c	**Red onion, chopped**
2	**Garlic cloves, pressed**
1 Tbl	**Olive oil**
1/2 Tbl each	**Lemon juice and aminos**
1 c	**Italian Arborio rice**
	Freshly cracked pepper and nutmeg to taste

1. Put broth into a skillet, bring to a boil and add asparagus. Cover, turn down to simmer for 2 minutes. Add peas, then turn off heat, return lid and let it sit a minute before straining. Reserve broth.
2. In a deep skillet, saute onion in olive oil, lemon juice and aminos until soft, add garlic and rice. Stir until well coated.
3. Stir in 1/2 cup broth into rice until absorbed, repeat until broth is used up. Stir in asparagus and peas when rice is done (approximately 20 minutes). The rice should be tender yet firm. Season to taste.

SERVING SUGGESTION:
Serve with Mainstream Romaine Salad (page 65).

SERVES: 2

Open your heart

and love as much as you can.

Stuffed Acorn Squash Americana

A beautiful presentation, satisfying to the visionary culinarist.
Perfect for Thanksgiving or other holiday meals.

1 large	**Acorn squash**
1/2 c	**Broth**
1 Tbl	**Lemon juice**
1/3 c	**Celery, diced**
1/2 c	**Bell pepper, diced**
1/3 c	**Green onions, minced**
1 c	**Cooked brown rice**
1/2 tsp	**Thyme**
1/2 tsp	**Cumin powder**
1/3 c	**Soy cheese, grated**
	(or Cheezy Sauce, page 121)
Dash	**Nutmeg and sea salt**
1 recipe	**Creamy Cashew Basil Sauce, page 114**

1. Slice squash lengthwise and scoop out seeds and pith. Place squash flesh side down onto a baking pan. Pour 1/2 cup or so of water in pan. Bake for 30 minutes at 375º. (Bake ahead of time and keep in fridge for quick assembly.)
2. In a large skillet, heat broth and lemon juice at medium and add vegetables. Saute until soft but still crunchy. Stir in the rice and the spices, coat evenly. Toss in soy cheese and turn off heat.
3. Press stuffing in squash cavity. Place on a baking pan in a pre-heated 350º oven, reheat stuffed squash for 20 minutes or until hot.

SERVING SUGGESTION:
Serve with hot gravy on the side.
Garnish with a few fresh herbs or parsley.

SERVES: 2

Divine Dolmas

Heavenly grape leaves stuffed with minted brown rice, currants, roasted pecans and herbs. Serve with a warm Greek lemon sauce (Avgolemono Sauce). The most flavorful Dolmas we've ever tasted!

1 c	**Long grain brown rice**
2½ c	**Pure water**
1/3 c	**Red onions, minced**
2 Tbl	**Lemon juice**
1 Tbl	**Aminos**
1/3 c	**Currants**
1/2 c	**Pecans, toasted and minced**
1/3 c	**Fresh mint, minced (or 1 Tbl dried)**
1 tsp each	**Thyme, coriander powder and oregano**
Dash	**Sea salt**
1/2 Tbl	**Olive oil**
1 oz jar	**Grape leaves**
1/4 c	**Water**
1 Tbl	**Olive oil**
1 recipe	**Avgolemono Sauce (page 120)**

1. Bring water to a boil, add washed rice, cover and cook on low for 35 minutes. Yields 2 cups cooked rice.
2. Saute the onion in lemon and aminos until soft. Stir into rice along with currants, pecans and spices. Spread out grape leaf, top part down. Put 1 Tbl stuffing in center, roll up by folding sides of leaf in over rice, roll up burrito style.
3. Heat 1/4 cup water in a deep heavy skillet; add oil and dolmas. Turn dolmas over after a minute, cover with extra grape leaves, then cover skillet and simmer for 15 minutes.
4. Refrigerate (with extra oil on top, if desired) or serve warm.

SERVING SUGGESTIONS:
Serve with warm Avgolemono Sauce, tomato wedges, Greek style salad and hummus dip with pita bread for a full feast!

MAKES: 30 Dolmas

Ecstasy is a prayer that has no words

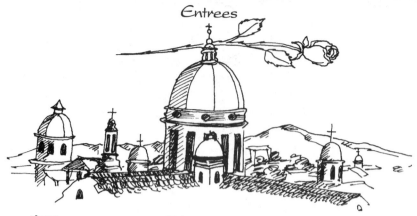

Notes:

Fettucini "Faux" Fredo

A scrumptuous lowfat version of a classic dish.
Add a fresh green salad and bon appetite!

1 lb	**Fettucine noodles (whole wheat)**
1 recipe	**Cheezy Sauce (page 121)**
	(delete turmeric and add 2 tsp basil or
	1/4 c fresh basil to sauce)
Garnish:	**Lightly toasted pine nuts**
	Italian parsley or basil

1. Cook pasta according to directions on package and strain.
2. Return pasta back to pot, stir in sauce.
3. Spoon onto a large preheated platter, garnish and enjoy!

SERVES: 4 - 6

Cheezy Noodle Bake

A more interesting, and certainly healthier version
of macaroni and cheese.

1 lb	**Macaroni**
2 c	**Cheezy Sauce (page 121)**
1 c	**Red bell pepper, minced**
	(try roasted peppers)
1/2 c	**Basil, cut into "ribbons"**
1/2 c	**Walnuts, toasted and minced**
1/2 c	**Soy cheddar, shredded**

1. Cook noodles al dente. Rinse and drain.
2. Mix sauce into noodles in a large pot, fold in the rest of the ingredients and put into a lightly oiled casserole dish. Top with soy cheese.
3. Bake in a preheated 350º oven for 30 minutes.

SERVES: 4 - 6

Kasha Nut Loaf

Whole buckwheat groats are featured in this savory mock meat loaf. Hearty and satisfying. This makes fine leftovers to use in sandwiches, or may be heated and crumbled into pastas or salads.

1 c	Kasha, rinsed
2 c	Boiling water
2 slices	Whole wheat bread, toasted and chopped
1 tsp	Basil
1/2 tsp	Sage
Dash	Cayenne
2 Tbl	Egg replacer mixed with 4 Tbl water
1 c	Onions, diced
1½ c	Mushrooms, chopped
1 c	Bell peppers, minced
2 Tbl	Lemon juice
1 Tbl	Liquid aminos (or "lite" soy sauce)
1/2 c	Sunflower seeds, toasted lightly
2 lrg	Garlic cloves, pressed

1. Bring water to a boil in a small pot. Add the kasha, stir and cover for 15 to 20 minutes. Put the kasha aside; half in a medium bowl and the other half in a food processor.
2. Add bread crumbs, spices and the egg replacer mixture to the food processor and pulse chop with kasha until it sticks together. Transfer into the bowl with the cooked kasha.
3. Saute onions, mushrooms and peppers in the lemon and aminos. Add garlic and sunseeds after 5 minutes. Stir well, then stir it into the kasha mixture until evenly blended.
4. Put into a lightly oiled bread pan, cover with foil, and bake for 30 minutes at 350º. Uncover and bake another 25 to 30 minutes. (Spread tomato paste on top for a nice addition.) Top with tomato sauce, or serve with a gravy or sauce of your choice.

SERVES: 4 - 6

Super Sensational Sesame Seeds

Unhulled sesame seeds contain ten times more calcium than cow's milk; one and a half times more iron than beef liver; more protein than chicken, beef liver or beef steak; three times more phosphorus than eggs; and more niacin than whole wheat bread.

Composition of Foods Handbook no. 8, U.S.D.A.

Notes:

Spicy Sesame Noodles with Chard

A quick and easy pasta dish that incorporates delicate vitamin-rich greens. Spicy and delicious.

7 oz	**Udon noodles**
2-3 c	**Chard, sliced thinly**
1	**Red bell pepper, julienne**
1	**Green onion, slivered at an angle**

Sauce:	**1 Tbl**	**Golden miso, dissolved into**
	2 Tbl	**Water**
	1/2 tsp	**Chile sesame oil**
	1 tsp	**Mirin (cooking sake) or honey**
	1	**Garlic clove, minced**
	1 tsp	**Rice vinegar**
	2 Tbl	**Sesame seeds, toasted**
	1 tsp	**Jalapeño chile, minced**

1. Cook noodles al dente, put the sliced chard leaves into the noodles right before draining. Transfer strained noodles and chard back into the empty cooking pot and add the peppers and onion.
2. Stir together sauce, then toss into noodles. Serve on a medium-sized platter.

SERVING SUGGESTION:
You can use spinach or bok choy instead of chard.
Serve with Marinated Hiziki (page 61) and a crisp salad.

SERVES: 2

Garlicky Zucchini with Bean Thread Noodles

This is a very simple and easy-to-prepare pasta dish. Bean thread noodles aren't as filling as other kinds of flour pastas.

2	Zucchinis (approx. 10" long)
6	Cloves garlic, sliced thinly
1 small	Red onion, sliced
2 tsp	Olive oil
1-2 Tbl	Water
1/2 Tbl	"Lite" soy sauce or tamari
1/2 c	Garbanzo beans
2	Roasted red bell peppers, peeled and diced
1/2 tsp	Chile sesame oil
1/2 pack	Bean thread noodles, soaked in water to soften

1. Steam zucchinis until just tender (only a few minutes).
2. Saute garlic and onions with the olive oil, water and tamari in a small skillet for a few minutes, then add the peppers and beans. Simmer and stir for a few more minutes, then turn off the heat. Stir in the sesame oil and zucchini.
3. Bring a medium pot of water to boil. Add bean thread noodles and cook 1 to 2 minutes until they soften. Strain.
4. Put noodles on a serving dish, toss in zucchini saute mixture and spoon over noodles. Season as desired.

SERVES: 2

Zucchini and other squash have been growing in the mountains of Mexico since 7,000 B.C. Both the flesh and the seeds were used as a food source. Squash has a high water content and thus adds moisture to baked goods. Try finely grated zucchini in salads, or cut zucchini into long strips for a nonfat "pasta": Steam gently and top with your favorite sauce.

Zucchini is an abundant crop in anyone's garden, and its versatility makes it a treasure to grow.

Pasta Fagiole

Pasta tossed with white beans and sauteed vegetables.

1/2 lb	Pasta (whole wheat),* cooked al dente
3 c	Bell peppers, cut into small strips
2 c	Mushrooms, quartered
2	Garlic cloves, minced
1½ Tbl	Olive oil
4 Tbl	Water
16 oz can	White beans, cooked with juice
1 c	Fire roasted or marinated red peppers, diced
1 tsp	Thyme
	Sea salt, cracked pepper to taste
	Fresh basil leaves, minced

1. Prepare the pasta, drain and set aside in large pot, cover.
2. Saute peppers, mushrooms and garlic in olive oil and water for 5 to 8 minutes, using a large skillet.
3. Stir in the beans, red peppers and spices; then add pasta and toss well to coat. Cover and simmer until thoroughly warmed.

*Try rotelli pasta (corkscrew shape) or penne (tubular shaped).

SERVING SUGGESTION:
Serve on a warm platter, garnish with fresh basil leaves.

SERVES: 2 - 4

Vegetable Lo Mein

A delicious Chinese Lo Mein without the oil.

1 pack	Lo Mein noodles, cooked according to package
1 medium	Bok choy, sliced
1 can	Bamboo shoots
1 can	Water chestnuts, sliced
1/4 c	Mirin (cooking sake)
8	Shiitake mushrooms, soaked 10 min., stemmed and sliced
1 pack	5-Spice baked tofu, cubed
1 recipe	Chinese Brown Sauce (page 117)
3-5	Green onions, slivered at an angle
Garnish: 1/4 c	Macadamia nuts (or cashews), toasted and chopped
1/4 c	Cilantro leaves

Lo Mein Sauce:

1/2 Tbl	Soy sauce
3 Tbl	Water
3 Tbl	Rice vinegar
1 tsp	Honey

1. In a wok saute bok choy, bamboo shoots and chestnuts in mirin on high flame. As bok choy softens, add mushrooms and tofu.
2. Fold noodles into wok, stirring all the while. Pour Chinese Brown Sauce on top and stir in the green onions.
3. Serve on a large heated platter with garnish on top. Serve the Lo Mein sauce on the side.

Mirin

A Japanese cooking wine made from rice (sake) that sweetens, tenderizes and enhances oriental stir frys.

Sake is made from the action of a yeast-like mold on rice. Mirin has less alcohol than regular sake.

NO VEGETABLE IS EVER A BURDEN

Hong Kong Pasta

A garden fresh soba noodle dish. The seasoned tempeh
and natural Szechuan sauce may be found in natural food stores.
A dash of hot pepper sauce can substitute for Szechuan sauce.

Veggie mix:	1 Tbl	Mirin
	1/2 Tbl	"Lite" soy sauce
	1/4 c	Water
	1/2 pack	Tempeh, cubed
	2	Garlic cloves, pressed
	2 tsp	Virgin olive oil
	1	Bell pepper, sliced
	3	Celery ribs, sliced
	1/2 head	Savoy cabbage, sliced (Chinese cabbage)
	1	Leek, cut 5" above base
	2 tsp	Szechuan sauce, to taste
	1	Tomato, chopped
Noodles:	1 pack	Buckwheat soba noodles
	2 Tbl	Fresh salsa
	1/2 Tbl	Virgin olive oil
	1 tsp each	Soy sauce and ginger, minced

1. In a wok, heat on high the mirin, "lite" soy sauce and water . Stir in the tempeh and garlic, then add the olive oil. Stir in the pepper, celery, cabbage, leek and Szechuan sauce and cook for a couple of minutes. Add the tomatoes and cover, then turn off wok. Do not overcook.
2. Cook Soba noodles according to package directions — al dente. Strain and reserve. Do not overcook.
3. Put the salsa, olive oil and ginger in a pot. Heat on medium and add the soba noodles, toss well. When noodles are hot, put onto a plate and top with veggies.

SERVES: 4

Glass Noodle Shiitake Surprise

A woked wonder of Asian delights, cooks in just 5 minutes.

7½ oz	Sai-fun noodles (bean thread noodles)
1 oz	Shiitake mushrooms, dried
1/2	Red bell pepper, julienne
1 bunch	Green onions, slivered
3 oz	5-Spice baked tofu

Seasonings:	1 Tbl	Garlic, thinly sliced
	1 tsp	Toasted sesame oil
	1 Tbl	Natural Szechuan sauce
	1 Tbl	Mirin cooking sake
	1/2 Tbl	Soy sauce

Garnish:	1/2 bunch Cilantro, chopped

1. Soak the sai-fun noodles and shiitake mushrooms in separate bowls of warm water for 30 minutes.
2. Stem and slice the mushrooms when soft. Heat the wok on high.
3. Add a bit of water to wok, stir in noodles and seasonings. Toss in vegetables quickly using wooden utensils in each hand. After a couple of minutes, add cilantro, cover, and turn off wok. Serve hot.

SERVES: 2

Eating with Chopsticks

Wooden chopsticks are fun to eat with. They encourage you to eat smaller portions and enhance the natural flavors of foods.

The vibrational frequency of wood resonates in harmony with our delicate skin and mouths and seem to have a calming influence as compared to processed stainless steel forks and spoons.

Fusilli Primavera

*A unique sauce of pureed yellow tomatoes, ginger,
garlic and chiles highlights this delightful garden pasta dish.
The vegetables are cooked in the same water pot after the pasta
has been strained out. Simple and delicious.*

1 lb	Fusilli pasta
2-3 c	Yellow round squash, chopped (or 14 baby squash)
5-6 c	Cauliflowerettes (1 head cauliflower)
1 small	Red onion, chopped
1 c	Carrot, sliced at an angle 1/4" thick

*Primavera Sauce:		
	2 Tbl	Golden miso
	1 Tbl	Tahini
	1½ c	Yellow tomato, chopped, seeded
	2 large	Garlic cloves
	1 c	Water
	2 tsp	Fresh ginger, chopped
	1	Serrano chile, chopped
	1 Tbl	Lemon juice

1. Blend the sauce ingredients together in a blender. Transfer to a saucepan and heat on low.
2. Cook pasta in a full pot of rapidly boiling water until al dente. Strain out the pasta with a slotted spoon into a colander, place in sink basin.
3. Return water to a boil, then add vegetables and cook another 8 to 10 minutes. Pour the vegetables over the pasta in the colander. Toss them gently together.
4. Put pasta and veggies on a large warmed platter and ladle the Primavera Sauce on top.

*Double the sauce recipe for sauce lovers.

SERVING SUGGESTION:
*Serve extra sauce on the side, garnish
with toasted pine nuts and Italian parsley.*

SERVES: 3 - 4 (sauce yields 2¾ cups)

Broccoli Bean Thread Saute

Spicy, fulfilling and easy to make. A combination of noodles, broccoli and a Southwestern-style sauce.

2 stalks	Broccoli
2 oz	Bean thread noodles
3 Tbl	Spicy Peanut Spread* (page 135)
1/4 c	Cilantro, fresh chopped

1. Rinse, trim and quarter each broccoli stalk. Put broccoli into a steamer basket and steam in 1" of water for 8 minutes, or until crisp-tender. Set aside steamer basket.
2. Put the bean thread noodles into steam water and cook for a couple minutes until soft. Strain away excess water.
3. Add Spicy Peanut Spread to noodles, stir to coat, then toss in the broccoli (you may want to cut the broccoli into smaller pieces). Serve hot. Top with cilantro.

*You may try Pueblo Pesto (page 133) for equally good results.

SERVES: 2

Notes:

Vegetable Eggless Fu Young

*An Oriental vegetable "frittata" that you cook on a griddle.
Serve with Chinese Brown Sauce (page 117)
or Mushroom Sauce (page 115).*

Vegetables:	1 Tbl	"Lite" soy sauce
	2 Tbl	Water
	1/2 c	Celery, minced
	1/2 c	Bell pepper, chopped
	1 c	Mushrooms, sliced
	1/3 c	Red onion, chopped
	1/2 c	Green onions, sliced
	1/2 Tbl	Garlic, minced
	2 c	Bean sprouts
Batter:	1 lb	Tofu
	1 Tbl each	"Lite" soy sauce, arrowroot powder, egg replacer
	2 Tbl	Water
	2 tsp	Baking powder
	1 tsp	Onion powder
	3/4 c	Flour
	1 recipe	Mushroom Sauce (page 115)

Preheat griddle on medium heat.

1. Put the soy sauce and water in a wok, heat on medium high and saute celery, peppers, mushrooms and red onions for 4 or 5 minutes. Stir in the green onions, garlic and bean sprouts, then turn off the heat and put the vegetables into a medium mixing bowl.
2. Put the batter ingredients into a food processor and puree until creamy. Stir into vegetables.
3. On a well warmed, lightly oiled griddle, spoon on the batter-vegetable mixture, flattening it out. Keep pancakes 4" in diameter so they will be easy to flip over with a spatula. Cook 4 to 5 minutes per side (or until set). (If your griddle isn't very hot, they may take up to 7 minutes per side.)

MAKES: 1 dozen pancakes, serving 4.

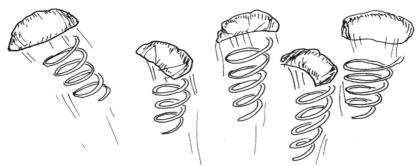

Spinach Spring Rolls

A steamed rice paper dumpling, stuffed with spinach and shiitake mushrooms.

Stuffing:

2 Tbl each	Lemon juice and water
1 Tbl	"Lite" soy sauce
1 oz	Dried shiitake mushrooms, soak to soften
1 Tbl	Fresh garlic, minced
1 bunch	Spinach, washed and dried, stemmed
1 c	Firm tofu, cubed small
1/4 c	Cilantro leaves, chopped
1 doz	Rice paper pancakes, rinse to soften

Sticky sesame sauce:

2 Tbl	Sesame seeds (unhulled)
2 tsp	Arrowroot powder
4 Tbl	Water
3 Tbl	Orange juice
1 Tbl	Honey and "lite" soy sauce
1" piece	Fresh ginger, peeled and minced

Spinach is rich in iron. Eat it uncooked for the best benefit to your body.

Spinach also contains phosphorus, calcium, potassium, vitamins A, C, E, B and K.

Serve it instead of lettuce for a more nutritional salad.

1. Heat lemon, water and soy sauce in a wok. Stem the shiitake mushrooms and slice them thinly. Stir in the mushrooms and garlic, then fold in the spinach and tofu. Cover and cook on low for 3 minutes. Turn off heat and stir in cilantro. Transfer to a small bowl.

2. Put the steamer tray in the wok, add water for steaming. Lightly oil the steamer tray so dumplings don't stick.

3. Place a spoonful of stuffing in the center of each soft rice paper pancake, roll up burrito style (tucking ends inward while rolling). Place on steam rack and cover wok. Turn to high heat until the water boils, then turn to low for 10 minutes.

4. Whisk the Sticky Sesame Sauce ingredients together, and heat in a small pan. Gently stir sauce as it thickens. Serve sauce on side with dumplings.

MAKES: 1 dozen, serving 4

Pizza!

By the proliferation of pizza parlors across the nation, clearly pizza is one of everyone's favorite foods. The emergence of healthier "gourmet" pizzas sweeping the California coast attests to the growing demand for a less fatty, fresher pie. You don't need a wood-fired oven, or lots of fatty cheese to make a great tasting pizza. Just use fresh vegetables and herbs, and a little imagination to create a sensational gourmet treat within your own oven. Here is a recipe for an easy whole wheat crust, and four different pizzas.

The "Spinizza" has fresh spinach and mushrooms. The "Pueblo" boasts black beans, salsa and peppers with a chile pesto sauce. The "California" is a primavera vegetable pizza using a cheezy sauce, and the "Pacific Rim" spices things up Thai-style with toasted sesame oil, cilantro, chiles, ginger, and veggies.

Whichever one you prepare, you can't beat-za a homemade pizza!

Viva Spinizza

A pizza with freshly steamed spinach, mushrooms and tomatoes.

Make 1 recipe	**Basic Wheat Pizza Dough (page 207)**
1 bunch	**Spinach, rinsed, stemmed**
3 c	**Mushrooms, sliced**
2 Tbl	**Fresh garlic, minced**
1 tsp	**Dried basil or 1/4 c fresh minced**
1 Tbl	**Olive oil**
1/2 c	**Grated soy cheese**
1/2 c	**Tomato sauce**

Preheat oven to 550º.

1. Roll out the pizza crusts and spread the olive oil and tomato sauce on top.
2. Steam the spinach leaves for a few minutes. Toss spinach with mushrooms, garlic, basil and olive oil.
3. Spread veggies on pizza crust and top with soy cheese. Bake in hot oven for 8 minutes.

The Birth of Pizza

When Roman soldiers occupied Israel, they tasted unleavened flat breads that had not been placed in the hearth to bake, and proclaimed it lacked "focus" (the latin word for hearth). So after crushing cheese on top, drizzling on olive oil and sprinkling the bread with herbs, they put this flat bread into a hot "focus" and decided it was worth repeating. Thus, unleavened flat bread became a "pizze" (the Italian name for flat pie).

The Romans' "focaccia" (another version of the flat bread) was learned from the Greeks, who in turn learned from the Egyptians. But truly we owe the pizza we love today to the Neapolitan women who perfected this wonderful food in their kitchens.

Food in History, by Reay Tannahill

Notes:

Disco Pizza

California Pizza

A fresh vegetable pizza.

1 recipe	Whole Wheat Pizza Dough (page 207)
3 tsp	Olive oil
9	Asparagus spears, trimmed, cut in thirds
1/2 c	Peas
1/2 c	Red onion, thinly sliced
1 c	Small mushrooms, sliced
1/2 c	Tomato sauce or Cheezy Sauce (page 121)
2/3 c	Soy cheese, shredded

Preheat oven to 550º.
1. Prepare pizza dough according to recipe. Roll out dough into 3 crusts, spread 1 tsp olive oil on each one.
2. Lightly steam asparagus till "al dente." Toss with veggies.
3. Spread sauce on crust, top with veggies and soy cheese. Bake 8 minutes.

Pueblo Pizza

*A lively Southwestern pizza using a Pueblo Pesto Sauce,
black beans and roasted peppers.*

1 recipe	**Whole Wheat Pizza Dough (page 207)**
2/3 c	**Pueblo Pesto (page 135)**
3/4 c	**Black beans, cooked**
1 c	**Roasted red or green peppers, sliced**
1 c	**Soy cheese, grated**
Garnish:	**Cilantro leaves and salsa**

Follow pizza dough recipe, dividing into 3 pizzas. Spread 1/3 of the
Pueblo Pesto on each crust. Sprinkle 1/3 of beans, peppers and soy
cheese on each pizza. Bake in hot 550º oven for 8 minutes. Garnish
with cilantro and salsa, or add avocado slices.

Other options: Top with corn, zucchini, or tomato slices.

Pacific Rim Pizza

Ginger, garlic and sesame spice up this Thai-style pizza.

1 recipe	**Whole Wheat Pizza Dough (page 207)**
3 tsp	**Toasted sesame oil**
3 tsp each	**Garlic and ginger (freshly minced), and sesame seeds (unhulled)**
Your choice of:	
Thinly sliced	**Broccoli florettes, zucchini, red pepper, bean sprouts, yellow squash, green onion**
Garnish:	**Cilantro leaves, sesame seeds (unhulled)**

Use sesame oil instead of olive oil to make crusts. Spread each
crust with 1 tsp toasted sesame oil, add spices and veggies. Bake
8 minutes in a 550º oven. Drizzle on a peanut sauce or dressing
(Green Thai Goddess [page 103] is tasty). Garnish with cilantro and
sesame seeds.

*When the
heart is full of
song, it sings ...*

Desserts

Introduction

♦ **Fruit Desserts**

Prune Purees (as fat replacers)   261

Raisin Puree   261

Apricot Puree   261

Prunicot Puree   261

Mandala Fruit Platter   262

Just Peachy   263

Mango Creme   263

Fresh Fruit Tart   264

Aphrodite's Freeze   265

Pineapple Delight   265

Peach Gel with Raspberry Sauce   266

Fruity Vanilla Banana Torte   267

Raw Berry Pie   268

Almond Pie Crust   268

Peachy Apricot Crumble   269

♦ **Cookies**

Chewy Double Carob Chip Cookies   270

Outrageous Oatmeal Cookies   271

Cherry Raisin Chews   272

Granola Chocolate Chippers   273

Sesame Applesauce Bran Cookies   274

Sprouted Carob Cookies   275

Sprouted Almond Croquettes   275

♦ **Cakes and Tortes**

Apple Spice Cake   276

Banana Orange Zest Cake   277

Carrot Ginger Cake   278

Raspberry Celebration Torte   279

Apricot Walnut Torte   280

♦ **Sauces**

Applesauce   281

Apple Cream   281

Orange Sauce   282

Raspberry Sauce   282

Tofu Pineapple Creme   283

Rhubarb Compote   283

Desserts

Ahhh, sweet morsels of life, how you
make living more enjoyable!

This chapter introduces some lowfat
and nonfat cookies, cakes, tortes, and fruit
desserts that are easy to prepare.

All of our no-bake fruit tarts,
gels and sorbets can be made in just
a few minutes — which is helpful when you
get the desire for something cool, sweet
and creamy after dinner.

To create your own great sorbets,
blend your favorite unsweetened frozen
fruits and a bit of fruit juice in your food processor.
Pulse chop the fruit to break it down into smaller
pieces, then cream it until smooth. Sorbets are the
perfect ending to a spicy meal, or a refreshing
repast on hot days. The most exciting aspect is
that fruit sorbets are fat free, which makes
them the "ultimate" dessert in our book.

Prunes in Baked Goods

Stewed prunes are best known for their natural laxative properties, especially when eaten in the morning. Recent studies show that prunes have other health-promoting benefits, such as the value of their fiber content. Eat prunes whole, rather than buying filtered or strained prune juice.

Prunes are high in calcium, magnesium, iron, potassium, and vitamins A and B. In fact, 1 cup of prunes contain 2.70 mcg of vitamin B_{12} — the same as in one pound of calves' liver.

Prunes add a slippery smooth sweetness to baked goods which replaces both fat and sugar in one step. Try raisins, apricots and figs for similar results. Put chopped, pitted, dried fruit into a food processor with water or juice and secure top tightly, then puree. Voila! A dynamic fruit puree!

Experiment by adding extracts, spices, and grated Orange or Lemon Zest (page 277) for some interesting creations.

Dried Fruit Purees

Use half of the water called for below if you use soaked dried fruit.
Pulse chop in food processor until pureed.

Prune Puree

1 c	Prunes, pitted and chopped
1 c	Water
1 tsp	Vanilla extract or orange zest

Apricot Puree

1 c	Dried apricots, chopped
3/4 c	Water
1/2 tsp	Orange zest
Dash	Nutmeg

Prunicot Puree

1/2 c	Dried apricots, chopped
1/2 c	Prunes, pitted and chopped
3/4 c	Water
1 tsp	Vanilla

Raisin Puree

1½ c	Raisins
1 c	Water
1 tsp	Vanilla
Dash	Cinnamon

The heavens are filled with the inspiration of the earth, both are reflections of the same heart.

Mandala Fruit Platter

*Soak dried organic fruit in separate bowls overnight
(or until rehydrated). Keep in the refrigerator until ready to use.
Soaking dried fruit makes them easier to digest.*

*Dried fruits supply lots of vitamins and minerals and satisfy a
sweet craving, while being a lowcal, nonfat treat. Mix them with
fresh orange and apple slices for texture and taste variation.
Oranges (vitamin C) help the body to efficiently utilize iron,
a prevalent nutrient in dried fruits. So remember to eat
an orange with iron-rich foods.*

Soak the following fruits:

12	**Pitted prunes**
1/3 c	**Raisins**
4-7	**Apricots, halved**
6-7	**Figs, sliced in half**

Fresh Fruit:

1	**Orange, cut in wedges**
1	**Apple, cut in wedges**
12	**Dates with an almond inside each**

Put apple wedges in line down center of platter. Put oranges in a
line crossing apples (to form an "X" shape). Place prunes in one
quadrant, figs in another, apricots and dates in the last 2 sections.
Sprinkle raisins on top or put them in the center.

SERVES: 4 - 6

Notes:

Just Peachy

A delightful frozen dessert — light, fragrant and delicious.
Substitute the papaya with mango for another nice treat.

> 2 c **Frozen peaches, or nectarines**
> 1/2 **Ripe banana**
> 1/3 c **Papaya pulp**
>
> **Topping:** 3 Tbl **Papaya, chopped**
> 1 **Lime wedge per person**

1. Partially defrost frozen fruit quickly by soaking bag in boiling water for a couple of minutes.
2. Put the peaches into a food processor and pulse chop until broken into small pieces. Add the remaining ingredients and continue to puree until smooth.
3. Spoon into dessert cups and top with fresh papaya and a squeeze of lime on top.

SERVES: 3 or 4

Mango Cream

A heavenly frozen ice cream made with just mangos and soy milk.
It whips up in seconds in your food processor.

> 8 oz **Frozen mango chunks**
> 5 Tbl **Vanilla soy milk**

Pulse chop mangos in your food processor with 2 Tbl of soy milk. When softened, add rest of soy milk and puree until creamy.

SERVES: 2

Life's inner melody is a soundless sound

A harmony
A rejoicing
A celebration

Notes:

Fresh Fruit Tart

A spiraling assortment of colorful fruit glistening under a fresh glaze. You can serve this on a raw crust or by itself as a jelled dessert — either way it's delicious.

6	Peaches or nectarines, peeled and sliced
8	Whole strawberries, tops trimmed
2	Kiwis, peeled and sliced
1 basket	Raspberries
2 c	Fruit juice
2 Tbl	Agar flakes
Optional	Almond Pie Crust (page 268) or Sprouted Wheat Carob Crust (page 267)

1. Prepare fruit, wash and pat dry. Arrange the fruit in a 9" to 10" glass pie or quiche dish (or, do this over a pie crust if desired): Peaches on perimeter, strawberries in next row, kiwis in third row and raspberries in the center of the circle (or any other way that alternates the colors with whatever fresh fruit is on hand).
2. Dissolve agar flakes in the fruit juice, then bring to a boil for 1 minute. Reduce and simmer a few minutes, then set aside for a couple of minutes. Pour glaze over fruit and chill to set.

YIELDS: 8 - 12 slices

Aphrodite's Freeze

The Greek Goddess of Love and Beauty would definitely be seduced by this dessert.

1 c	Frozen apricots
1	Frozen banana
1/2 c	Orange juice

Pulse chop everything in food processor, then blend well until smooth. Serve immediately in small dessert cups or goblets.

SERVES: 2

Pineapple Delight

Topped with Raspberry Applesauce, this nonfat jelled dessert with pineapple chunks is quite a delight!

2 c	Pure water
3 Tbl	Agar flakes
1 tsp	Ascorbic acid (vitamin C crystals)
1/2 tsp	Grated orange zest
2 tsp	Honey
8 oz can	Pineapple tidbits
1	Banana, sliced
1 c	Raspberry Applesauce (page 281) or Raspberry Sauce (page 282)

1. Bring water, agar flakes, vitamin C, orange zest and honey to a boil in a small saucepan. After 2 minutes with occasional stirring, remove from heat.
2. Add pineapple and banana to the pot. Spoon into 3 to 4 dessert cups and chill 1 hour.
3. To serve: Pour Apple Raspberry Sauce on bottom of the dessert plate, unmold jelled dessert in center of plate. Decorate with strawberry slices and a mint leaf.

YIELDS: 3 - 4 servings

A is for Apricots

Most orange-colored fruits and vegetables, wild greens as well as green leafy vegetables, contain high quantities of vitamin A.

Vitamin A is essential to the growth and repair of body tissue, improvement in the quality of the skin, overall eye health, and to create strong bones and teeth.

Here is a list of some excellent sources of vitamin A: Steamed dandelion greens, 21,060*; Steamed lambs-quarters, 14,550*; Steamed carrots, 15,750*; Steamed spinach, 8,100*; Dried apricots, 16,350*; Half a cantaloupe, 6,800; 1 small sweet potato, 8,100. *I.U. supplied in 1 cup (RDA of vitamin A for adults is 5,000 I.U.)

Notes:

Peach Gel with Raspberry Sauce

Naturally sweet, refreshing and simple to make.
Equally grand with frozen peaches.

3½ c	**Pureed peaches (fresh or frozen)**
2	**Peaches, peeled and sliced**
1/4 c	**Agar flakes**
1/2 c	**Water**
1 tsp	**Lemon juice**
1/2 c	**Apple or other juice**
1 recipe	**Raspberry Sauce (page 282)**

1. Put pureed peaches into a medium bowl. Arrange peach slices on bottom of pie dish in a spiraling circular pattern.
2. Dissolve agar in water and juices, heat on high in a small saucepan until boiling, reduce and let bubble for 1 minute.
3. Pour agar juice mixture into pureed peaches, stir or whisk together, then pour into the pie dish. (You can top with peaches if you don't want to invert the pie dish.) Chill for a minimum of 3 hours. Slice like a pie, and serve the Raspberry Sauce on top, or underneath the pie.

YIELDS: 6 - 8 servings

Fruity Vanilla Banana Torte

A celebration of flavors! Cool, sweet fresh fruit tops a vanilla banana pudding, served on a sprouted wheat carob crust. Fun to make and eat! Better yet, it contains no flour, margarine or eggs.

Sprouted Wheat Carob Crust

1½ c packed	Sprouted wheat berries (see page 275)
1/4 c	Roasted carob powder
1/3 c	Raisins
2 Tbl	Tahini
1/2 Tbl	Orange juice

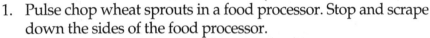

1. Pulse chop wheat sprouts in a food processor. Stop and scrape down the sides of the food processor.
2. Add the remaining ingredients and continue to blend, stopping to scrape down the sides as needed.
3. Press with wet hands into a 9" lightly oiled pie dish. Bake 1 hour at 250º. Let cool before filling.

Vanilla Banana Pudding Filling

A creamy pudding; freeze for half an hour before using for a pie filling.

10.5 oz	Soft silken tofu
1 medium	Banana, ripe
2 Tbl	Kuzu (or arrowroot powder)
2 Tbl	Honey
2 tsp	Vanilla extract
4 Tbl	Soy milk (vanilla)
2 tsp	Agar flakes

1. Put ingredients into a blender and puree until smooth.
2. Pour into a medium saucepan and whisk at medium heat until mixture thickens (about 2 to 3 minutes).
3. Pour into a pie shell (or dessert glasses) and top with fruit slices. Chill 3 hours before serving.

Fruit Topping

2	Kiwis, peeled and sliced
1/2	Banana, sliced
	Raspberries or sliced strawberries.

Arrange in spiral pattern on top.

YIELDS: 6 servings

Sprouting wheat berries

converts its starch into simple sugars, the vitamin E content triples, the vitamin B content increases from 20 to1200 percent, and the vitamin C content increases by a factor of 6*.

The ultimate way to eat wheat (aside from sprouting the berries) is in the form of wheat grass juice, which acts as a cellular healer, rejuvenator and oxygenator.

Love Your Body, by Victoras Kulvinskas

Notes:

Raw Berry Pie

*A simple, no-bake, fresh fruit torte that can be served with
frozen Mango Cream (page 263), non-dairy ice cream or
accented with Tofu Pineapple Creme (page 283).*

1 basket	**Strawberries, stems trimmed**
1 basket	**Raspberries**
1 c	**Fruit juice**
1 Tbl	**Agar flakes**
1 recipe	**Almond Pie Crust (see below)**

1. Trim and wash the berries, put them on paper towels to drain.
   Arrange on the Almond Pie Crust.
2. Mix the fruit juice with the agar flakes in a small pot, bring to
   a boil for 1 minute, then simmer for another minute. Let stand a
   couple of minutes before pouring over the fruit. Chill to set.

SERVES: 6

Almond Pie Crust

*Soaking almonds overnight, or for a few days in water, makes them
easier to digest. A very delicious pie crust.*

1 c	**Soaked almonds**
1/3 c	**Raisins or currants**
2 Tbl	**Tahini**
1/2 tsp	**Vanilla extract**

1. Pulse chop ingredients together in a food processor until a paste
   forms. You may need to stop and scrape down the sides of the
   food processor a couple of times while processing.
2. Spread into a 9" pie dish using wet fingers. Freeze an hour to set,
   or you can bake it at 250º for 30 minutes, before filling.

YIELD: 1 pie crust 9" diameter

Peaches

originated in China between 2,000 to 1,000 B.C. Originally called the "Persian Apple," their name has evolved to peach over the centuries. A fresh peach is mostly water by weight, and contains about 1,516 I.U. of vitamin A!

A sweet peach has many sensual references, and is one of the most heavenly fruits around.

Peachy Apricot Crumble

A quick dessert to make in the summer when peaches and apricots are plentiful.

2 c	**Apricots, pitted and sliced**
5 c	**Peaches, pitted, peeled and sliced**
3/4 c	**Fructose**
3 Tbl	**Flour**
1 tsp	**Cinnamon**
1 tsp	**Lemon juice**
2 tsp	**Arrowroot powder**
Topping: 1 c	**Granola, partially ground**

Preheat oven to 350º.

1. Put the sliced fruit and lemon juice into a bowl. Stir the dry ingredients together, then toss them into the fruit.
2. Put the granola into a food processor and pulse chop 3 times to break the granola up a bit.
3. Place fruit mixture in a glass baking dish and top with granola. Bake for 20 minutes.

SERVES: 6

Notes:

Beyond the Cookie

Our cookies go beyond the traditional concept of what ingredients make a good cookie recipe.

We use dried fruit, fruit purees, and fruit juice to sweeten; nut butter and/or tahini as a binder and lots of whole grains such as oats, wheat, and bran for a fiber-rich treat that will rival the "traditional" cookie in a much healthier, less caloric, less fatty way.

The health stars of these cookie recipes are the Sprouted Almond Croquettes, and the Sprouted Carob Cookie. Both are fiber and enzyme rich, made from sprouted wheat berries ground up with raisins to sweeten and slowly baked at a low temperature to ensure their nutritional benefits.

Chewy Double Carob Chip Cookies

A scrumptuous carob chip cookie, fruit sweetened and packed with lots of bran.

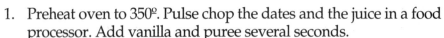

1/2 c (packed)	Honey dates, pitted
1 c	Fruit juice (apple, berry, etc.)
2 tsp	Vanilla extract
1/2 c each	Oat bran and wheat bran
1/2 c	Whole wheat pastry flour
1/2 Tbl	Baking powder
1/2 c	Carob chips
30	Walnut halves (optional)

1. Preheat oven to 350º. Pulse chop the dates and the juice in a food processor. Add vanilla and puree several seconds.
2. Stir together the bran, flour and baking powder, then pulse chop them in the processor with the juice mixture. Transfer to a medium bowl.
3. Stir in the carob chips and roll the cookie dough into 1" balls. Press down the walnut half in the center, if desired. Bake at 350º for 12 to 15 minutes.

Store in airtight bag, otherwise these soft, chewy cookies get hard after 2 to 3 days because they are made without oil.

YIELDS: 30 cookies

Outrageous Oatmeal Cookies

As their name implies, these are outrageous!
Chewy and full of goodies inside.

1 Tbl	Egg replacer
4 Tbl	Water
1/3 c	Honey
1 c	Prunes, pitted and cut in half
1/4 c	Orange juice
1 c	Walnuts, lightly toasted (optional)
1 c	Oat flakes
1/2 c	Oat bran
1/4 c	Whole wheat pastry flour
1 tsp	Cinnamon
1 Tbl	Baking powder
1 Tbl	Arrowroot powder

Preheat oven to 350º.

1. Put egg replacer and water in a food processor and beat until fluffy. Add in the honey and blend.
2. Pulse chop in the prunes and orange juice, beat well until prunes are chopped fine. Pulse chop in walnuts briefly.
3. Mix the rest of the dry items separately in a medium bowl. Mix wet mixture into the dry mixture bowl. Stir until evenly distributed.
4. Drop the cookie dough by tablespoon onto a lightly oiled pan. Bake for 13 to 15 minutes at 350º.

YIELDS: 28 - 30 medium-sized cookies

Since the birth of civilization, oats have been a staple food. First harvested as a weed by Northern Europeans, oats are now one of the finest whole foods one can eat at breakfast.

To make your own muesli, try soaking oats in an equal quantity of water for a couple of hours, or overnight. (You can also add dried fruit and flax seeds to this.) Top with fresh fruit or some soy milk before serving.

The bran in oats is said to help reduce cholesterol and is an excellent source of fiber in your diet.

Notes:

Cherry Raisin Chews

A soft cereal-based cookie with a sweet-tart chewy taste.

1/2 c	Dried cherries
1 c	Raisins
1 c	Hot water
1 tsp	Lemon Zest, loosely packed (page 277)
1/2 tsp	Almond extract
1/2 c	Honey
2 Tbl	Peanut butter
1 tsp	Vanilla
1 Tbl	Lecithin granules
1 c	Water
1/4 c	Farina (instant cereal)
1¾ c	Whole wheat pastry flour

1. Preheat oven to 350º. In a large bowl, soak the cherries and the raisins in water until plump (about 10 minutes). Then add the lemon zest and the almond extract.
2. In a food processor, cream together the honey, peanut butter, vanilla and lecithin. Add to the bowl with the raisins.
3. Bring water to a boil. Whisk in cereal, turn to low, then cook cereal until thick, pour into the bowl with the raisins. Sift in flour, fold together.
4. Drop cookie dough by tablespoon onto a pre-oiled baking sheet. Bake for 15 minutes.

Try adding 1/2 cup walnuts to mixture for more crunch.

YIELDS: 36 cookies

Granola Chocolate Chippers

*If you love a nutty-crunchy-chocolaty cookie,
this one's a must. The applesauce gives it a moist flavor and
the tahini holds it together. Quick and easy!*

1/4 c	Tahini
1/4 c	Water
1/3 c	Whole wheat pastry flour
1/3 c	Applesauce
1/2 c	Granola of choice
1 tsp	Vanilla extract
1/2 c	Granola
1/2 c	Walnuts, toasted and chopped
1/2 c	Chocolate or carob chips*

Preheat oven to 350º.

1. Put the first 6 items in a food processor and blend for a few seconds until creamy. Scrape mixture into a medium bowl.
2. Stir in the granola, walnuts and chips. Drop cookie dough in tablespoonfuls onto a baking sheet and press down. Bake 18 minutes at 350º.

*Look for unsweetened carob chips.

YIELDS: 20 - 22 cookies

Chocolate comes from the cacao tree pod in South America. These pods are fermented, roasted, hulled and ground into cocoa powder.

Hot chocolate was consumed by Aztec royalty with gusto, and later brought to Europe through the Conquistadors of Spain.

Carob powder comes from the carob pod (also called St. Johns Wort). It is roasted and ground, similar to chocolate and has a natural sweetness. Carob powder is healthier than cocoa powder, because it contains no caffeine and has more nutrients.

Both carob and cocoa powder have a delicious taste, but keep in mind that fats and sugars are added when they are processed into chips or bars.

Notes:

Sesame Applesauce Bran Cookies

Moist and delicious with a down-home cinnamon apple flavor.
These cookies are loaded with fiber.

1/2 c packed	Honey dates, pitted
1¼ c	Applesauce
1 tsp	Cinnamon
1 tsp	Vanilla extract
1 c	Whole wheat pastry flour
1/2 c	Wheat bran ⎫
1/2 c	Oat bran ⎭ mixed with 1/2 c hot water
1/2 c	Sesame seeds (unhulled)
3/4 c	Raisins

Preheat oven to 350º.

1. Blend honey dates in a food processor with applesauce, cinnamon and vanilla, blend well. Pour water over wheat and oat brans in a medium bowl.
2. Add the flour and bran, then pulse chop several seconds. Put in the sesame seeds and raisins, then pulse chop briefly.
3. Drop by tablespoonsful onto a lightly oiled baking sheet, flatten slightly using your wet fingers. Bake for 20 minutes in a 350º oven.

YIELDS: 45 cookies

Sprouted Almond Croquettes
"The Healthiest Cookie Around"

A whole grain sprouted-wheat cookie. The natural sweetness comes from the maltose sugar in the sprouted wheat berries, with a little help from almond extract, currants and applesauce. Once you've sprouted the wheat berries, just grind the ingredients together for a delicious, crunchy fiber- and vitamin-rich treat. Then slow bake at a low temperature which preserves the vitamins.

1 c	Sprouted wheat berries
1/2 c	Apple sauce
1/3 c	Raw cashews
3/4 c	Currants
1/2 tsp	Almond extract
1/4 c	Almonds, toasted and minced

Preheat oven to 250º.

1. To sprout wheat (see right margin).
2. Pulse chop the sprouted wheat in a food processor, stop and scrape down the sides. Pulse chop in applesauce and cashews, then add the currants and almond extract, blending for another 30 seconds.
3. Stir in almonds and drop cookie dough by tablespoonful onto a lightly oiled cookie sheet and bake 1½ hours at 200º.

YIELDS: 20 cookies

Sprouted Carob Cookies

A sprouted cookie naturally sweetened from the maltose sugar in the sprouted wheat, the raisins and the toasted carob powder.

1 c	Sprouted wheat berries
1 tsp	Vanilla
1/3 c	Raw cashews (or soaked)
1/3 c	Unsweetened coconut flakes
1/4 c	Carob powder (roasted)
1/3 c	Soaked raisins (soak in water to soften)

1. Grind sprouted wheat in a food processor with vanilla and cashews. Stop and scrape down the sides. Puree to a paste.
2. Add the coconut and the carob powder, and pulse chop again. Pulse chop in raisins for 3 seconds.
3. Roll between your wet palms into 1" balls, flatten onto a baking sheet. Bake at 200º for 1 to 1½ hours.

YIELDS: 21 cookies

Basic Wheat Berry Sprouting Procedure

Put wheat berries in a bowl or jar and cover the wheat berries with water; let soak for 24 hours.

Drain out the water, then rinse with fresh water, and drain again.

Rinse and drain morning and night for 2 more days or until white sprout tails appear.

Notes:

Apple Spice Cake

All fruit sweetened and delicious!
This recipe also makes wonderful muffins.

3 c	Apple, grated
2 Tbl	Lemon juice
3/4 c	Applesauce
1/2 c	Frozen concentrated apple juice
4 tsp	Egg replacer
1/2 c	Water
1/2 c	Mashed ripe banana
1¹/₃ c	Walnuts, chopped fine
2 c	Whole wheat pastry flour
1 tsp	Baking soda
1 tsp	Cinnamon
1/4 tsp each	Cloves and nutmeg

Preheat oven to 350º.

1. Mix the grated apple and lemon juice together in a medium bowl.
2. Blend the next 5 ingredients in a food processor.
3. Stir blended ingredients into apple/lemon juice mixture. Fold in the walnuts.
4. Sift the whole wheat pastry flour with baking powder and spices in a separate bowl, then fold into apple mixture. Put into a large, lightly oiled cake pan. Bake at 325º for 1 hour. Unmold after cake has cooled a bit and drizzle Orange Sauce (page 282) on top, then refrigerate.

YIELDS: 12 - 16 slices

Banana Orange Zest Cake

A moist cake that doesn't need frosting. Serve for dessert with fresh fruit or a non-dairy ice cream. Simple to prepare.

1½ c	Mashed ripe banana
1 Tbl	Egg replacer
3 Tbl	Water
3 Tbl	Safflower or canola oil
1/2 c	Honey
1 tsp	Orange zest, grated (see right margin)
1½ c	Whole wheat pastry flour
1/2 Tbl	Baking powder
1/2 tsp	Baking soda
1/4 tsp	Cinnamon
2 Tbl	Coconut flakes (optional)

Preheat oven at 350º.

1. Mash banana with a whisk in a large bowl. Add the next 5 ingredients and whisk well.
2. Separately sift the dry ingredients, then fold them into the wet mixture just until mixed. Do not overmix. Pour into a lightly oiled round cake pan or a bread loaf pan. Sprinkle the coconut on top and bake 50 minutes — or until knife inserted comes out clean. Let cool before slicing.

YIELDS: 12 slices

How to Make Orange and Lemon Zest

Make your own delicious dried orange or lemon peel by saving the skins of organic oranges or lemons. Wash and dry the peel, then shave off the outer layer of the rind (colored part only) with a knife or vegetable peeler. To dry the peel, place in the top part of a (toaster) oven at 250° for 30 minutes or until crisp but not brown. Then place in a food grinder and pulverize into a fine powder. Store in a glass jar.

Add to baked goods, brewed beverages, soups or sauces, hot cereals or stir frys. It will add a rich orange (or lemon) flavor and aroma to your favorite foods.

Notes:

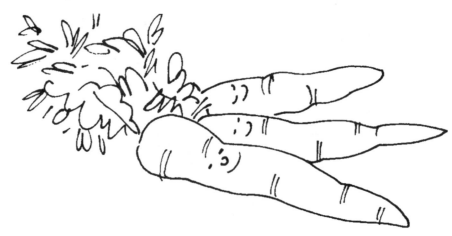

Carrot Ginger Cake

A moist and fluffy cake, softly spiced with ginger. For variation, top with Tofu Pineapple Creme (page 283). For a very festive flair, use as a cake base for the Raspberry Celebration Torte (page 279).

Sift together: 1½ c Whole wheat pastry flour with:

2½ tsp	Baking powder
1 tsp	Baking soda
1 Tbl	Egg replacer
3/4 tsp	Cinnamon
1/2 tsp	Nutmeg, freshly grated

Mix in wet items:

2 Tbl	Cold pressed safflower oil
3/4 c	Soy milk (vanilla)
1/2 c	Honey
1 Tbl	Fresh ginger root, grated
1 c	Carrots, finely grated
1/2 c	Raisins

Preheat oven to 375º.

1. Sift the first 6 ingredients into a large bowl.
2. Mix the next 4 items separately in a blender, fold or whisk them into the dry mixture (do not overmix).
3. Stir in the carrots and raisins* and spoon the batter into a prepared (oiled and floured) cake pan. Bake for 35 minutes at 350º (or until toothpick inserted comes out clean). Let stand in pan for 15 minutes before inverting onto a platter. Chill.

*Optional additions: 1 cup pineapple chunks, 3/4 cup walnuts, chopped.

YIELDS: 8 - 12 servings

Raspberry Celebration Torte

A stunning birthday or special occasion cake that is easy to make. A vanilla almond pudding ices the cake, which is then topped with fresh raspberries.

1 recipe	**Carrot Ginger Cake* (page 278)**	
Pudding:	**1 pack**	**Soft silken tofu**
	1 c	**Vanilla ("lite") soy milk**
	1/4 c	**Agar flakes**
	2 Tbl	**Raspberry topping (fruit sweetened)**
	1/4 tsp each	**Vanilla and almond natural extracts**
	1½ Tbl	**Honey**
Glaze:	**1 c**	**Natural fruit juice****
	1 Tbl	**Agar flakes**
	2 tsp	**Kuzu powder**
	1 box	**Fresh raspberries**

1. Prepare carrot cake according to recipe.
2. Blend the pudding ingredients in a blender, then pour into a medium size pan. Whisk until thick at medium heat. Remove from heat and chill till firm (1 to 2 hours). This will "set" the pudding.
3. Whisk up the pudding until it's smooth (it will resemble tapioca pudding). Spread thickly on cake top. Put glaze in the blender, then heat for 1 minute. Let cool.
4. Press raspberries all over the cake top. Pour glaze on top and chill till ready to serve.

 *Can use Banana Orange Zest Cake (page 277).
**Any red-colored berry blend.

YIELDS: 8 - 12 slices

Every vision of celebration is a love story.

Notes:

Apricot Walnut Torte

A layered pie of glazed fresh fruit, and creamy apricot filling on top of a walnut torte crust. Walnuts are a good source of both of the essential fatty acids (linoleic and linolenic acid).

Filling: 1 recipe Apricot Puree (page 261)
10 oz pack Soft silken tofu
1 tsp Orange Zest (page 277)
1 Tbl Egg replacer
1 Tbl Water } mix together
1 Tbl Orange juice

Crust: 1 c Walnut pieces, toasted
1/2 c Whole wheat pastry flour
2 Tbl Oat bran
1/2 tsp Lemon juice

Topping: 4 Apricots, halved, peel if desired
2 Peaches, sliced, peel if desired
1/4 c Blueberries
Or use fresh or frozen fruit in season

Glaze: 1 Tbl Agar flakes mixed with 3/4 c juice

Preheat oven to 350º.
1. Prepare the apricot puree in a food processor, then add the tofu and orange zest. Blend in egg replacer mixture while the food processor is running. Put into a bowl.
2. Put the crust mixture into the food processor and grind well. Pat into a glass pie pan, evenly distributing the crust on the bottom and the sides. Prick with a fork a few times and prebake for 10 minutes at 375º.
3. Pour the filling inside the pie crust and bake for 25 minutes more.
4. Arrange the fresh fruit on the top of the pie in a swirl pattern, put blueberries around the perimeter. To make glaze: heat agar flakes with juice to a boil, then reduce for a minute on low heat. Pour thick glaze over fruit and refrigerate.

YIELDS: 8 - 12 slices

Applesauce

A smooth sauce to spoon over Apple Spice Cake (page 276) or fresh fruit. Blend in 1/2 cup raspberries or strawberries to bring out a fruitier taste and a luscious red color. Use as an ingredient in baked goods to make them moist.

7 c	**Apples, chopped (about 6-8 apples)**
1½ c	**Water or apple juice**
4 tsp	**Concentrated fruit sweetener**
1 tsp	**Cinnamon**
1/2 tsp	**Grated Lemon Zest (page 277)**

1. Peel the apples (if not organic), otherwise just core and chop. Bring water or juice to a boil in a pot and add the apples. Cover and return to a boil, then simmer on low for about 10 minutes.
2. Drain off the excess liquids. Transfer apples to a food processor and puree. Add the spices and pulse a bit more. Chill.

SERVING SUGGESTION:
Garnish with cinnamon.

YIELDS: 3 cups

Apple Cream

Tofu and applesauce blend to create a creamy topping on pancakes or desserts.

5 oz	**Silken tofu**
1 c	**Applesauce (see above)**
2 Tbl	**Maple syrup**
Dash	**Cinnamon**

1. Pulse chop all the ingredients in a food processor, then blend it to a smooth, creamy consistency.
2. Pour over Apple Spice Cake (page 276) or pumpkin pie or even over breakfast cereal or granola.

YIELDS: 1¼ cups

An Apple a Day Keeps the Doctor Away

Apples are an excellent source of fiber, carbohydrates and pectin. Pectin is a carbohydrate which yields a gel that helps to keep your intestines and bowels clear and healthy.

Fresh raw apples and apple juice are cleansing to your body, and when combined with lemon juice, their cleasning value is enhanced.

Notes:

Orange Sauce

A thick orange fruit sauce to top cakes, flan and non-dairy ice creams. Easy to prepare and delicious.

1/2 c	Orange juice
2 Tbl	Frozen orange juice concentrate
1 tsp	Kuzu
1/2 tsp	Grated orange rind

Whisk together ingredients in a small saucepan, heat on medium high and let gently boil for a few minutes as it thickens. Pour sauce into a small container and keep in the refrigerator.

YIELDS: 1/2 cup

Raspberry Sauce

Spoon over cakes or nondairy ice creams, or serve on the bottom of a slice of cake for a fruity accent to desserts.

1½ c	Frozen raspberries
4 Tbl	Fruit juice
1 Tbl	Honey, if desired

Puree in a food processor until smooth, add juice to attain the desired consistency.

Tofu Pineapple Creme

*A creamy whipped topping, delicious over cakes
or to top a chilled fruit soup.*

5 oz	Soft silken tofu
1 Tbl	Tofu mayonnaise
2 Tbl	Pineapple juice concentrate, frozen
1 Tbl	Lime juice
1 Tbl	Maple syrup

Blend in a blender or a food processor until creamy smooth;
refrigerate.

YIELDS: 1/2 cup

Rhubarb Compote

*A ravishing stewed rhubarb, good hot or cold. Serve over vanilla
soy ice cream, on a thin piece of cake, or even on your pancakes or
oatmeal. Serve in the spring, or as rhubarb appears in your market.*

5 c	Rhubarb, cut into 2" pieces (1 lb)
1/3 c	Honey
1/2 tsp	Orange or Lemon Zest (page 277)
1/4 c	Water
1/4 c	Currants
1 c	Apple, peeled and sliced

Put all the ingredients into a medium saucepan, cover and bring to
a boil. Reduce heat, cook on low for 5 minutes, just until rhubarb is
soft. Stir and sweeten to taste. Serve hot or cold.

YIELDS: 8 — 1/2 cup servings

Did you know ...

Rhubarb is loaded with calcium? There is 211 mg of calcium per 1 cup of stewed rhubarb, and 216 I.U. of vitamin A.

Rhubarb began appearing in Asia Minor and the Eastern Mediterranean in 2,700 B.C., making it a very ancient plant!

800 mg R.D.A. for calcium

Bibliography

Cousens, Gabriel, M.D. *Conscious Eating*. Vision Books International, 1992.

Editors of Prevention Magazine Health Books. *Everyday Health Tips*. Rodale Press, 1988.

Elkort, Martin. *The Secret Life of Food*. Jeremy P. Tarcher, Inc., 1991.

Erasmus, Udo. *Fats and Oils*. Alive Books, 1986.

Kirshchmann, John D. *Nutrition Almanac*. McGraw Hill Books, 1975.

Kulvinskas, Viktoras, M.S. *Love Your Body*. OMango d'Press, 1972.

Meyerowitz, Steve. *Juice Fasting and Detoxification*. The Sprout House, 1992.

Robbins, John. *Diet for a New America*. Stillpoint Publishing, 1987.

Robbins, John. *Realities for the 90's*. Earth Save, 1992.

Tannahill, Reay. *Food in History*. Crown Publishers, 1988.

Menus

7 Days of Breakfasts

Day 1
Pineapple Date Shakes   13
Vibrant Oatmeal   20

Day 2
Pumpkin Walnut Pancakes   23
Syrup of Choice
Orange Banana Flips   11
Grain Beverage

Day 3
Blue Corn Griddle Cakes
with Strawberries   26
Fresh Squeezed Orange Juice
Herbal Tea

Day 4
Sliced Kiwis and Berries
Banana French Toast   27
with Maple Syrup
Grain Beverage

Day 5
Super C Salad   55
Breakfast Burritos   25
Herbal Tea

Day 6
Vanilla Rice Cream with
Blueberries   21
Orange Slices
Mint Tea

Day 7
Whole Grain Toast
Matzo Scrambler   24
Herbal Tea

(See also Live Energy Morning Meals, page 293)

Bountiful Brunch

Apricot Spritzers   10
Fresh Fruit Kabobs   53
Bagel and Paté Platter   44
Apple Spice Muffins   28

❤

Picnic Fare

Cranberry Gingerales   9
Tuscan Tomato Rice Salad   83
Rice Paper Salad Rolls   46
Sunseed Arugula Rolls   49
Melon Slices
Chewy Double Carob Chip
Cookies   270

❤

Backyard Barbecues

Garlic Roasted Corn   189
A Grilled Affair   220
Sprouted Frijoles   206
Watermelon Triangles
Apricot Spritzers   10

Seasonal Meals

Spring Flings

Tomato Mushroom Vinaigrette   65

Asparagus Tofu Pie   230
with Mushroom Sauce   115

Aphrodite's Apricot Freeze   265

❤

Green Salad of Choice

Eggplant Tomato Boats   218

Bread Sticks   209

Crisp Pear Slices
with Lime Wedges

Fall Fancifuls

Fennel Asparagus Bisque   172

Harvest Hiziki Salad   69

Golden Nugget Squash Pockets   216

Silken Chile Ginger Sauce   112

Carrot Ginger Cake   278

❤

Golden Squash Bisque   162

Confetti Salad   56

Cheezy Broccoli Stuffed
Potatoes   219

Sesame Applesauce
Bran Cookies   274

Summer Sashay

Orange Fennel Salad   57

Grilled Pesto Kabobs   221

Polenta Triangles   204

Raw Berry Pie   268

❤

Gazpacho   151

Presto Pesto Caps   133

Pasta Fo' Y'All   89

Peach Gel with Fruity Sauce   266

Winter Warming

Chilled Endive
with Tomato Vinaigrette   63

Carrot Flower Puree   164

Wild 'n' Cheezy Casserole   228

Cherry Raisin Chews   272

Mint Tea

❤

Wild Greens Salad   67

Chunky Tomato Mushroom Sauce
over Spaghetti Squash   116

Bread Sticks   209

Apricot Walnut Torte   280

Worldly Evenings

Mexican Fiestas

Jicama Appetizers   59

Marinated Cucumbers
and Red Onions   65

Cheezy Corn
and Zucchini Enchiladas   233
or
Pronto Enchilada Casserole   229

Sprouted Frijoles   206

Warm Tortillas

Papaya and Mango Slices
with Lime
♥
Fiesta Coleslaw   68

Tamale Pie   232

Creamy Green Chile Potato Soup   169

Pineapple and Orange Wedges
♥
Chopped Green Salad

Avocado Lime Sauce   98

Tofu Mole over Cumin Rice   226

Just Peachy   263

Native Dinners

Wild Greens Salad   67

Pozole and Squash Stew   168

Hot Tortillas and Spicy Pinto Dip   125

Peach Gel and Raspberry Sauce   266
♥
Warm Tortillas

Ruby Slaw   76

Anasazi Beans
with Roasted Garlic   201

Roasted Corn   189

Watermelon Wedges

French Feast

Celery Victor   64

Braised Onion Soup   180

Mushrooms La Jolla   194

Chard Ribbon Salad   72

Red Rogue Dressing   102
♥
Green Beans Almandine   200

Chilled Ratatouille   198
on Bibb Lettuce Leaves
with Olives and Tomatoes

Fresh Fruit Tart   264

Russian Repast

Purple Cabbage Puree   162

String Beans in Walnut
Vinaigrette   80
or
A Better Beet Salad   73

Mushroom Seitan Stroganoff   222

Nondairy Vanilla Ice Cream
with Rhubarb Compote   283

Indian Impressions

Confetti Salad   56

Green Bean Curry
with Condiments   223

Brown Basmati Rice

Mango Cream   263

❤

Wild Greens Salad   67

Indian Cauliflower   193

Brown Basmati Rice
with Condiments

Papaya Slices

Oriental Occasions

Thai Broccoli Salad   79

Spicy Sesame Noodles
with Chard   242

Spinach Spring Rolls with
Sticky Sesame Sauce   252

Orange Slices

❤

Orange Palm Heart Delight   59

Bok Choy Bliss Soup   154

Hong Kong Pasta   246

❤

Asparagus Puree   160

Imperial Salad   82
with Ginger Cashew Sauce   102

Vegetable Lo Mein
with Brown Sauce   245

❤

Edamame Beans   61

Daikon Carrot Salad   60

Miso Soup with
Mushrooms and Peas   184

Sea Sprout Nori Rolls   47

❤

Marinated Hiziki   61

Glass Noodle Shiitake Surprise   247

Steamed Yellow Squash
Wedges

Greek Dinner

Minted Corn Salad   74

Toasted Pita with Babaganush   125
or Cucumber Dip   127

Divine Dolmas   239

Avgolemono Sauce   120

Apple Spice Cake   276

Italian Evenings

Focaccia   208

Grilled Eggplant, Mushroom
and Pepper Salad   77

Risotto with Asparagus and Peas   237

Fresh Fruit Kabobs   53

❤

Gazpacho   151

Wild Greens Salad   67

Fettucine "Faux" Fredo   240

Panne con Pomodore   209
or Bread Sticks   209

Chilled Grapes

Southwest Soirees

Oven-Baked Tortilla Chips
with Corn Salsa   128

Mainstream Romaine   66

Santa Fe-an Sauce   99

Green Chile Quiche   231

❤

Wild Greens Salad   67

Oven-Baked Tortilla Chips   128

Creamy Tomato Chilé Soup   175

Corn Souffle Stuffed Chiles   217

Outrageous Oatmeal Cookies   271

Dinner on the Nile

Garbanzo Nile Salad   71

Warm Pita Triangles
and Cucumber Dip   127

Egyptian Red Stew   183

Mint Tea and Honey

African

Leafy Green Salad

African Eggplant Peanut Stew   178

Cous-Cous with Peas

Mandala Fruit Platter   262

Holiday Feasts

Vegetable Crudités, Nonfat Crackers and Tomato Red Pepper Mouse   140

Creamy Grilled Eggplant Soup   173

Braised Carrots with Apricots   192

Steamed Broccoli

Stuffed Acorn Squash Americana   238

Peachy Apricot Crumble   269

Mandala Fruit Platter   262

♥

Chilled Endive with Tomato Vinaigrette   63

Celery Root Salad   72

A Better Beet Salad   73

Kasha Nut Loaf   241

Mushroom Sauce   115

Mashed Potatoes

Tangerines

Raspberry Celebration Torte   279

Live Energy Meals

Energy meals feature live soups and other uncooked savories for revitalizing your body. All fruits, vegetables, fresh juices, herbal teas, live soups and cleansing purees promote health and vitality.

Begin your day with warm lemon water followed by the Orange Flush (page 5). Drink lots of pure water, herbal teas and fresh squeezed juices throughout the day.

Morning Meals

Cantaloupe Cleanser   19

Mint Tea

❤

Pink Tropic   19

Fruity Flax Smoothie   11

❤

Vibrant Oatmeal with
Raw Applesauce   20

Pineapple Date Shake   13

❤

Golden Mandala   19

Strawberry Nut Milk Smoothie   12

❤

Fresh Fruit Kabobs   53

Banana Blueberry Shake   11

❤

Sprouted Wheat and Date Loaf   31

Orange Banana Flips   11

Afternoon/Evening Meals

Chilled Papaya Mint Bisque   152

Sea "Pasta" Vegetable Salad   70

Besto Pesto Stuffed Celery   129
or Mushrooms

❤

Gazpacho   151

Wild Greens Salad with   67
Alfalfa Sprouts and Carrot Sticks

Seed Cheese   136

❤

Garden Ginger Energy Soup   149

Jicama Sticks   59

Chard Ribbon Salad   72

❤

Euphoria Soup   150

Spicy Sprout Salad with   76
Cucumber Wedges

❤

Seed Cheese Cabbage Rolls   48

Confetti Salad   56

❤

Sprouted Sunseed Sushi   49

Orange and Fennel Salad   57

Sprouts of choice

Fire-Roasted Red Pepper
Spa Dressing   96

Alphabetical Index

A

Agar-Agar, xvi, xx
Almonds
  Almond Milk, 12
  Almond Pie Crust, 268
  Basic Creamy Seed Cheese, 136
  Crunchy Honey Almond Stars, 35
  Green Bean Almandine, 200
  Nutty Salad Sauce, 94
  Sprouted Almond Croquettes, 275
Apples, facts, 281
  Apple Nutbutter-wiches, 35
  Apple Spice Cake, 276
  Apple Spice Muffins, 28
  Apple Cream, 281
  Applesauce, 281
  Confetti Salad, 56
  Granola Chocolate Chippers, 273
  Rhubarb Compote, 283
  Raw Applesauce, 20
  Spiced Vegetable Puree, 158
  Sesame Applesauce Bran Cookies, 274
Apricot, facts, 265
  Apricot Spritzers, 10
  Apricot Puree, 261
  Apricot Walnut Torte, 280
  Aphrodite's Freeze, 265
  Braised Carrots with Apricots, 192
  Fresh Fruit Kabobs, 53
  Peachy Apricot Crumble, 269
Aromatherapy, 87
Arrowroot Powder, xxi, xx
Arugula
  Sunseed Arugula Rolls, 49
  Wild Greens Salad, 67
Asparagus
  Asparagus Puree, 160
  Asparagus Tofu Pie, 230
  Fennel Asparagus Bisque, 172
  Risotto with Asparagus and Peas, 237
  Spicy Asparagus in Black Bean Sauce, 224
Avocado
  Avocado Lime Sauce, 98
  Chile Tempeh Tacos, 40
  Euphoria Soup, 150
  Garden Ginger Soup, 149
  Sprouted Sunseed Sushi, 49

B

Bamboo Shoots
  Oriental Pantry, xxii
  Vegetable Lo-Mein, 245
Bananas, facts, 27, 29
  Apple Spice Cake, 276

Aphrodite's Freeze, 265
Banana Blueberry Shake, 11
Banana Walnut Cornbread, 29
Banana Orange Zest Cake, 277
Banana French Toast, 27
Crunchy Honey Almond Stars, 35
Elephant Spread, 36
Fresh Fruit Kabobs, 53
Fruity Vanilla Banana Torte, 267
Honolulu Toss Salad, 54
Mocha Date Shake, 14
Monkey Toast, 36
Orange Banana Flips, 11
Pineapple Date Shakes, 13
Sweet Oatmeal Corn Muffins, 30
Universal Tofu Pancake, 23
Vanilla Banana Pudding, 267
Basil
  A Grilled Affair, 220
  Basil, Lime and Pumpkin Seed Pesto, 134
  Basil Broccoli California Puree, 163
  Besto Pesto, 129
  Cheezy Noodle Bake, 240
  Eggplant Tomato Boats, 218
  Focaccia, 208
  Fresh Herb Zitistrone, 182
  Panne con Pomodore, 209
  Ratatouille, 198
Beans
  Anasazi Beans with Roasted Garlic, 201
  Black Bean Chapati Burritos, 45
  Creamy Tomato Chilé, 175
  Garden Stew, 153
  Green Beans Almandine, 200
  Green Bean Curry, 223
  Marinated Bean Salad, 86
  Montezuma's Black Bean Sauce, 113
  Nachoz, 37
  Navy Bean Salad, 84
  Pasta Fagiole, 244
  Pasta Fo' Y'All, 89
  Spicy Asparagus in Black Bean Sauce, 224
  Spicy Pinto Dip, 125
  Sprouted Frijoles, 206
  String Beans in Walnut Vinaigrette, 80
  Tamale Pie, 232
  Thai Navy Bean Soup, 177
  Tostadas, 38
Bee Pollen
  Bee-Better Butter, 36
  Orange Banana Flips, 11
Beet
  A Better Beet Salad, 73
  Basil Beet Dressing, 95
  Euphoria Soup, 150
  Ruby Fennel Salad, 58
  Ruby Slaw, 76

Bell Pepper, (*see also* Red Peppers)
A Grilled Affair, 220
Fresh Tomato Coulis (Mex-Style), 110
Gazpacho, 151
Green Bean Curry, 223
Hong Kong Pasta, 246
Italian Peppers and Links, 225
Kasha Nut Loaf, 241
Oyster Mushroom Saute, 236
Pasta Fagiole, 244
Pasta Fo' Y'All, 89
Ratatouille, 198
Sprouted Peas and Minted Peppers, 206
Blueberries
Apricot Walnut Torte, 280
Banana Blueberry Shake, 12
Strawberry Nut Milk Smoothie, 12
Vanilla Rice Cream with, 21
Bluecorn
Bluecorn Cakes with Strawberries, 26
Bok Choy
Bok Choy Bliss Soup, 154
Sweet Sesame Bok Choy, 74
Vegetable Lo-Mein, 245
Breads (*see also* Wheat)
Banana Walnut Cornbread, 29
Bread Sticks, 209
Panne con Pomodore, 209
Sprouted Wheat and Date Loaf, 31
Whole Wheat Pizza Dough, 207
Breakfast Ecstasies
Apple Spice Muffins, 28
Banana French Toast, 27
Banana Walnut Cornbread, 29
Bluecorn Cakes with Strawberries, 26
Breakfast Burritos, 25
Cantaloupe Cleanser, 19
Golden Mandala, 19
Matzo Scrambler, 24
Pink Tropic, 19
Pumpkin Walnut Muffins, 28
Pumpkin Walnut Pancakes, 23
Sprouted Wheat and Date Loaf, 31
Swedish Oatmeal Pancakes, 22
Sweet Oatmeal Corn Muffins, 30
Universal Tofu Pancake, 23
Vanilla Rice Cream with Blueberries, 21
Vibrant Oatmeal with Raw Applesauce, 20
Breathing Exercises, 5
Brewers Yeast, (*see* Nutritional Yeast)
Broccoli, facts, 75, 163
Basil Broccoli California Puree, 163
Broccoli Bean Thread Saute, 249
Broccoli Eggplant Pesto Salad, 75
Cheezy Broccoli Potatoes, 219
Thai Broccoli Salad, 79
Brown Rice (*see* Rice)

C

Cabbage
Chinese 5-Spice Tempeh Salad, 85
Chile Tempeh Tacos, 40
Da Kine Tahini Mint Salad, 92
Fiesta Coleslaw, 68
Green Supreme Puree, 157
Hong Kong Pasta, 246
Imperial Salad, 82
Purple Cabbage Puree, 162
Ruby Slaw, 76
Seed Cheese Cabbage Rolls, 48
Spiked Cabbage Puree, 158
Cakes (*see* Desserts)
Calcium, facts, 79, 249
Cantaloupe
Cantaloupe Cleanser, 19
Carob, facts, 273
Chewy Double Carob Chip Cookies, 270
Sprouted Carob Cookies, 275
Sprouted Wheat Carob Crust, 267
Carrot, facts, 111
Basil Beet Dressing, 95
Braised Carrots with Apricots, 192
Carrot Apple Juice, 7
Carrot Flower Puree, 164
Carrot Garlic Red Sauce, 111
Carrot Ginger Cake, 278
Carrot Juice, 7
Chard Ribbon Salad, 72
Chinese 5-Spice Tempeh Salad, 85
Confetti Salad, 56
Daikon Carrot Salad, 60
Euphoria Soup, 150
Fiesta Coleslaw, 68
Fusilli Primavera, 248
Garbanzo Nile Salad, 71
Garden Blend Juice, 7
Garden Steamers, 195
Gentle Stew, 152
Harvest Hiziki Salad, 69
Imperial Salad, 82
Minted Corn Salad, 74
Orange Blossom Carrots, 192
Oyster Mushroom Saute, 236
Purple Cabbage Puree, 162
Risotto Verde Stew, 179
Seed Cheese Cabbage Rolls, 48
Spiced Vegetable Puree, 158
Sprouted Sunseed Carrot Dip, 124
Sunset Cashew Bisque, 171
Tomato Garden Minestrone, 181
Cashews
Banana Blueberry Shake, 12
Basic Creamy Seed Cheese, 136
Classic Cashew Nut Milk, 15
Creamy Cashew Basil Sauce, 114
Creamy Corn and Red Pepper Chowder, 176
Creamy Cauliflower Puree, 170

Ginger Cashew Sauce, 102
Imperial Salad, 82
Strawberry Nut Milk Smoothie, 12
Sunset Cashew Bisque, 171

Cauliflower
Careflower Bisque, 159
Carrot Flower Puree, 164
Cauliflower Okra Stew, 155
Caulipeño Sauce, 118
Creamy Cauliflower Cashew Puree, 170
Creamy Green Chile Potato Soup, 169
Desert Cauliflower, 196
Egyptian Red Stew, 183
Fusilli Primavera, 248
Golden Nugget Squash Pockets, 216
Indian Cauliflower, 193
Mexican Cauliflower Puree, 156
Tempeh Cauliflower Pie, 235
Tomato Garden Minestrone, 181

Cayenne, facts, 135
Celery
Braised Onion Soup, 180
Carrot Flower Puree, 164
Celery Root Salad, 72
Celery Victor, 64
Chinese Woked Vegetables, 227
Cucumber Dip, 127
Hong Kong Pasta, 246
Oyster Mushroom Saute, 236
Ruby Fennel Salad, 58
Thai Navy Bean Soup, 177

Chapatis, 45
Chard (*see* Swiss Chard)
Cheezy Sauce, 121
Jalapeño Cheezy, 122
Cheezy Sauces, used in
Cheezy Broccoli Stuffed Potatoes, 219
Cheezy Corn and Zucchini Enchilada, 233
Cheezy Noodle Bake, 240
Curried Lentils and Tomatoes, 205
Fettuccine "Faux" Freddo, 240
Nachoz, 37
Tostadas, 38
Wild 'n' Cheezy Casserole, 228

Cherry
Cherry Raisin Chews, 272
Chocolate/Cocoa, facts, 273 (*see also* Carob)
Granola Chocolate Chippers, 273
Tofu Mole, 226

Cilantro
Broccoli Bean Thread Saute, 249
Besto Pesto, 129
Cauliflower Okra Stew, 155
Caulipeño Sauce, 118
Cilantro Walnut Pesto, 131
Corn Salsa, 128
Desert Cauliflower, 196
Euphoria Soup, 150
Gingered Cashew Pesto, 131
Glass Noodle Shiitake Surprise, 247

Pozole and Squash Stew, 168
Pueblo Pesto, 133
Sesame Cilantro Dressing, 100
Southwest Steamers, 191
Spinach Spring Rolls, 251

Coconut
Thai Navy Bean Soup, 177
Color, 59
Condiments (*see* Mousses, Patés, Pestos, Seed Cheeses)
Cookies
Cherry Raisin Chews, 272
Chewy Double Carob Chip Cookies, 270
Granola Chocolate Chippers, 273
Outrageous Oatmeal Cookies, 271
Sesame Applesauce Bran Cookies, 274
Sprouted Almond Croquettes, 275
Sprouted Carob Cookies, 275

Corn (*see also* Pozole)
Banana Walnut Cornbread, 29
Cheezy Corn and Zucchini Enchiladas, 233
Corn Salsa, 128
Corn Souffle Stuffed Chiles, 217
Creamy Corn and Red Pepper Chowder, 176
Creamy Tomato Chilé, 175
Euphoria Soup, 150
Fiesta Coleslaw, 68
Garden Ginger Energy Soup, 149
Garlic Roasted Corn, 189
Green Corn Chowder, 174
Minted Corn Salad, 74
Pasta Fo' Y'All, 89
Polenta Triangles, 204
Pronto Enchilada Casserole, 229
Southwest Cornbread Quiche, 234
Southwest Corn Stew, 165
Sweet Oatmeal Corn Muffins, 30
Tamale Pie, 232

Cranberry
Cranberry Gingerale, 9
Cucumber
Cucumber Dip, 127
Cucumber Dressing, 98
Garbanzo Nile Salad, 71
Garden Ginger Energy Soup, 149
Gazpacho, 151
Mainstream Romaine, 66
Marinated Cucumbers, 65

Currants
Divine Dolmas, 239
Rhubarb Compote, 283
Sprouted Almond Croquettes, 275

Curry
Curried Lentil Mushroom Sauce, 117
Curried Lentils with Tomatoes, 205
Curried Sunny Dulse Dressing, 93
Green Bean Curry, 223

D

Daikon Carrot Salad, 60
Date
    Mandala Fruit Platter, 262
    Mocha Date Shakes, 14
    Pineapple Date Shakes, 13
    Sesame Applesauce Bran Cookies, 274
    Sprouted Wheat and Date Loaf, 31
Desserts
    Cakes and Tortes
        Apple Spice Cake, 276
        Apricot Walnut Torte, 280
        Banana Orange Zest Cake, 277
        Carrot Ginger Cake, 278
        Raspberry Celebration Torte, 279
    Cookies
        Cherry Raisin Chews, 272
        Chewy Double Carob Chip Cookies, 270
        Granola Chocolate Chippers, 273
        Outrageous Oatmeal Cookies, 271
        Sesame Applesauce Bran Cookies, 274
        Sprouted Carob Cookies, 275
        Sprouted Almond Croquettes, 275
    Fruit Desserts
        Almond Pie Crust, 268
        Aphrodite's Freeze, 265
        Apricot Puree, 261
        Fresh Fruit Tart, 264
        Fruity Vanilla Banana Torte, 267
        Just Peachy, 263
        Mandala Fruit Platter, 262
        Mango Creme, 263
        Peach Gel with Raspberry Sauce, 266
        Peachy Apricot Crumble, 269
        Pineapple Delight, 265
        Prune Purees (as fat replacers), 261
        Prunicot Puree, 261
        Raisin Puree, 261
        Raw Berry Pie, 268
    Sauces
        Apple Cream, 281
        Applesauce, 281
        Orange Sauce, 282
        Raspberry Sauce, 282
        Rhubarb Compote, 283
        Tofu Pineapple Creme, 283
Dill
    Careflower Bisque, 159
    Creamy Ranchero Dressing, 92
    Fennel Asparagus Bisque, 172
    Purple Cabbage Puree, 162
Dips
    Babaganush, 125
    Corn Salsa, 128
    Cucumber Dip, 127
    Green Goddess Guacamole, 126
    Pesto Dips, 128
    Spicy Pinto Dip, 125
    Sprouted Sunseed Carrot Dip, 124

Dr. Bronner's Bouillon, 161
Dressings (salad)
    Avocado Lime Sauce, 98
    Basil Beet Dressing, 95
    Creamy Ranchero, 92
    Cucumber Dressing, 98
    Curried Sunny Dulse Dressing, 93
    Fire-Roasted Red Pepper Spa Dressing, 96
    Ginger Cashew Sauce, 102
    Green Thai Goddess, 103
    Magic Slaw Sauce, 96
    Nutty Salad Sauce, 94
    Papaya Lime, 97
    Raspberry Vinaigrette, 101
    Red Rogue Dressing, 102
    Royal Orange Thai Dressing, 103
    Santa Fe-an Sauce, 99
    Sesame Cilantro, 100
    Sesame Miso, 100
    Tahini Mint, 92
    Tomato Vinaigrette, 101
Dry Brush Massage, 55

E

Edible Flowers, 83
Eggplant, facts, 63
    African Eggplant Peanut Stew, 178
    Afro Rumba Sauce, 109
    A Grilled Affair, 220
    Broccoli Eggplant Pesto Salad, 75
    Creamy Grilled Eggplant Soup, 173
    Eggplant Tomato Boats, 218
    Egyptian Red Stew, 183
    Grilled Eggplant Mushroom Pepper Salad, 77
    Grilled Garlic and Vegetables, 189
    Japanese Eggplant Salad, 78
    Ratatouille, 198
    Sesame Eggplant Tacos, 39
Egg Replacer, xx, Pantry, xxii
Endive
    Chilled Endive with Tomato Vinaigrette, 63
Entrees
    Casseroles, Quiches and Pies
        Asparagus Tofu Pie, 230
        Cheezy Corn and Zucchini
          Enchiladas, 233
        Green Chile Quiche, 231
        Pronto Enchilada Casserole, 229
        Southwestern Cornbread Quiche, 234
        Tamale Pie, 232
        Tempeh Cauliflower Quiche, 235
        Wild 'n' Cheezy Casserole, 228
    Dishes with Grains
        Divine Dolmas, 239
        Kasha Nut Loaf, 241
        Oyster Mushroom Saute, 236
        Risotto with Asparagus and Peas, 237
        Stuffed Acorn Squash Americana, 238

Meals in a Skillet
   Chinese Woked Vegetables, 227
   Green Bean Curry, 223
   Italian Peppers and Links, 225
   Mushroom Seitan Stroganoff, 222
   Spicy Asparagus and Black Beans, 224
   Tofu Mole, 226
Other Delights
   California Pizza, 254
   Pacific Rim Pizza, 255
   Pizza!, 252
   Pueblo Pizza, 255
   Spinach Spring Rolls, 251
   Vegetable Eggless Fu Young, 250
   Viva Spinizza, 253
Pasta Dishes
   Broccoli Bean Thread Saute, 249
   Cheezy Noodle Bake, 240
   Fettucine "Faux" Freddo, 240
   Fusilli Primavera, 248
   Garlicky Zucchini with Bean Thread
      Noodles, 243
   Glass Noodle Shiitake Surprise, 247
   Hong Kong Pasta, 246
   Pasta Fagiole, 244
   Spicy Sesame Noodles with Chard, 242
   Vegetable Lo-Mein, 245
Vegetables in the Spotlight
   A Grilled Affair, 220
   Cheezy Broccoli Stuffed Potatoes, 219
   Eggplant Tomato Boats, 218
   Golden Nugget Squash Pockets, 216
   Pesto Kabobs, 221
   Corn Souffle Stuffed Chiles, 217
Exercise, 149

F

Fatty Acids, 11
Fennel, facts, 57
   Fennel Asparagus Bisque, 172
   Orange Fennel Salad, 57
   Ruby Fennel Salad, 58
Flax, facts, 11
   Classic Cashew Nut Milk, 15
   Fruity Flax Smoothie, 11
Fruit (*see specific fruits*)
Fruit Salads
   Confetti Salad, 56
   Fresh Fruit Kabobs, 53
   Honolulu Toss Salad, 54
   Orange Fennel Salad, 57
   Orange Palm Heart Delight, 59
   Ruby Fennel Salad, 58
   Super "C" Salad, 55
Fusilli (*see* Pasta)

G

Garbanzo Beans, facts, 71
   Da Kine Tahini Mint Salad, 92
   Egyptian Red Stew, 183
   Fresh Herb Zitistrone, 182
   Garbanzo Nile Salad, 71
   Garlicky Zucchini Bean Thread Noodles, 243
   Grilled Veggie Pasta Salad, 88
   Minted Corn Salad, 74
Garlic, facts, 141
   Anasazi Beans with Roasted Garlic, 201
   Braised Onion Soup, 180
   Carrot Garlic Red Sauce, 111
   Desert Cauliflower, 196
   Eggplant Tomato Boats, 218
   Focaccia, 208
   Fusilli Primavera, 248
   Garlic Herb Seed Cheese, 139
   Garlic Roasted Corn, 189
   Garlic Seed Cheese Sauce, 138
   Garlicky Soba Noodles, 200
   Garlicky Zucchini Bean Thread Noodles, 243
   Glass Noodle Shiitake Surprise, 247
   Green Chile and Garlic Mousse, 141
   Green Chile Sauce, 119
   Green Supreme Puree, 157
   Grilled Garlic and Vegetables, 189
   Oven Roast Potatoes with Garlic, 190
   Ratatouille, 198
   Roasted Garlic, 189
   Soup'r Fresh Parsley Vegetable Soup, 185
   Spinach Spring Rolls, 251
   Tempeh Cauliflower Quiche, 235
   Viva Spinizza, 253
Ginger, facts, 9
   Carrot Ginger Cake, 278
   Chinese 5-Spice Tempeh Salad, 85
   Cranberry Gingerale, 9
   Fresh Ginger Concentrate, 9
   Fusilli Primavera, 248
   Garden Ginger Energy Soup, 149
   Ginger Soy Seed Cheese, 139
   Ginger Cashew Pesto, 131
   Ginger Cashew Sauce, 102
   Orange Flush, 5
   Pueblo Pesto, 133
   Sesame Miso Dressing, 100
   Silken Chile Ginger Sauce, 112
   Thai Navy Bean Soup, 177
Grains (*see specific grains:* Rice, Kasha, Lentils, Pasta)
Granola
   Granola Chocolate Chippers, 273
   Peachy Apricot Crumble, 269
Grapes
   Orange Fennel Salad, 57
   Ruby Fennel Salad, 58
Green Beans (*see* Beans)
Green Chiles (*see also* Jalapeños")
   Basil Broccoli California Puree, 163

Corn Souffle Stuffed Chiles, 217
Creamy Green Chile Potato Soup, 169
Fusilli Primavera, 248
Green Chile and Garlic Mousse, 141
Green Chile Quiche, 231
Green Chile Sauce, 119
How to Roast, 119
Mexican Cauliflower Puree, 156
Minted Pepita Sauce, 114
Riso Verde Stew, 179
Santa Fe-an Sauce, 99
Green Onions
Asparagus Puree, 160
Corn Salsa, 128
Cheezy Corn and Zucchini Enchiladas, 233
Glass Noodle Shiitake Surprise, 247
Green Thai Goddess, 103
Vegetable Lo-Mein, 245
Green Peas
Green Goddess Guacamole, 126
Homestyle Split Pea, 166
Mushroom Seitan Stroganoff, 222
Miso Soup with Mushrooms and Peas, 184
Sprouted Peas and Minted Peppers, 206
Risotto with Asparagus and Peas, 237
Grilling Vegetables, basics, 39

H

Herbs and Herbal Brews, 8
Fairy Tea, 10
Hiziki
Harvest Hiziki Salad, 69
Imperial Salad, 82
Marinated Hiziki, 61
Sea Sprout Salad Rolls, 47
Hot Side Dishes (*see also* Vegetable Side Dishes)
Other Side Dishes
Anasazi Beans with Roasted Garlic, 201
Bread Sticks, 209
Cumin Rice, 204
Curried Lentils with Tomatoes, 205
Focaccia, 208
Garlicky Soba Noodles, 200
Panne con Pomodore, 209
Polenta Triangles, 204
Sprouted Frijoles, 206
Sprouted Millet, 203
Sprouted Peas and Minted Peppers, 206
Twice as Wild Rice, 202
Whole Wheat Pizza Dough, 207
Wild Tofu Jasmine Rice, 203

J

Jalapeño Pepper
Bok Choy Bliss Soup, 154
Caulipeño Sauce, 118
Creamy Cauliflower Cashew Puree, 170
Cucumber Dip, 127

Egyptian Red Stew, 183
Green Goddess Guacamole, 126
Spicy Pinto Dip, 125
Spinach Pesto, 132
Montezuma's Black Bean Sauce, 113
Jicama
Fiesta Coleslaw, 68
Jicama Sticks, 59
Juices, 6, 7

K

Kale
Kale Mushroom Leek Puree, 161
Tomato Garden Minestrone, 181
Wild 'n' Cheezy Casserole, 228
Kasha
Kasha Nut Loaf, 241
Kiwi
Fresh Fruit Kabobs, 53
Fresh Fruit Tart, 264
Honolulu Toss Salad, 54
Super "C" Salad, 55
Kuzu, xx

L

Lecithin, facts, 15
Classic Cashew Nut Milk, 15
Strawberry Nut Milk Smoothie, 12
Leek
African Eggplant Peanut Stew, 178
Hong Kong Pasta, 246
Kale Mushroom Leek Puree, 161
Lemon, facts, 93
Avgolemono Sauce, 120
Bok Choy Bliss Soup, 154
Cheezy Sauce, 121
Cilantro Walnut Pesto, 131
Ginger Cashew Sauce, 102
Jalapeño Cheezy, 122
Lemon Zest, 277
Magic Slaw Sauce, 96
Morning Cleanser, 5
Mushroom Seitan Stroganoff, 222
Nutty Salad Sauce, 94
Pueblo Pesto, 133
Lentil, facts, 205
Bagel and Paté Platter, 44
Curried Lentils and Tomatoes, 205
Curried Lentil Mushroom Sauce, 117
Harvest Hiziki Salad, 69
Lentil Paté, 145
Lentil Paté Tomato-wiches, 41
Lettuce (*see* Salads)
Mainstream Romaine, 66
Wild Greens Salad, 67
Lime
Avocado Lime Sauce, 98
Basil, Lime and Pumpkin Seed Pesto, 134

Chilled Papaya Mint Bisque, 152
Green Chile Sauce, 119
Green Goddess Guacamole, 126
Green Thai Goddess Dressing, 103
Papaya Lime Dressing, 97
Liquid Aminos, xx
Liquid Delights
Almond Milk, 12
Apricot Spritzer, 10
Banana Blueberry Shake, 12
Cranberry Gingerale, 9
Classic Cashew Nut Milk, 15
Fairy Tea, 10
Fresh Fig Vanilla Shake, 13
Fresh Ginger Concentrate, 9
Fruity Flax Smoothie, 11
Herbs and Herbal Brews, 8
Hot 'Eggless' Nog, 15
Iced Mochas, 14
Juice Combos, 7
Juice of Life, 6
Mocha Date Shake, 14
Morning Cleanser, 5
Orange Banana Flips, 11
Orange Flush, 5
Pineapple Date Shake, 13
Strawberry Nut Milk Smoothie, 12
Strawberry Spritzer, 10

M

Mango
Fresh Fruit Kabobs, 53
Honolulu Toss Salad, 54
Mango Creme, 263
Maple Syrup
Butternut Maple Bake, 197
Classic Cashew Nut Milk, 15
Pumpkin Orange Muffins, 28
Massage, 19
Meditation, 113
Mint
Cauliflower Okra Stew, 155
Chilled Papaya Mint Bisque, 152
Confetti Salad, 56
Divine Dolmas, 239
Garbanzo Nile Salad, 71
Minted Corn Salad, 74
Minted Pepitas Sauce, 114
Tahini Mint Dressing, 92
Mirin, cooking rice wine, 245
Miso
Chinese Brown Sauce, 117
Garlicky Soba Noodles, 200
Miso Soup with Mushrooms and Peas, 184
Mousses
Green Chile and Garlic Mousse, 141
Spinach Mushroom Mousse, 144
Tomato Red Pepper Mousse, 140
2-Tier Fiesta Mousse, 142-3

Muffins
Apple Spice Muffins, 28
Pumpkin Orange Muffins, 28
Sweet Oatmeal Corn Muffins, 30
Mushrooms (*see also* Shiitake *and* Oyster
Mushrooms), facts, 65, 115
A Grilled Affair, 220
Cauliflower Okra Stew, 155
Chinese Woked Vegetables, 227
Chunky Tomato Mushroom Sauce, 116
Curried Lentil Mushroom Sauce, 117
Golden Nugget Squash Pockets, 216
Grilled Eggplant Mushroom Pepper Salad, 77
Grilled Veggie Pasta Salad, 88
Imperial Salad, 82
Italian Links and Peppers, 225
Kale Mushroom Leek Puree, 161
Kasha Nut Loaf, 241
Miso Soup with Mushrooms and Peas, 184
Mushrooms La Jolla, 194
Mushroom Seitan Stroganoff, 222
Pasta Fagiole, 244
Pesto Kabobs, 221
Presto Pesto Caps, 133
Pronto Enchilada Casserole, 229
Ratatouille, 198
Spinach Mushroom Mousse, 144
Tomato Garden Minestrone, 181
Tomato Mushroom Vinaigrette, 65
Viva Spinizza, 253
Wild 'n' Cheezy Casserole, 228
Woked Chard and Mushrooms, 195

N

Nori (*see also* Seaweed)
Sea Sprout Salad Rolls, 47
Seed Cheese Sushi Rolls, 48
Sprouted Sunseed Sushi, 49
Nut Milk (*see also* Soy Milk), facts, 23
Almond Milk, 12
Banana Blueberry Shake, 11
Classic Cashew Nut Milk, 15
Pumpkin Walnut Pancakes, 23
Southwest Cornbread Quiche, 234
Strawberry Nut Milk Smoothie, 12
Nutritional Yeast
Cheezy Sauce, 121
Fresh Herb Zitistrone, 182
Green Chile and Garlic Paté, 141
Jalapeño Cheezy, 121
Lentil Paté, 145
Mushroom Seitan Stroganoff, 222
TNT Super Sauce, 112
Tomato Red Pepper Mousse, 140
2-Tier Fiesta Paté, 142-3

O

Oats (*see also* Granola), facts, 271
Cheezy Sauce, 121
Outrageous Oatmeal Cookies, 271
Sweet Oatmeal Corn Muffins, 30
Vibrant Oatmeal, 20
Swedish Oatmeal Pancakes, 22
Okra, facts, 155
Cauliflower Okra Stew, 155
Olive Oil
Cilantro Walnut Pesto, 131
Onions (*see also* Red Onion), facts, 173, 193
African Eggplant Peanut Stew, 178
Afro Rumba Sauce, 109
Anasazi Beans with Roasted Garlic, 201
Braised Onion Soup, 180
Carrot Garlic Red Sauce, 111
Eggplant Tomato Boats, 218
Indian Cauliflower, 193
Kasha Nut Loaf, 241
Lentil Paté, 145
Montezuma's Black Bean Sauce, 133
Orange Blossom Carrots, 193
Spinach Mushroom Mousse, 144
Oranges
Aphrodite's Freeze, 265
Banana Orange Zest Cake, 277
Carrot Flower Puree, 164
Fresh Fruit Kabobs, 53
Orange Banana Flips, 11
Orange Fennel Salad, 57
Orange Flush, 5
Orange Palm Heart Delight, 59
Orange Zest, 277
Orange Sauce, 282
Royal Orange Thai Dressing, 103
Sprouted Wheat and Date Loaf, 31
Super "C" Salad, 55
Sweet Chile Chutney, 130
Sweet Oatmeal Corn Muffins, 30
Oyster Mushroom, facts, 62
Oyster Mushroom Shooters, 62
Oyster Mushroom Saute, 236

P

Palm Hearts
Orange Palm Heart Delight, 59
Pancakes
Blue Corn Cakes with Strawberries, 26
Pumpkin Walnut Pancakes, 23
Swedish Oatmeal Pancakes, 22
Universal Tofu Pancake, 23
Pantothenic Acid, 65
Papaya, facts, 97
Chilled Papaya Mint Bisque, 152
Fresh Fruit Kabobs, 53
Honolulu Toss Salad, 54
Just Peachy, 263
Papaya Lime Dressing, 97

Parsley, facts, 185
Fennel Asparagus Bisque, 172
Focaccia, 208
Fresh Herb Zitistrone, 182
Soup'r Fresh Parsley Vegetable Soup, 185
Thai Navy Bean Soup, 177
Pasta
Cheezy Noodle Bake, 240
Fettucine "Faux" Freddo, 240
Fresh Herb Zitistrone, 182
Fusilli Primavera, 248
Garlicky Soba Noodles, 200
Garlicky Zucchini and Bean Thread
Noodles, 243
Grilled Vegetable Pasta Salad, 88
Holy Mole Pasta Salad, 87
Pasta Fo' Y'All, 89
Risotto Verde Stew, 179
Spicy Sesame Noodles and Chard, 242
Patés (*see also* Mousse)
Lentil Paté, 145
Peach, facts, 269
Apricot Walnut Torte, 280
Fresh Fruit Kabobs, 53
Fresh Fruit Tart, 264
Just Peachy, 263
Peach Gel with Raspberry Sauce, 266
Peachy Apricot Crumble, 269
Peanut/Peanut Butter
African Eggplant Peanut Stew, 178
Afro Rumba Sauce, 109
Green Thai Goddess Dressing, 103
Miso Soup with Mushrooms and Peas, 184
Pueblo Pesto, 133
Thai Navy Bean Soup, 177
Tofu Mole, 226
Yellow Tomato Nut Bisque, 174
Pecans
Divine Dolmas, 239
Pepitas (pumpkin seeds)
Basil, Lime and Pumpkin Seed Pesto, 134
Minted Pepitas Sauce, 114
Peppers (*see* Bell Peppers *or* Red Peppers)
Pesto, ideas, 129
Basil, Lime and Pumpkin Seed Pesto, 134
Besto Pesto, 129
Cilantro Walnut Pesto, 131
Gingered Cashew Pesto, 131
Presto Pesto Caps, 133
Pueblo Pesto, 133
Seed Cheese Pesto Caps, 139
Spinach Pesto, 132
Sweet Chile Chutney, 130
Pineapple
Honolulu Toss Salad, 54
Pineapple Delight, 265
Pineapple Date Shake, 13
Tofu Pineapple Creme, 283
Pine Nuts
Besto Pesto, 129

Pizza, 252, the birth of, 253
    California Pizza, 254
    Pacific Rim Pizza, 255
    Pueblo Pizza, 255
    Viva Spinizza, 253
Potassium, 219
Potatoes, caring for, 153
    Bok Choy Bliss Soup, 154
    Breakfast Burritos, 25
    Cheezy Broccoli Stuffed Potatoes, 219
    Corn Souffle Stuffed Chiles, 217
    Creamy Green Chile Potato Soup, 169
    Garden Steamers, 195
    Garden Stew, 153
    Oven Roasted Potatoes with Garlic
      and Herbs, 190
    Tamari Spicy Fries, 190
Pozole
    Holy Mole Pozole, 168
    Native Pozole, 167
    Pozole and Squash Stew, 168
Protein, facts, 25
Prune
    Mandala Fruit Platter, 262
    Outrageous Oatmeal Cookies, 271
    Prune Puree, 261
    Prunicot Puree, 261
    Pumpkin Orange Muffins, 28
Pumpkin
    Pumpkin Orange Muffins, 28
    Pumpkin Walnut Pancakes, 23
Puree (*see* Soups)

Q

Quick Meal Ideas, 215

R

Raisin (*see also* Currants)
    Almond Milk, 12
    Butternut Maple Bake, 197
    Carrot Ginger Cake, 278
    Cherry Raisin Chews, 272
    Mandala Fruit Platter, 262
    Sesame Applesauce Bran Cookies, 274
    Sprouted Carob Cookies, 275
    Sweet Chile Chutney, 130
    Sweet Oatmeal Corn Muffins, 30
    Tofu Mole, 226
Raspberries
    Fresh Fruit Tart, 264
    Peach Gel with Raspberry Sauce, 266
    Raspberry Celebration Torte, 279
    Raspberry Sauce, 282
    Raspberry Vinaigrette, 101
    Raw Berry Pie, 268
Red Chiles (*see also* Green Chiles *and* Jalapeños)
    Anasazi Beans and Roasted Garlic, 201
    Corn Salsa, 128

    Creamy Grilled Eggplant Soup, 173
    Creamy Tomato Chilé, 175
    Desert Cauliflower, 196
    Pronto Enchilada Casserole, 229
    Red Chile Enchilada Sauce, 108
    Silken Chile Ginger Sauce, 112
    Southwest Corn Stew, 165
    Sweet Chile Chutney, 130
    Tofu Mole, 226
Red Onion
    Broccoli Eggplant Pesto Salad, 75
    Curried Lentils and Tomatoes, 205
    Fusilli Primavera, 248
    Garden Steamers, 195
    Garlicky Zucchini and Bean Thread
      Noodles, 243
    Gentle Stew, 152
    Pesto Kabobs, 22
    Red Onion Pickles, 60
    Tomato Mushroom Vinaigrette, 65
Red Peppers
    A Grilled Affair, 220
    Broccoli Bean Thread Saute, 249
    Broccoli Eggplant Pesto Salad, 75
    Chard Ribbon Salad, 72
    Cheezy Noodle Bake, 240
    Creamy Corn and Red Pepper Chowder, 176
    Fire-Roasted Red Pepper Spa Dressing, 96
    Fusilli Primavera, 248
    Garlicky Zucchini and Bean Thread
      Noodles, 243
    Glass Noodle Shiitake Surprise, 247
    Grilled Eggplant Mushroom Pepper Salad, 77
    Grilled Garlic and Vegetables, 189
    Hong Kong Pasta, 246
    Marinated Bean Salad, 86
    Pasta Fagiole, 244
    Pasta Fo' Y'All, 89
    Polenta Triangles, 204
    Thai Broccoli Salad, 79
    Tomato Red Pepper Mousse, 140
    Vegetable Lo-Mein, 245
Rhubarb, facts, 283
    Rhubarb Compote, 283
Rice (*see also* Wild Rice)
    Cumin Rice, 204
    Divine Dolmas, 239
    Risotto with Asparagus and Peas, 237
    Stuffed Acorn Squash Americana, 238
    Tuscan Tomato Rice Salad, 83
    Vanilla Rice Cream with Blueberries, 21
    Wild 'n' Cheezy Casserole, 228
    Wild Tofu Jasmine Rice, 203
Romaine (*see* Lettuce)
    Mainstream Romaine Salad, 66
Rosemary
    Fresh Herb Zitistrone, 182
    String Beans with Walnut Vinaigrette, 80
    Tomato Garden Minestrone, 181
    Tuscan Tomato Rice Salad, 83

S

Saffron
 Egyptian Red Stew, 183
 Southwest Corn Stew, 165
Salad Dressings
 Avocado Lime Sauce, 98
 Basil Beet Dressing, 95
 Creamy Ranchero, 92
 Cucumber Dressing, 98
 Curried Sunny Dulse Dressing, 93
 Fire-Roasted Red Pepper Spa Dressing, 96
 Ginger Cashew Sauce, 102
 Green Thai Goddess, 103
 Magic Slaw Sauce, 96
 Nutty Salad Sauce, 94
 Papaya Lime, 97
 Raspberry Vinaigrette, 101
 Red Rogue Dressing, 102
 Royal Orange Thai Dressing, 103
 Santa Fe-an Sauce, 99
 Sesame Cilantro, 100
 Sesame Miso, 100
 Tahini Mint, 92
 Tomato Vinaigrette, 101
Salads
 Appetizer Salads
 Celery Victor, 64
 Chilled Endive Vinaigrette, 63
 Daikon Carrot Salad, 60
 Edamame Beans, 61
 Eggplant Arugula Disks, 63
 Jicama Sticks, 59
 Marinated Cucumbers, 65
 Marinated Hiziki, 61
 Oyster Mushroom Shooters, 62
 Red Onion Pickles, 60
 Tomato Mushroom Vinaigrette, 65
 Fruit Salads
 Fresh Fruit Kabobs, 53
 Honolulu Toss Salad, 54
 Super "C" Salad, 55
 Hearty Salads
 Chinese 5-Spice Tempeh Salad, 85
 Grilled Vegetable Pasta Salad, 88
 Holy Mole Pasta Salad, 87
 Imperial Salad, 82
 Marinated Bean Salad, 86
 Navy Bean Salad, 84
 Pasta Fo' Y'all, 89
 Spicy Tofu Mushroom Salad, 81
 Tuscan Tomato Rice Salad, 83
 Light Salads
 A Better Beet Salad, 73
 Broccoli Eggplant Pesto Salad, 75
 Celery Root Salad, 72
 Chard Ribbon Salad, 72
 Fiesta Coleslaw, 68
 Garbanzo Nile Salad, 71
 Grilled Eggplant, Mushroom and Pepper Salad, 77
 Harvest Hiziki Salad, 69
 Japanese Eggplant Salad, 78
 Mainstream Romaine, 66
 Minted Corn Salad, 74
 Ruby Slaw, 76
 Sea "Pasta" Vegetable Salad, 70
 Spicy Sprout Salad, 76
 String Beans with Walnut Vinaigrette, 80
 Sweet Sesame Bok Choy, 74
 Thai Broccoli Salad, 79
 Wild Greens Salad, 67
 Salads with Fruit
 Confetti Salad, 56
 Orange Fennel Salad, 57
 Orange Palm Heart Delight, 59
 Ruby Fennel Salad, 58
Salsa
 Corn Salsa, 128
 2-Tier Fiesta Mousse, 142-3
Salt Glow, 53
Sauces
 Saucy Ideas, 107
 Afro Rumba Sauce, 109
 Avgolemono Sauce (Greek Lemon Sauce), 120
 Carrot Garlic Red Sauce, 111
 Caulipeño Sauce, 118
 Cheezy Sauce, 121
 Chinese Brown Sauce, 117
 Chunky Tomato Mushroom Sauce, 116
 Creamy Cashew Basil Sauce, 114
 Curried Lentil Mushroom Sauce, 117
 Fresh Tomato Coulis (Mex-Style), 110
 Green Chile Sauce, 119
 Jalapeño Cheezy, 122
 Lemon Grass Sauce, 118
 Minted Pepita Sauce, 114
 Montezuma's Black Bean Sauce, 113
 Mushroom Sauce, 115
 Red Chile Enchilada Sauce, 108
 Silken Chile Ginger Sauce, 112
 TNT Super Sauce, 112
Seaweed (*see* Hiziki *and* Nori), facts, 69, 47
 Sea "Pasta" Vegetable Salad, 70
Seed Cheese
 Basic Creamy Seed Cheese, 136
 Garlic and Herb Seed Cheese, 139
 Garlic Seed Cheese Sauce, 138
 Ginger Soy Seed Cheese, 139
 Seed Cheese Cabbage Rolls, 48
 Seed Cheese Sushi Rolls, 48
 Vegetable Seed Cheese, 138
Seitan
 Mushroom Seitan Stroganoff, 222
Sesame (*see also* Tahini), facts, 241
 Garlicky Soba Noodles, 200
 Ginger Soy Seed Cheese, 139
 Pacific Rim Pizza, 255
 Sesame Applesauce Bran Cookies, 274

Sesame Cilantro Dressing, 100
Spicy Sesame Noodles and Chard, 242
Sticky Sesame Sauce, 251
Sweet Sesame Bok Choy, 74
Shiitake Mushrooms
Boy Choy Bliss Soup, 154
Chinese 5-Spice Tempeh Salad, 85
Glass Noodle Shiitake Surprise, 247
Rice Paper Salad Rolls, 46
Spinach Spring Rolls, 251
Vegetable Lo-Mein, 245
Smoothies (*see also* Drinks)
Banana Blueberry Shake, 11
Fruity Flax Smoothie, 11
Fresh Fig Vanilla Shake, 13
Orange Banana Flips, 11
Pineapple Date Shakes, 13
Mocha Date Shake, 14
Strawberry Nut Milk Smoothie, 12
Snacks and Sandwiches
Kid Stuff
Apple Nutbutter-wiches, 35
Bee-better Butter, 36
Crunchy Honey Almond Stars, 35
Elephant Spread, 36
Monkey Toast, 36
Mexican
Chile Tempeh Tacos, 40
Nachoz, 37
Sesame Eggplant Tacos, 39
Tostadas, 38
Salad Rolls
Rice Paper Salad Rolls, 46
Sea Sprout Salad Rolls, 47
Seed Cheese Cabbage Rolls, 48
Seed Cheese Sushi Rolls, 48
Sprouted Sunseed Sushi, 49
Sunseed Aragula Rolls, 49
Sandwiches
Bagel and Paté Platter, 44
Black Bean Chapati Burrito, 45
Classic Tofu Sandwich, 43
Lentil Paté and Tomato-wiches, 41
Tofu Salad Chapati Rollups, 45
Vegetable Mousse Sandwiches, 42
Soba Noodles (*see* Pasta)
Hong Kong Pasta, 246
Soups
Cleansing Purees
Asparagus Puree, 160
Basil Broccoli California, 163
Carrot Flower Puree, 164
Cauliflower Bisque, 159
Golden Squash Bisque, 162
Green Supreme Puree, 157
Kale Mushroom Leek, 161
Mexican Cauliflower, 156
Purple Cabbage Puree, 162
Spiced Vegetable, 158
Spiked Cabbage, 158

Cleansing Soups
(nonfat, oil-free, vegetables only)
Bok Choy Bliss, 154
Cauliflower Okra Stew, 155
Garden Stew, 153
Gentle Stew, 152
Fortifying Soups
(with grains, nuts, tofu or soy milk)
African Eggplant Peanut Stew, 178
Braised Onion Soup, 180
Creamy Cauliflower Cashew, 170
Creamy Corn and Red Pepper Chowder, 176
Creamy Green Chile Potato, 169
Creamy Grilled Eggplant Soup, 173
Creamy Tomato Chile, 175
Egyptian Red Stew, 183
Fennel Asparagus Bisque, 172
Fresh Herb Zitistrone, 182
Green Corn Chowder, 174
Holy Mole Pozole, 168
Homestyle Split Pea, 166
Miso Soup with Mushrooms and Peas, 184
Native Pozole, 167
Pozole and Squash Stew, 168
Risotto Verde Stew, 179
Soup'r Fresh Parsley Vegetable, 185
Southwest Corn Stew, 165
Sunset Cashew Bisque, 171
Thai Navy Bean Soup, 177
Tomato Garden Minestrone, 181
Yellow Tomato Nut Bisque, 174
Live Energy Soups
(live and uncooked, a liquid salad, the revitalizers!)
Chilled Papaya Mint Bisque, 152
Euphoria Soup, 150
Garden Ginger Soup, 149
Gazpacho, 151
Soy Beans, *facts, 61, 233, 235*
Edamame Appetizer, 61
Soy Milk
Banana French Toast, 27
Banana Walnut Cornbread, 29
Bluecorn Cakes and Strawberries, 26
Creamy Grilled Eggplant Soup, 173
Fruity Vanilla Banana Torte, 267
Hot "Eggless" Nog, 15
Pumpkin Walnut Pancakes, 23
Raspberry Celebration Torte, 279
Riso Verde Stew, 179
Southwest Cornbread Quiche, 234
Universal Tofu Pancake, 23
Spinach, *facts, 251*
Garden Ginger Soup, 149
Green Supreme Puree, 157
Spinach Mushroom Mousse, 144
Spinach Pesto, 132
Spinach Spring Rolls, 251
2-Tier Fiesta Mousse, 142-3
Viva Spinizza, 253

Spreads (*see also* Patés, Mousses, Pestos, Dips)
Bee-better Butter, 36
Elephant Spread, 36
Spicy Peanut Spread, 135
Sprouts, facts, 49
Chinese 5-Spice Tempeh Salad, 85
Harvest Hiziki Salad, 69
Imperial Salad, 82
Lentil Paté Tomato-wiches, 41
Rice Paper Salad Rolls, 46
Sea Sprout Salad Rolls, 47
Seed Cheese Sushi, 48
Sesame Eggplant Tacos, 39
Spicy Sprout Salad, 76
Sprouted Peas and Minted Peppers, 206
Sprouted Sunseed Sushi, 49
Sunseed Arugula Rolls, 49
Tofu Salad Chapatis, 45
Vegetable Eggless Fu Young, 250
Squash, facts, 197
Butternut Maple Bake, 197
Fusilli Primavera, 248
Golden Nugget Squash Pockets, 216
Golden Squash Bisque, 162
Grilled Vegetable Pasta Salad, 88
Pozole and Squash Stew, 168
Southwest Steamers, 191
Spaghetti Squash, 199
Stuffed Acorn Squash Americana, 238
Sunset Cashew Bisque, 171
Strawberries
Bluecorn Cakes with Strawberries, 26
Fresh Fruit Tart, 264
Raw Berry Pie, 268
Strawberry Nut Milk Smoothie, 12
Strawberry Spritzer, 10
Super "C" Salad, 55
Sunflower Seeds
Basic Creamy Seed Cheese, 16
Curried Sunny Dulse Dressing, 93
Kasha Nut Loaf, 241
Nutty Salad Sauce, 94
Sprouted Sunseed Carrot Dip, 124
Sprouted Sunseed Sushi, 49
Sunseed Arugula Rolls, 49
Swiss Chard, facts, 195
Chard Ribbon Salad, 72
Spicy Sesame Noodles and Chard, 242
Woked Chard and Mushrooms, 195

Tahini, Sesame Tahini facts, 143
Cheezy Sauce, 121
Da Kine Tahini Mint Salad, 92
Granola Chocolate Chippers, 273
Green Chile and Garlic Paté, 141
Jalapeño Cheezy, 122
Sesame Cilantro Dressing, 100
Sesame Miso Dressing, 100

Spinach Mushroom Mousse, 144
Soup'r Fresh Parsley Vegetable Soup, 185
Sprouted Sunseed Carrot Dip, 124
Tahini Mint Dressing, 92
Tomato Red Pepper Mousse, 140
TNT Super Sauce, 112
2-Tier Fiesta Paté, 142-3
Tempeh, facts, 85
Chile Tempeh Tacos, 40
Chinese 5-Spice Tempeh Salad, 85
Hong Kong Pasta, 246
Tempeh Cauliflower Quiche, 235
Tofu, facts, 81
Apple Cream, 281
Apricot Walnut Torte, 280
Asparagus Tofu Pie, 230
Avgolemono Sauce, 120
Breakfast Burritos, 25
Cheezy Corn and Zucchini Enchiladas, 233
Classic Tofu Sandwich, 43
Creamy Cashew Basil Sauce, 114
Creamy Grilled Eggplant Soup, 173
Creamy Ranchero Dressing, 92
Creamy Tomato Chilé, 175
Cucumber Dip, 127
Fennel Asparagus Bisque, 172
Fruity Vanilla Banana Torte, 267
Glass Noodle Shiitake Surprise, 247
Green Chile Quiche, 231
Matzo Scrambler, 24
Miso Soup with Mushrooms and Peas, 184
Mocha Date Shake, 14
Pesto Dips, 128
Pesto Kabobs, 221
Pronto Enchilada Casserole, 229
Raspberry Celebration Torte, 279
Rice Paper Salad Rolls, 46
Silken Chile Ginger Sauce, 112
Southwest Cornbread Quiche, 234
Spicy Tofu Mushroom Salad, 81
Spinach Spring Rolls, 251
Sweet Oatmeal Corn Muffins, 30
Tempeh Cauliflower Quiche, 235
TNT Super Sauce, 112
Tofu Mole, 226
Tofu Pineapple Creme, 283
Tofu Salad Chapati Rollups, 45
Universal Tofu Pancake, 23
Vegetable Eggless Fu Young, 250
Vegetable Lo-Mein, 245
Wild Tofu Jasmine Rice, 203
Tomato, facts, 109
African Eggplant Peanut Stew, 178
Afro Rumba Sauce, 109
Besto Pesto, 129
Carrot Garlic Red Sauce, 111
Cauliflower Okra Stew, 155
Chunky Tomato Mushroom Sauce, 116
Creamy Tomato Chilé, 175
Creamy Tomato Nut Cheese Sauce, 137

Curried Lentils and Tomatoes, 205
Curried Lentil Mushroom Sauce, 117
Eggplant Tomato Boats, 218
Egyptian Red Stew, 183
Fresh Herb Zitistrone, 182
Fresh Tomato Coulis (Mex-style), 110
Fusilli Primavera, 248
Garden Stew, 153
Gazpacho, 151
Gentle Stew, 152
Green Bean Curry, 223
Indian Cauliflower, 193
Panne con Pomodore, 209
Pozole and Squash Stew, 168
Ratatouille, 198
Red Rogue Dressing, 102
Spicy Cocktail Sauce, 62
Tamale Pie, 232
Tomato Mushroom Vinaigrette, 65
Tomato Red Pepper Mousse, 140
Tomato Vinaigrette, 101
Tuscan Tomato Rice Salad, 83
Yellow Tomato Nut Bisque, 174

Tortillas
Chile Tempeh Tacos, 40
Nachoz, 37
Pronto Enchilada Casserole, 229
Tostadas, 38

Udon Noodles (*see* Pasta)

Vegetable Broth, 231
Vegetable Mousse Sandwiches, 42
Vegetable Salads (*see* Salads)
Vegetable Side Dishes
Braised Carrots with Apricots, 192
Butternut Maple Bake, 197
Desert Cauliflower, 196
Garden Steamers, 195
Garlic Roasted Corn, 189
Green Beans Almandine, 200
Grilled Garlic and Vegetables, 189
Indian Cauliflower, 193
Mushrooms La Jolla, 194
Orange Blossom Carrots, 192
Oven Roasted Potatoes with Garlic and
    Herbs, 190
Ratatouille, 198
Roasting Garlic, 189
Southwest Steamers, 191
Spaghetti Squash, 199
Tamari Spicy Fries, 190
Woked Chard and Mushrooms, 195

Walnut
Apple Spice Cake, 276
Apple Spice Muffins, 28
Apricot Walnut Torte, 280
Banana Walnut Cornbread, 29
Butternut Maple Bake, 197
Cilantro Walnut Pesto, 131
Granola Chocolate Chippers, 273
Nutty Salad Sauce, 94
Spinach Pesto, 132
String Beans with Walnut Vinaigrette, 80
Tuscan Tomato Rice Salad, 83
Water, facts, 73, 151
Water Chestnuts
Vegetable Lo-Mein, 245
Wheat Berries, how to sprout, 275, facts, 267
Sprouted Almond Croquettes, 275
Sprouted Carob Cookies, 275
Sprouted Wheat and Date Loaf, 31
Wheat Flour
Apple Spice Cake, 276
Banana Orange Zest Cake, 277
Basic Whole Wheat Pizza Dough, 207
Bread Sticks, 209
Carrot Ginger Cake, 278
Cherry Raisin Chews, 272
Focaccia, 208
Kasha Nut Loaf, 241
Panne con Pomodore, 209
Wheat Grass Juice, 7
Wild Rice, facts, 203
Twice as Wild Rice, 202
Wild 'n' Cheezy Casserole, 228
Wild Tofu Jasmine Rice, 203

Zucchini, facts, 243
A Grilled Affair, 220
Cheezy Corn and Zucchini Enchiladas, 233
Fresh Herb Zitistrone, 182
Garden Ginger Soup, 149
Garden Steamers, 195
Garlicky Zucchini and Bean Thread
    Noodles, 243
Golden Squash Bisque, 162
Grilled Vegetable Pasta Salad, 88
Pozole and Squash Stew, 168
Ratatouille, 198
Riso Verde Stew, 179
Soup'r Fresh Parsley Vegetable Soup, 185
Southwest Cornbread Quiche, 234
Southwest Steamers, 191
Tamale Pie, 232